2020:

THE YEAR
THAT CHANGED
AMERICA

2020: THE YEAR THAT CHANGED AMERICA

Blogs/Essays • Poetry • Fiction • Journal Entries

EDITED BY
KEVIN POWELL'S WRITING
WORKSHOP

kepo Inc.
49 Flatbush Avenue
Suite 1024
Brooklyn, New York 11217

 Copyright © 2020 by kepo Inc.

For information, please address:
kepo Inc.
49 Flatbush Avenue
Suite 1024
Brooklyn, New York 11217
ATTN: **REPRINT REQUEST**

Manufactured in the United States of America

10 9 8 7 6 5 4 3 2 1

Library of Congress Cataloging-in-Publication Data
is available.

ISBN **978-1-7351997-4-0** (paperback)

ISBN **978-1-7351997-3-3** (e-book)

This book is dedicated to the memory of Miguel Algarín,
principal founder of the Nuyorican Poets Cafe.

It is also dedicated to victims and survivors of COVID-19,
and to essential workers everywhere—

Proceeds from this book will be donated to
Urban Word NYC

ACKNOWLEDGEMENTS

We want to thank, first and foremost, all the writers who contributed to this anthology. You are a writer, you are amazing, we thank you for trusting us with your words, and your spiritual and artistic energy. Definitely also want to acknowledge the many writers who participate in Kevin Powell's Writing Workshop, via Zoom, and also via our Facebook group. None of this would exist without you all. Thank you to art directors Rodney Clancy (front and back covers) and Hilary VanWright (interior layout) for the great design work, and to photographer Kay Hickman for the magnificent images. We appreciate you too, The Nuyorican Poets Cafe (Daniel Gallant, Jason Quinones, and Chris Lopez) and you, Sadia James, and John Wesley for your work. Must thank Valenti Phillips for coming up with the main title of this book, and so quickly. Also want to shout out Andrew Skerritt and Ritza Yana both, who on separate occasions suggested the writing group do a book like this. Finally, we want to salute, by name, the volunteer editors, copyeditors, and managing editors who made this anthology happen, quite literally, in two months.

They are the Editors:

Andre Canty
Lujira Cooper
Jeannine Etter
Wanda E. Green
Kahlil Hernandez
Dara Kalima
Evangeline Lawson
David P. Martin
Andrea Price
Regan Richardson
Michele Simms-Burton
Andrew Skerritt
Lauren Summers
Gladira Velázquez

They are the Copyeditors:

Alexis Coleman
Jenine Corneal
Thomas Gerbasi
Eunice Hudak
Yolanda Jones
Regan Kelso-Spells
Vinnie Manginelli
Padmini Persaud-Obasi
Carla Vega

**And they are the
Managing Editors:**

Rishaunda Poole Robinson
Gerie Ventura

TABLE OF CONTENTS

we them people *by Kevin Powell* 1

PART I: BLOGS/ESSAYS

2020: The "Worst Year Ever" *by Alexandria Esplana*..........................5

The Moment The Monster Lost *by Alexis Davina Coleman* 6

A Virtual Farewell *by Allen Callaci* 9

How Huey Freeman Got Us to 2020 *by Andre Canty* 11

See New Hope with Tired Eyes *by Andrea D. Price* 14

Hopes & Fears On Election Eve 2020 *by Andrew J. Skerritt*................18

Educational COVID Crisis *by Antonio Tijerino* 20

Refund the People *by asha bandele* 23

Does Grief Expire? *by Barbara N. Owens* 27

Sorting out the Mess: An Uncle to His Niece on the
Democratic Primaries *by Bob Salzman* 29

I Lost My Twin Sister to COVID *by Bummi Niyonu Anderson* 32

Stacey Abrams "And That Says What?" *by C. Liegh McInnis* 33

"I Am Speaking" and Why Black and Brown Voices Matter
by Clinnesha D. Sibley 36

On Louisville, Breonna Taylor, and Muhammad Ali
by Dave Zirin 39

E-Note *by E. Ethelbert Miller* 41

The NFL And Trump Both Reek Of Hypocrisy
After George Floyd Murder *by Etan Thomas* 43

We Voted, So Now What? *by Evangeline Lawson* 47

"Belinda" *by Felicia S.W. Thomas* 49

50 Years Ago, Gloria Steinem Wrote an Essay
for TIME About Her Hopes for Women's Futures.
Here's What She'd Add Today *by Gloria Steinem* 52

Children of Revolution – Biden and Harris Won't be Saviors
(But We'll Take 'Em) *by Haydée Cuza, Ed.D.* 59

Red Wine, Chicken Nuggets and Zoom:
A Working Mom's Pandemic Tale *by Heidi M. Barker* 63

Why Black Trans Women Are Essential to Our Future
by Imara Jones 66

What Donald Trump Understands About American Men
by Jackson Katz 68

A Brief Celebration *by James Phoenix* 73

2020: A Loss of Balance and Innocence *by Jeannine Etter* 75

Letter To My Daughter *by Jerome Hurt* 78

What is Your Final Answer? *by John Agnelli* 80

Joe Who *by Jorjina Koffi* 84

Love Thy Christian Neighbor *by Judith Malveaux-Ellerbe* 85

Not Today! *by Kayinde Harris* 88

2020 is a Waiting Room *by Kendra Stoll* 91

The Principles I Stand For *by Kimberly Milton* 93

Exploring the relationship between imaginative language
and belonging *by Luis J. Rodriguez* 96

Teaching in an Age of Corona *by Dr. Mark Naison* 100

Crimes Against Humanity, or The Changing Same
by Michele L. Simms-Burton, PhD 101

Build Back Better *by Mona J. Eskridge* 104

Houseguest *by Padmini Persaud-Obasi* 106

My Rant on Control (or the lack of) during 2020
by Quentin Walcott (Chey's Son) 109

Patriarchy's Post Election End Days *by Rob Okun* 111

50 Years Ago, Police Fired on Students at a Historically
Black College *by Dr. Robert Luckett*..114

Clean, create and educate. A COVID-19 survival guide!
by Sadia James 117

Motherhood, Journalism, and Storytelling in The Age
of COVID-19 and Racial Unrest *by Taigi Smith* 121

On Election Day, There are a Few Things We Know
for Certain *by Tim Wise*..126

The Breath of Black Folk and the Carceral State
by Tonya Lovelace..129

Touch saved me from loneliness. What will we become
without it? *by V (formerly Eve Ensler)*....................................132

An Elegy For Better Times *by Vicki Meek* 135

Just Me. 2020 The Year That Tried To Drag Me,
But I'm Still Here! *by Wanda Elizabeth Green* 137

White America is Eating its Own Tail *by Zenzile Greene-Daniel* 140

PART II: POETRY

While Black *by Aaliyah C. Daniels* 145

Star Light *by Aaron "SpazeCraft" Lazansky-Olivas* 146

Tyranny of Mirrors *by Absolute Nsyte* 148

SKIN *by Andrea "Kelli" Higgs* 151

The Great Divide *by Angelina Rivera* 153

Tax Evasion *by Benin Lemus* 156

March 30 Year of the Plague *by Bob Holman* 158

Last day I could smell: March 16, 2020 *by Brian Shaw* 160

HALF IS STILL WHOLE *by Carla Vega* 165

Guns For Hire *by CeLillianne Green* 172

COVID Poem *by Charlie R. Braxton* 174

2020 Election *by Dara Kalima* 175

SEARCHING FOR ANSWERS *by Darryl King* 180

A Nation of Weavers *by de'Angelo Dia* 184

SCARLET TRIANGLE *by Dee Allen.* 187

Kneeling *by Dorothy Randall Gray* 189

THE PINK SLIP *by D.P. Martin* 190

Silence *by Elle Cee* 192

2020 What a Year It Has Been? *by Eric "E-Elevates" Nelson* 195

Dump Trump ¿Y ahora qué? *by Gladira Velázquez*......................196

My Story Ending *by Gladys Dae Weeks*.....................................199

LOVE AND HATE *by Glenn Hodge*.......................................202

Cock of the Crow *by Grace Beniquez*......................................204

Social Working *by Dr. Helena D. Lewis*..................................206

The Beginning, or The End? *by Jacob Edwards* 207

Protect your family *by Jenine Corneal*....................................209

UNDER THE CLOCK *by Jerry W. Ward, Jr.* 212

Ramadan 20 VS COVID-19 The call to prayer is
louder than the death toll *by jessica Care moore* 213

The Not So Hidden Agenda *by J. Hammad* 218

A Sign Is Just A Start *by Joseph Powell* 219

Black and Blue *by Josephine Basch*..223

Constitutional Hardball *by Josephine Williams*.......................225

Not Going Gently *by Keina Fields-Small*.................................227

Remember *by Keisha-Gaye Anderson* 229

This Muvfucka *by Kenneth Carroll*..231

COVID-19th Street *by Kim Yaged*...234

Revelation 23 *by KS Hernandez*...235

October Surprise *by Lauren Summers*......................................238

Conversations with Black Conservatives *by Lawrence Chan*.........239

ELECTION 2020 *by Lenard D. Moore*....................................241

What You Told Me *by Lois Elaine Griffith* 242

Strange Fruit *by Makissa Lewis*.......................................244

Shift *by Manuel Gonzalez*...245

The Count Is Still Out *by Martina Green McGowan, MD* 249

Election Anxiety *by Maya Goss* 251

Within Walls *by Michael Sindler* 253

me, immigrant, me *by Michele Rannie* 255

Plagued America *by Nancy Mercado* 256

2020 Vision Means Nothing in The Dark *by Nathaniel Swanson* 258

Thank God for the Internet *by Nicole Jocleen* 260

2020 *by Nikki Giovanni* 264

America, you're beautiful. *by Nina Brewton* 266

This New America *by Noel A. Figueroa* 271

The World is Closed *by Peter D. Hehir* 273

Soldier of Solitude *by Peter M. Schepper aka PMS* 275

Continuity *by Randi McCreary* 277

Impotent Gods Are Their Own Devils *by RaShell R. Smith-Spears* 279

#45 *by Regina Head* 281

The Urban Wall *by Robert Vazquez* 283

White Wrong Right *by Sean Hill* 285

Journal Entry: Tuesday April 2nd, 2020
by Shanelle Gabriel 292

VOTE *by Suzen Baraka* 294

Normally *by Terri L. Bailey* 298

A Haiku for SOME Writers *by Thandisizwe Chimurenga* 303

CHAINS *by Valenti Phillips* 308

PART III: FICTION

A Glorious Win *by Gwendolyn Cahill* 310

When the Bubble Bursts *by Jolon McNeil* 313

The Legend of Sweetie Mae Brown *by Kathy Henry* 320

Make Plans *by Kevin Scott* 322

Bad Dream *by London Lome'* 326

A KHARIZMA VALENTINE *by Lujira Cooper* 328

Floodlight *by Lulu Alicea* 332

A COVID Birth: Interrupted Life Lessons *by Marcy Best* 335

Sunny *by Pauline Bertholon* 338

Goodbye 2020, My Old Friend *by Rishaunda Poole Robinson* 341

PART IV: JOURNAL ENTRIES

A Tale of Two Pandemics *by Andrea Ward*.............................344

I Am Not a Training Facility *by April Carter* 345

Faith from a Distance *by Avery Danae Williams* 347

Inside 2020-Excerpts from a Journal *by CeCelia Falls* 349

Why??? *by Crystal P. Anthony* 355

So, We Are Here *by Dana Sanabria* 356

DOWN AT THE SWAMP *by Durwin Brown aka Brotha D* 358

Untitled *by Elaina T. Dariah* 360

Election Time Observations: Heart v. Mind
by Erzsébet Karkus 363

Protests *by Jason Rhodes* 367

Tree Rings *by Jenina Podulka*...369

Faith. Hope. Action. *by Katrina Hayes* 370

20/20 Love: A "No Outside Interference in My Relationship"
Writing *by Kephra Amen* 372

Journal Entry *by Kerika Fields Nalty* 374

From My Heart to God's Ears *by Lindsey "LynMarie" Morales* 377

Before and After 2020 *by Lisa T. Daughtrey* 379

A Letter to Donald Trump *by Lolita Maeweathers* 381

"Pan Damn It and Unnatural Causes!" *by Melba Joyce Boyd* 383

My Mom and COVID-19 *by Melinda Lightburn* 385

The Freedom To Be Me *by Michele Jones*..387

"Make Me Wanna Holler" Journal
by Ominira (Chiquita Camille) 389

Collateral Damage *by Pauline DeNise*..390

Flight of The Solo Traveler *by Qurell-Amani Wright*............................391

Untitled *by Regan Kelso-Spells*..395

Challenging, Beautiful, Breathtaking *by Regina Davis* 397

COVID Chronicles *by R. Ummi Modeste* 399

"Voter Registration Déjà Vu" *by Safiya E. Bandele*................................401

2020 Showed Out *by Sherring Dartiguenave* 403

gleaning election history *by S. Pearl Sharp* 405

ELECTION EVE *by Tara D. Smith* 407

Dear Nova *by Tatiana Richardson-Narell & Elijah Narell*.....................410

2020: This Makes No Sense *by Tony Thompson* 412

Happy Birthday, Happy Birthday to Me!!! *by Tracy Carness*................415

An (Now) Open Letter to My Father *by Tracy MacDonald* 418

20/20 election : Blk Wmn save amerika . . . AGAIN
Or
We good, we been here before
Or
It's levels to this thing
Or
Always centering ourselves in our existence daily long form bullet
journal entries *by veronica precious bohanan*..423

WE THEM PEOPLE
BY KEVIN POWELL

dream on
dreamer
the way Alvin Ailey
and Maya Angelou
and George Floyd
and Breonna Taylor
dreamed of
southern-baked
pilgrims
dancing and
slow marching
their sorrows
down the yellow
brick roads
of
second-line members
humming from
the heels of their dirt-kissed feet:
i wanna be ready/ to put on my long white robe....
we are survivors
we are survivors
we are survivors
of people
who were free
and became slaves
of people
who were slaves
and became free
we know why the caged bird sings
we know what a redemption song brings
we them people
we the people
we are those people

who shall never forget
our ancestors all up in us as we sleep
our grandmother all up in us as we weep
because we are native american
black irish welsh french german polish italian
jewish puerto rican mexican greek russian
dominican chinese japanese vietnamese
filipino korean arab middle eastern
we are biracial and we are multicultural
we are bicentennial and we are new millennial
we are essential and we are frontline
we are everyday people and we are people everyday
we are #metoo we are #metoo we are #metoo
we are muslim christian hebrew too
we are bible torah koran atheist agnostic truer than true
we are rabbis and imams and preachers and yoruba priests
tap-dancing with buddhists and hindus and rastafarians
as the Nicholas Brothers
jump and jive and split the earth in half
while Chloe and Maud Arnold
them syncopated ladies
twist and shout and stomp and trump
hate
again—
again—
again—
yeah
still we rise still we surprise
like we got Judith Jamison's crying solo in our eyes
every hello ain't alone every good-bye ain't gone
we are every tongue every nose every skin every color every face
mask
we are mattered lives paint it black
we are mattered lives paint it black
we are mattered lives paint it black
we are every tattoo every piercing every drop of blood every global flood
we are straight queer trans non-gender conforming
we are she/he/they

we are disabled abled poor rich
big people little people in between people
we are protesters pepper-sprayed with knees on our necks
we are protesters pepper-sprayed with knees on our necks
we are protesters pepper-sprayed with knees on our necks
we them people
we the people
we are those people
who will survive
these times
because we done
survived
those times
where pandemics were
trail of tears and lynchings and holocausts
where pandemics were
no hope and no vote and no freedom spoke
we them people
we the people
we are those people
while our planet gently weeps
we bob and bop
like hip-hop
across the tender bones
of those tear-stained photographs
to hand to
this generation
the next generation
those revelations
yeah
that blues suite
yeah
that peaceful dance
inside a raging tornado
we call
love

Originally published in When We Free The World

PART I: BLOGS/ESSAYS

2020: THE "WORST YEAR EVER"
BY ALEXANDRIA ESPLANA

The year 2020 has brought such an array of struggles and pain for many, but it is important in these times of sorrow to reflect on the positive growth that circumstances like this forces out of us.

It would be effortless for me to solely focus on the negative impacts COVID-19 has brought upon me. My senior year was cut short, and I consequently lost out on many memories some people cherish as they look back on their teenage years.

Going into college was nothing like anything I could have ever imagined. Since my first day of high school, I was already looking ahead at my college experience. My principal at the time instilled "college starts now" into my young mind. Younger me never anticipated starting college as millions die around the world in the midst of a global pandemic.

As if the pandemic wasn't enough, my home state of California burst into flames early in my first semester of college. I was lucky enough, however, to only be affected by the smoke and consequent poor air quality that ensued, and my pandemic mask had an even more important responsibility.

2020, being an election year, brought its own set of anxieties as well. The hate and gross injustice that lives in this country awoke a movement for people who have been discriminated against and silenced for way too long. The horrific police brutality against the black community, my community, was a wake-up call for millions of Americans that something had to change. This change started with getting a hateful president, who refuses to condemn White supremacy, out of office.

But throughout all of the challenges I have faced this year, I still feel lucky. I am thankful for the health of my family and me, I am thankful the fires did not displace my family as it did to so many others, and I am thankful for the growth and maturity this year has forced upon me.

The things I have struggled with this year helped me to be more mindful of what is going on in the world and to truly count my blessings. Being a young black woman in this country will never be easy, and 2020 especially made this brutally clear for me. A disproportionate amount of COVID-19 deaths, police violence, incarceration rates, and poverty plagues the black community. Seeing how people who look like me are treated in this country pushes me to work harder to go against the odds systematic racism lays out for me.

I think this year will have lasting effects for the following years to come. I believe my generation who experienced these fundamental young-adult years of our lives in lockdown will come out of this more mature and have a better outlook on the world than we did going into this year. The character development the year 2020 forced Generation Z to have better equips us to make the world a better place in the future.

Alexandria Esplana is currently a freshman at California State University, Chico and is majoring in Animal Sciences. She has a passion for civil rights activism and empowering the underprivileged.

THE MOMENT THE MONSTER LOST
BY ALEXIS DAVINA COLEMAN
NOVEMBER 2020

I took three days off from my horrid job to rest. Even working from home in a pandemic, I wasn't going to sacrifice my mental health by interacting with my co-workers who I knew were voting for Trump. Especially not this week. Then the time finally came. I voted; and then, went numb. The numbness was in the satisfaction of knowing my part was now done. I can exhaust myself with something else now, or remain numb. I then volunteered at the polls and with the unhoused to keep myself busy and positive. I was elated to see some familiar faces who were almost foreign to me now because of this pandemic.

The night hours of the election approached and with it, my own darkness. With a whiskey cocktail in hand, texting friends and crying. The numbness was waning. The rush of feeling was slowly ebbing back to me. But I definitely preferred the numbness. My mother didn't answer my calls to avoid my angst as she maintained her own sense of peace. I watched horror movies in between news reports.

I was sinking deep into a rage I never used to understand when coming from others. Every day feels like the 1960s all over again but like being on some strong edible. As humans, we use almost any forward-moving kinetic energy we generate to implode; and from there, we explode. It's this tragic tendency to destroy good worlds rather than sustain them. Suppressing our love, hiding our insecurities, deflecting responsibility, not being willing to unpack all the feelings we feel about ourselves just so we can blame others. All that hate. The explosion of it. We sit on all of those things, letting it become toxic. It becomes hate, and it finally explodes. That venom reaches far and wide. Explosions are not containable.

So as a nation, here we are: wading through feelings we know are there but without the arsenal to name them. How do you name the feelings behind seeing 21st century lynchings turn into digital postcards via social media? How do you cry when you've laughed to survive it all for so long?

My people are not sociopaths. The sociopaths bank on good people being good. And when that isn't enough, they gaslight us in Jesus' name to be peaceable. They don't bank on us to rebel; and if we do, they bank on it not lasting for long. They don't expect us to finally pull the knives out from their sheaths.

I thought of Trump winning, and I immediately felt Haitian, but outnumbered. I did the math, and I remembered it all: my empathy, my fear, my other dreams, and my comfort.

The morning finally came. And with a new tide of blue, I gave myself the courage to write the first lines of a story that was buried inside; and a song I was writing finally started to make sense to me.

As soon as the blue numbers really started to rise, I was able to completely forget the wave of rage that had previously come over me. And not until Georgia went blue did I believe it could happen.

I had just hung up with my mother and we didn't know. I looked online once again and there it was. People were crying, but I laughed loudly in schadenfreude, with a turmeric honey mask on my face, the moment I knew the monster lost. And I videotaped it. No tears.

I know the Lord and His universe is filled with irony and jokes, and that they resonate down to the earth and vibrate high enough for us to rebel against our darker natures. Most of the people of the African diaspora have learned to tap into and master this rebellion for centuries. This rebellion is hope. I am grateful to have been shown this even when I'm in my own dark space.

In the days coming, it may still get violent. In reality, I'm not as comfortable as I dream. I just don't want it to get worse than what I know. We hang on to every thread of luxury, like raising a teacup to the lips with a loaded gun under it for balance. I will not ever welcome violence. But after this win, if it comes, I'm okay.
It won't be me who draws first.

St. Louis native Alexis Coleman is a multidisciplinary artist, finding expression as a vocalist, songwriter, essayist, poet, photographer, and actor. You can find her work highlighted at alexiscoleman.com, and her social media via Twitter and Instagram at @only1alexis.

A VIRTUAL FAREWELL
BY *ALLEN CALLACI*

The last time we spoke was late October. I joked with you that the best thing anyone could say about this sour year was that at least it couldn't get any worse.

Then, just like that, it got worse.

The phone on the nightstand buzzed like a rudely awakened hornet.

It was your ex.

"Allen, he's gone. . . I'm sorry . . . no one will ever know how sorry . . . how broken. . . how lost and empty . . .I'm sorry . . . I'm sorry . . ." she cried. These were the only words she could manage in her despondency. They were far more words than I could muster in my late night stupor of brokenness and disbelief.

The years long battle you'd been stoically waging with Parkinson's Disease had come to a quiet early dawn conclusion.

A few days following that phone conversation I'd find myself recording a 5-minute shakey-cam video remembrance punctuated with quiet sobs and heavy sniffling to be broadcast along with many others at your virtual service. My cracked-voice reflection centered on how much you despised "The Ents" from "The Lord of the Rings." Your exact words were: "The Ents are pointless. Just a bunch of slow walking, slow talking do-nothing trees that do nothing to advance the plot." And the more caffeine you drank, the more animated and impassioned your "anti-Ent" diatribes became.

There aren't many things on this earth that could make me laugh like your raging tirades at the Ents. I was always jokingly threatening to record one of those Ent rants for posterity. God, how I wish I would have.

Of course you hated the Ents. They were quiet, passive, and deliberate. And you were loud, passionate, and burned for each moment. And you know what? You were right about those apathetic Ents. There are so many Ents in this universe and so few of us with the reckless and sometimes foolish abandon to even dare attempt to live our lives to their fullest.

Maybe I should have shared a more profound anecdote for your service. It's ridiculous to be mentioning Ents at someone's service, I know . . . but I thought it pretty much captured you. To you there was no middle ground to this life. When it came to friends, family, lovers and Ents you went all in.

A life without guardrails.

A life well lived.

When I look back on this most trying of years, like everyone else, I will flashback to the micro and macro cornerstones of the age – the selfishness, the sacrifice, the rage, the faith, the scratching my beard underneath my Etta James facemask, and the weekly Instacart drop offs at the door.

But the wave that will crash strongest when I think of 2020, is the wave that bears your name. When I think of 2020 I will think of this first, you lighting your cigar as you loudly and declaratively proclaim that if you could come back as anyone it would be Prince, and challenging anyone at the table to dare and question your choice. The Star Wars facemask you dropped off at my door the last time I saw you and told you, "Well, at least this year can't get any worse." And the flashback to myself on Labor Day weekend 2020 slumped on my sofa, numb, and grief stricken in front of a hazy laptop screen streaming tears at your virtual farewell.

I am ready for 2020 to be over. I am ready for a clean slate, a new beginning, the promise of putting it behind, and moving ahead. This is not the most original thought, I know. It's tired, trite, and clichéd. But as this year crawls to its close, it's all I've got left.

Your friend,
Allen

Allen Callaci is the author of the 2016 memoir Heart Like a Starfish *and the e-book* Louder Than Good-Bye *on Pelekinesis Press. He has also blogged for BK Nation, The Huffington Post, and Inland Weekly and sings with the lo-fi pioneer band Refrigerator.*

HOW HUEY FREEMAN GOT US TO 2020
BY ANDRE CANTY

"Since when are millions of Americans ready to wake up to the rantings of an angry Black kid?"- Caesar from "The Boondocks."

The year was 2007. The place was Middle Tennessee State University and a group of Black students packed into a stadium-sized classroom to discuss a funeral for the word "Nigger," after the NAACP declared the word as the worst thing to happen to Black America. The word has been the monster du jour since the 80s from questioning Eazy-E to Dave Chappelle. The debate over the word "Nigger" reemerges like Dracula. It can be subdued, but not killed.

In the classroom full of FUBU and Baby Phat labels, we all sat to watch the burial on a primitive YouTube clip. Some believed that the word "Nigger" was the Red Dragon from The Book of Revelation while others saw the word very low on the list of issues harming Black people. I was in the latter. Frustrated by most of the opinions shared a mere thirty minutes into the event, I raised my hand to give my thoughts on the controversy. With a confident voice that I've yet to master I said,

"If burying the word would lead to curing AIDS, freeing us from prison, and putting food on the table then let's bury it. If not, let it be. You know, this is something trivial and trifling to hold onto, and who holds onto trivial and trifling things? Niggas."

How I articulated the issue, while using the word, reflected a quiet separation from set beliefs on social justice that became louder in 2020. The Boondocks had a part to play in that from what it illustrated and what it predicted.

Created by Aaron McGruder, the adult animated sitcom The Boondocks first appeared in 2005 on Cartoon Network. The first episode started with a bang that featured one of its main characters, Huey Freeman, declaring that Ronald Reagan was Satan. Huey, named after Black Panther Party leader Huey P. Newton, was both a parody and a symbol of radical politics. McGruder described Huey as 'ultimately the blackest character ever to be popular in mainstream media, other than maybe Chuck D and Flavor Flav." The characters were revolutionary in how they portrayed the complexities of Black culture and set the stage for 2020 in many ways through the episode "Return of the King." This episode, which first aired in January 2006 (season 1; episode 9), provided a "what if" scenario of Martin Luther King, Jr. surviving his assassination. The fictional King wakes up from a 32-year long coma to a post 9/11 America. One of the key points of the episode was how King witnesses the commercialization of his beliefs with an undertone of how the Civil Rights movement has been whitewashed.

After the deaths of George Floyd, Ahmaud Arbery, and Breonna Taylor, protests erupted worldwide and detractors used King as a talking point to delegitimize the movement, while using intellectual dishonesty to paint the current movement as antithetical to protests held decades before. It's a common talking point that has been used to downplay how radical leaders like Muhammad Ali were because it's easy to gentrify a message when the physical container of it is gone. Many corporations took up the battle cry of "Black Lives Matter" with nothing more than a change in their bios, without structural change. Some of them even banned employees from wearing anything related to the movement, an irony worthy of its own "The Boondocks" episode.

In this Boondocks episode King was declared a traitor after first not supporting the Afghanistan war after the 9/11 attacks, as he did not support the war in Vietnam. He founded a new political party under the influence of Huey and faced scenarios activists in 2020 faced while organizing. In the system's view to stand up to established "law and order" is to be un-American... though only people of color have had that label placed on them when they stand up. Towards the end of the episode, after people mistook his invitation to his political party as a dance party, King said what he thought was the truth and disappeared again.

King's fictional departure could be interpreted as elder leaders stepping aside and making space for younger people to continue the fight. The next few scenes of the episode, set in 2006 led to change in the very last scene of the episode, which was set in 2020. These fictional scenes foreshadowed factual events in 2020 as Black people marched en masse to the White House, like they did this year. In the cartoon, NBA athletes refused to play unless the US pulled troops out of the Middle East. In 2020, actual NBA players like LeBron James and others addressed racial injustice just like the WNBA's Minnesota Lynx and Colin Kaepernick did four years prior. In a generation that was still trying to define themselves, "The Boondocks" gave us an outlet to carve our own path that led to history's largest protest.

Aaron McGruder himself couldn't have foreseen its impact and how we shifted from the colorblind education of the 2000s. McGruder was considered one of the most Leftist voices in the country from a comic strip and was sought out to be the Green Party Presidential candidate in 2003. His response to that was,

"I'm not trying to be that guy, the political voice of young Black America, because then you have to sort of be a responsible grownup, for lack of a better word. And it's like—you know, Flip Wilson said this, he said, 'I reserve the right to be a nigger.' And I absolutely do, at all times."

His indifference of being "the voice" reflected the "leaderless" movement a decade later. In 2020, people felt the wrath of not just a selected few, but from a collective many just like the ending scene of "Return of the King."

As Huey Freeman said in 2006, 2020 was when "The Revolution Began."

Andre Canty is from East Knoxville and serves as Associate of Planning and Programs at Cities United. Andre was also a co-founder of several social justice organizations and has been featured in the Knoxville News-Sentinel, The Tennessean, *and Huffington Post.*

SEE NEW HOPE WITH TIRED EYES
BY ANDREA D. PRICE

This year, I am grateful for the lesson I learned about focus. This lesson didn't come from taking a class or watching "how-to" videos about focus. This lesson did not come from talking to a therapist about my need to focus because of distractions. This lesson came from Virginia's COVID-19 face mask mandate.

Masks force me to focus on people's eyes with a newfound intensity. I even feel people's emotions in a new way since I focus on their eyes. I looked into the eyes of a woman at the grocery store as she frantically cleaned her shopping cart with a disinfectant wipe. I noticed her caution-filled eyes. I locked eyes with a stranger on the street. Our eyes said, "Hello" and I recognized his friendly smile because of the eyes. I glanced into the eyes of a masked, crying toddler. I saw her frustration.

Oddly, I learned that I hear people better when I focus on their eyes. When I talk to masked cashiers in stores, I focus on their eyes to hear them. If my eyes stray away from theirs, I often respond with, "Huh?" "Can you repeat that?" or some variation of "I didn't understand you."

During the 2020 election season, I watched a lot of campaign events and attended many campaign events online. I noticed that when I watched these events, I focused more on the eyes of the people on the other side of the screen than before the mask mandate. One candidate, President-Elect Joe Biden's eyes often looked dark and squinty during his hopeful stump speeches. The eyes of this elder statesman were so tight that I barely saw his crow's feet. His eyes looked tired. As I focused on his eyes, I asked myself, "How can he see new hope with tired eyes?"

The more I thought about the question, the more I thought about this year, 2020. I then asked myself, "How can I see new hope with tired eyes?"

As I travel down 2020's memory lane, I realize my tears flowed incessantly throughout this entire year. My eyes grew tired.

Kobe Bryant, Gigi, and the rest of the helicopter passengers and crew.

I cried.

Ahmaud Aubrey, George Floyd, Breonna Taylor, and many more victims of violent crime.

I cried.

Protests, Protests, Protests.

I cried.

The Explosion in Beirut.

I cried.

Canceled Olympics.

I cried.

Canceled School.

I cried.

The deaths of Chadwick Boseman, Justice Ruth Bader Ginsburg, and Rep. John Lewis.

I cried.

West Coast and Australian Wildfires.

I cried.

Over 20 Million People Unemployed.

I cried.

At least 15 Million American COVID Cases.

I cried.

Over 280,000 COVID deaths.

I cried.

My family witnessed someone get shot while we attended a protest.

I cried.

I spent eight months in physical therapy after Achilles tendon repair surgery.

I cried.

I felt the stress of my family adjusting to a new way of life...a pandemic life.

I cried.

Most of my tears flowed into a sea of lament. I desperately needed to see new hope with my tired eyes, so I cried out to God relentlessly. I even wrote prayers to connect more deeply with God.

One prayer I wrote is:

"Dear God,

You sent me into exile

Into a land I've never known

I kneeled in prayer and worship

Trying to understand what's going on

You said you have plans for me

And they will prosper too

You give me hope and a future

That you want me to use

I feel alone and helpless

In this land I've never known

I pray and seek to find you

My love for you I've shown

Help me to make meaning

Of a world that is so cold

Release me from captivity

And make me a new home.

Amen."

Soon after writing this prayer, I read "Lamentations, Chapter 3." This chapter helped me realize that my tears and lament are filled with dignity. A sacred dignity that allows me to show up at God's altar with all of my concerns and feelings. My tears and lament free me to accept that grace and mercy are intertwined in my DNA. My tears and lament liberate me from the weight of grief. My tears and lament rescue me from the barbed wire of life's challenges. My tears and lament make my heavy, tired eyes a lot lighter.

I am grateful because my newfound focus on people's eyes led to the question, "How can I see new hope with tired eyes?" I am also grateful because I discovered that although I don't totally understand what God is doing in the middle of my human experiences, I fully understand that God welcomes, hears, and answers my lament. My lament helps me see new hope with tired eyes.

Previously published on andreadprice.com.

Andrea D. Price is a native of Monticello, AR. She is the author of Everyday Prayers for Servant Leaders *and* Montongo Roads. *Follow her on Instagram at @iamandreaprice.*

HOPES & FEARS ON ELECTION EVE 2020
BY ANDREW J. SKERRITT

Tallahassee, Florida, 9 p.m.

Monday, Nov. 2, 2020

I write this on the eve of Election Day. I write this knowing that 24 hours from now, the results of the election will begin coming in. Then, America, and the rest of the world, will be watching anxiously to see if Donald Trump will be re-elected to a second term.

The world will be holding its collective breath to see if Americans will rescue them from the nightmare of despair and disillusionment of the past four years. They've asked themselves for four years – how could the United States of America, the richest, most powerful nation on earth, elect somebody like Donald Trump to be president?

How could a failed businessman with multiple bankruptcies and loan defaults con so many people about his business acumen?

Four years later, very smart people still search for answers. The complexity of the problem makes it even harder.

I spent much of 2016 telling my friend from college, "America deserves Donald Trump." But each time I made that admission, I followed with a question, "Do I deserve Donald Trump?" The answer equivocally is "Yes." In a democracy, guilt and punishment are collective. The hand of one is the hand of all.

Fears

And so on the eve of the most consequential election since 1932 when FDR tried to unseat Herbert Hoover, I ponder the fate of my country. I shudder to imagine life under Trump for another four years. I shudder to imagine the levers of executive power in the hands of a president whose only interest is self-interest, who has no regard for the Constitution and is unbound because he is no longer answerable to voters.

I fear for our Democratic institutions.

I fear for federal civil servants who must suffer under the tyranny of unqualified political hacks who have signed nondisclosure agreements and have sworn an oath of loyalty, not to the United States or to the Constitution but to Donald J. Trump.

I fear for scientists whose knowledge and insight have been discarded in exchange for political expediency – for one sole purpose of re-electing Donald Trump.

I fear for those who say they worship the one true God but who have bent the knee before the orange calf that is Trumpism.

I fear for justice, hijacked and abused by judges who are unqualified, inexperienced, and unjust. They are political hacks in black robes.

I fear for my country.

I fear for our children.

But even as I write this, a glimmer of hope flickers within me.

Hope

I hope the millions of Americans who braved the coronavirus pandemic and stood for hours in line to vote send a message to take their country back.

I hope Americans say they are tired of the lies, the fraud, the deceit, and the incompetence.

I hope Americans will once again affirm their belief in the inherent goodness of their neighbors and co-workers, even if they disagree politically.

I hope that brothers and sisters, parents and children can be reconciled after the nightmare of the past four years has ended.

I hope friendships can be rekindled now that the divider-in-chief will no longer occupy our White House.

I hope Donald Trump is not just defeated but repudiated by voters.

I hope Joe Biden & Kamala Harris are elected.

I hope America wins.

I hope for my children and your children.

I hope for America.

The world hopes for America.

Andrew J. Skerritt, who grew up on the Caribbean island of Montserrat, is author of Ashamed To Die: Silence, Denial and the AIDS Epidemic in the South. *His essays and reportage have been published in the* Michigan Quarterly Review, *the* Caribbean Quarterly *and elsewhere. He lives in Tallahassee, Florida.*

EDUCATIONAL COVID CRISIS
BY ANTONIO TIJERINO

By mid-March, as most schools in America were closing down, the pandemic's disruption was nearly complete. The health and economic crisis were prioritized but another crisis was becoming more and more apparent as we headed into summer, the educational crisis of 2020.

And for certain students – Latinx, Black, Native, rural – what I call the TechEquity Gap just got bigger and bigger as students had to learn from home, while teachers scramble to add IT to their capabilities and parents had to add being a teacher's assistant to their duties while working from home. That is, if the parents were lucky enough to work from home during the worst pandemic in over 100 years. For example, five out of six Latinx aren't able to work from home, creating a retrofitted, 21st Century "latchkey" kid.

Black, Latinx, and Native students have dealt with bias and bigotry throughout their young lives from being most likely to be suspended to facing lower academic expectations and being least likely to have access to adequate wifi or a device, which have become vital to their basic education, and later, workforce development.

We have to meet the moment. This is not the time to be patient. We need a sense of urgency. A tech triage if you will.

The Hispanic Heritage Foundation did a national study which found that Latinx and Black students were most likely to say their grades suffered because of a lack of access to broadband. These students were also most likely to say they couldn't finish their homework because of a lack of access to wifi, and they were most likely to use a smartphone to complete homework or fill out a college application. One of the findings was that teachers said Latinx parents were most difficult to communicate with because of the parents' lack of access to the Internet for email communication It was NOT a language barrier. It was an Internet barrier.

And this was BEFORE the pandemic.

As a parent, I worried about the "summer slide" when students would lose about 25% of what they learned over about two months of summer vacation. That two months has turned into at least nine months and that's if schools open in January. How much are they and other students losing during this pandemic?

Actually, Latinx students are at risk of falling 9.2 months behind in their schoolwork by the end of the year. How long will it take to come back from that? What lasting implications will that have going forward in their educational career?

Additionally, the future of work is dependent on how quickly we can get everyone connected to broadband. If this digital gap persists, studies show it will have negative consequences with 76% of Blacks and 62% of Latinx being shut out or under-prepared for 86% of U.S. jobs by 2045.

And then you wonder why Black and Latinos are so dramatically underrepresented in tech jobs … yeah, mystery solved.

But now we need to solve the problem. It's not just a problem for the Black and Latinx community, it's an American problem considering they make up nearly half of the K-12 population.

According to the Pew Research Center's COVID-19-era findings on Internet & Technology, 43% of lower-income parents say it is very or somewhat likely their children will have to do schoolwork on their cellphones and 40% said the same likelihood of their child having to use public wifi to finish schoolwork because of lack of access to reliable Internet connection at home. More than one out of three say it is somewhat likely their children will not be able to complete schoolwork because they do not have access to a computer at home.

Teachers have also seen the need for better wifi and access to computers to be able to teach. According to a RAND Corporation survey of teachers, 75% find "students' lack of access to technological tools and students' lack of access to high-speed Internet" are serious obstacles to effective implementation of remote learning.

And according to Bellwether Education Partners' Missing in the Margins: Estimating the Scale of the COVID-19 Attendance Crisis report, approximately 3 million of the most educationally-marginalized students in the country, March of this year might have been the last time they experienced any formal education — virtual or in-person.

In my hometown of Washington, DC, "back-to-school" family surveys found that 60% of students lacked the devices and 27% lacked the high-speed Internet access needed to successfully participate in virtual school.

Adan Gonzalez was a high school student in the rough Oak Cliff neighborhood in Dallas, TX with dreams of going to college, being a boxer, and launching a national effort to support disenfranchised youth through education, empowerment, and networking. At one time, Adan shared one bedroom with six others while his father worked long hours as a custodian and mother held odd jobs to help feed the family. Unfortunately, there was no Internet in his apartment or apartment complex, and too often no electricity. To complete homework requiring online access, he would walk late at night, after sports practices, to a McDonalds or Starbucks and lean up against the building to catch enough of the sporadic wi-fi signals to finish his assignments on a borrowed laptop. When he had to research and apply for colleges, he hit the streets in search of a signal that didn't have a password attached to it.

Fortunately, Adan was able to hurdle the TechEquity Gap and went to Georgetown University for undergrad, Harvard's Graduate School for Education, and Columbia's Teaching College and yes, he's the founder and runs the Puede Academy in his hometown where he educates hundreds of children. Unfortunately, the kids under his tutelage are facing the same issues he did when he was a kid, except with greater force because of the pandemic. The gap has gotten bigger which Adan never would have imagined when he was dealing with it 10 years ago as a high school student.

Even beyond education, at a time that our communities need to have social impact, a tech equity gap is looming. Think about it, a 15- year-old Black, Latinx or Native with access to a laptop and wifi can reach more people in a split second than Martin Luther King, Jr., Cesar Chavez, and Gandhi could in their iconic lifetimes combined. That is unprecedented potential for social impact …if they have the tools.

Antonio Tijerino heads the Hispanic Heritage Foundation and is an activist, writer, and artist.

REFUND THE PEOPLE
BY ASHA BANDELE

There's an evolving check-list I've run through every day since the August afternoon 21 years ago when I learned I was pregnant. And everything on that list is tied to a single question: what do I need to do to keep my child safe?

In the beginning it meant abandoning the financially loose life I'd chosen as poet for a stable job and healthcare. After Nisa, my daughter, was born, I included other urgencies: a stable, secure home; a school that would undergird her both academically and culturally; activities that were spiritually and culturally grounded, parks where we could take off our shoes and feel the earth beneath our feet. Today, I am left breathless by her accomplishments as a scholar and an activist, and comforted that the safety measures that my education and other privileges allowed me to put in place, worked. Although Nisa is 20 years old now, I still cling to that check-list and with particular care in this moment of rebellion, rage and grief, making note that of all the items on it, the one never included to keep my daughter safe was, "police."

When the Movement for Black Lives recent demand to defund the police went viral over the last week, there were who thought it a bridge too far. Yes, police were antagonistic and even dangerous, and yes, they'd had "the talk," with their children, but look at the crime in our communities, they'd also argue. Look at the rioting! Untethering ourselves from the police sounded good in theory but unrealistic and dangerous in practice. But if the goal is actual safety and security, you cannot reverse engineer it into a police budget.

Here's why.

Over the last decade, and in particular during the Obama Administration, there was a spectacular breadth of reform initiatives, which have just as spectacularly, failed: anti-bias trainings, diversified departments, body cams and particularly cynical, in Minneapolis, an early-warning system so that problem officers could be identified. The cop who killed George Floyd had nearly 20 complaints filed against him. Maybe the early-warning system beeper thingamajig gave out after the first 10 and the information was lost? Whatever the case, what was true at the birth of Black Lives Matter in 2013, is true today: African Americans are at least three times as likely to be killed by police as our White counterparts.

This is because the idea of reforming the institution of policing--and it's important to understand them as an institution as opposed to the one bad apple scenario--has a critical design flaw. It ignores the fundamental role of police in Black communities. For us, their role as first responders is not heroic, but harmful, when not outright deadly.

Consider the White child in the middle-income or wealthy community who is clearly disrupted but before police are asked to intervene, school counselors, special programming and mental health professionals are called upon. They know that only as a final resort, should police be involved, which is entirely appropriate. It's hard to remember, with all the cop television shows that serve as PR campaigns, that only recently have police been considered heroic. Most often they were broadly considered to be what Black people have generally never backed away from calling them: corrupt thugs. Attempts to reform them began a century ago, although it would be Lyndon Johnson who really put heft behind the pro-police push as Black communities were in the throes of the Civil Rights and Black Power Movements. For what it's worth, one place where there's been little discrimination is in how Democrats and Republicans chose to respond to Black communities. Leaders of both parties, from Johnson, to Nixon to Reagan to Clinton, called for our lockdown.

For Black people, though, police are first responders--often the only responders but not in the way we're spoon-fed the concept in the media. As our first responders, their role is not and never has been to care for and protect us, but to do what police in America have always been instructed to do with Black people: contain us. We're a problem to be controlled. What isn't thought to be problematic enough to do everything possible to fix are all the things that we know undercut lives: the absence of jobs, quality schools, healthcare, green spaces--you know, what parents everywhere put on their checklists as critical to their children living a successful life.

Nationwide, more than 100 billion dollars are spent on police departments, with some cities spending fully 50 percent of their budgets on law enforcement--even when crime levels are historically lower. And of those dollars, billions are spent to further militarize local law enforcement. Local police agencies are literally trained to go to war against the very people their public relations teams say that they are sworn to protect. It's the most basic conflict of interest. And while all of this is happening, the institutions that are proven to provide security, from schools to hospitals, from parks to arts centers, have contracted. Which is to say that the funding of police and the defunding of critical social needs has, rather than creating safety, created danger--and this would be true even if no cop ever killed another Black person again.

Can you imagine with me a world where there was a true commitment to repair the harm done to Black people, from slavery to Jim Crow to being targeted for incarceration; from voter disenfranchisement to work and housing discrimination? It's absolutely possible and one way for us to realize it is to recalibrate budget priorities. The M4BL call is less about defunding police than it is about refunding the people. Or, as Martin King said so beautifully on that Mall two generations ago: we are here to collect on the promissory note written into the collective American covenant of the right to life, liberty and the pursuit of happiness.

As a parent, I have a duty to scrutinize my budget in order to ensure my daughter. I take care of what is needed before anything else is purchased. That was true before the COVID-19 pandemic and it's true now. And while the idea of government being cast in the parental role is not what I would ever argue for, it's also true that there is a fundamental duty of care it owes us. We elect and fund a government whose responsibility it is to ensure baseline care for all the people. To that extent, their charge, like mine as a mother, is to set fiscal priorities that align with that elemental responsibility. Demand your legislator prove that they are spending public is spending dollars in actual service of the public--the whole public. Demand that they prove that proper dollars have been allocated for evidence-based safety and prosperity initiatives. Demand that with every dollar spent, government leaders are doing what I and parents across this nation are called to do with every dime and every decision: put our children's real-world needs, their lives, at the center.

An original version of this article first appeared on Essence.com

asha bandele is a New York Times best-selling and award-winning author and journalist.

DOES GRIEF EXPIRE?
BY BARBARA N. OWENS

2020 has been the year from hell. Unfortunately, resting was not easy because of the lack of a government plan to control the pandemic and the recurrent cases of unarmed African-American men and women being killed by law enforcement and vigilantes. I lost two of my personal warriors this year; my brother passed on March 9, 2020, and my first cousin who I called "aunt" passed on November 9, 2020. My brother died after being struck by a vehicle. I am not able to confirm my aunt's cause of death, but it's suspected that a heart attack might have been the culprit. Like many people who have lost loved ones to COVID-19 and violence, I grieved. But my heart broke when I lost my brother and aunt. My heart was not ready for them to leave this earth and their unexpected deaths were hard for me to accept.

My childhood experiences with death and memories of attending funerals of close family members were marked more by ritual than intimacy. I felt like I stood on the outside of a glass box while looking at the dead person; a person I wish I'd known better. There was a distance between me and that person, and grief could not connect us. But now, the sting of death is much more intense.

Although I have experienced grief before, the grief I feel this year is unrecognizable. This grief feels like someone stole something from me. I also feel entitled because I question why my warriors received their wings. Who am I to question? I have no control over death. Unfortunately, every time I see updates on COVID deaths and see stories about unarmed African-American men and women who are killed, the grief I feel from losing my warriors is reactivated. Is there an expiration date on grief?

I feel the presence of my brother and aunt inside of me. They live through me. I am who I am because of them. Their deaths made that clear to me. During their homegoing celebrations, I had the honor of hearing and seeing written testimonies of the positive influence and impact that they left on this earth. Their stories motivate me to try to achieve the same impact.

Because they are a part of my life story, I have a duty to share their stories and my memories of them with my children and generations to come. Memories are all I have. My last memory of my brother is him jokingly telling my children they were going to lose at a video game match with him this year at Christmas. They went back and forth trash-talking each other. They were laughing so hard that they couldn't catch their breaths. The uncontrollable smiles on my children's faces during this exchange was heartwarming. A memory of my aunt is this message that she often shared: "Your present circumstance does not determine your future potential."

My warriors were my role models, but they were also educators, preachers, leaders, entrepreneurs, and legacy trendsetters. My love for my warriors will never expire, but will my grief?

My warriors are my forever keepsakes. I now walk with more confidence because I keep them close. Their spiritual presence makes me a warrior too. I just wish I knew them better: their hopes, their dreams, and their stories, through their eyes.

Their deaths make me feel like I am now standing on the inside of that glass box I saw as a child. There is no distance between me and my warriors. We are bound to one another. Deep love connects us. Grief also connects us. Grief that never expires.

Barbara N. Owens is a native of Houston, TX and she is persistent in all of her pursuits.

SORTING OUT THE MESS: AN UNCLE TO HIS NIECE ON THE DEMOCRATIC PRIMARIES
BY BOB SALZMAN

She wrote, "I'm worried as well and can't seem to decide which Democrat I think can win! Who do you think?" This was my response.

Thanks for the excuse of trying to unpack your question that's on everyone's mind.

From inside my Upper West Side liberal bubble it's hard to get a picture of what's going on west of the Hudson. The prospect of Trump winning a second term is real, horrifying, and sickening.

The thing about being retired is that I can schmooze about politics on a Thursday morning before starting my "workday. I'll spend the rest of today writing unpublished letters to the editor and inquiries to various disinterested authors, talking for hours to tech support, then rejecting requests to complete a brief survey on how well John Smith in Manila addressed my issues, or trying to get an airline to waive the $60 charge to reserve an aisle seat because of my knee. Then there's lunch somewhere between 12 p.m. and 12:03 p.m. to provide me with the energy to try, unsuccessfully, to make sense of endless Medicare forms before my beloved afternoon nap.

Now on to your question. The interesting overarching mystery to me is why any sane person would want to be president. The answer is that only someone who is bat shit crazy would want that job, even those who were really good at hiding it like Obama was.

The other factor and the only glimmer of hope is the extent of damage Trump and the Republican brand are suffering as the impeachment process exposes Trump as a grifter without a soul.

And more Americans inside the ReFoxican smoke machine are getting a look at the man behind the curtain and the corrosive damage he has done to the country.

The mobs of screaming Trump ReFoxicans, channeling their political ancestors from 1939 Berlin who wanted to make Germany "great again," are hopelessly beyond the gravitational pull of Earth's fact-based atmosphere. The big question is whether any sectors of Republican voters, who are not knuckle scraping Neanderthals, can be peeled away. [See my Warren wildcard prediction below].

As of Nov 1, 2019, there are 17 Democrats still standing.

Ugh.

The short list of key "holy grail" voting sectors that the Democrats need to mobilize to beat Trump seem to be:

1. The Republican "Colin Powell' middle — who are nauseous at what has become of their party, still have a sense of right and wrong, and will never vote for Trump. The Democrat needs to be someone who will make them want to come out from under the covers on election day.

2. Black people --- Motivating Black people to vote for another White politician who suddenly shows up in their churches to hug the minister is a major problem for the Dems.

There is also the impact of the republican decades long Jim Crow 2.0, full court press to stop Black and Brown people from voting;

3. Suburban women — college educated and physically revolted by Trump, but hard to predict because they have internal bullshit detectors that are well honed from years of wrangling their kids to do their homework. There is also the fact that keeping a job and running a family often leaves them too exhausted to do anything but have a glass of wine and go to bed.

4. Bernie's army--- active, angry, young people. It's inspiring but I'm worried that they are quasi- cultish and not big picture, eyes on the prize, flexible types who will join the fight when Bernie is not the nominee.

Now, for my predictions on which candidates will secure which voting blocks.

Warren is the best candidate although increasingly personally annoying. She is the only one I can see knocking the Orange Godzilla off his feet in the professional wrestling ring of a national debate. She also has an SNL problem because when she talks I keep seeing Kate McKinnon.

Now she has thrown her Hail Mary "Medicare for All" pass which may be the reason she wins or loses.

Maybe she will get votes from suburban women and Bernie's army, but less from Black people. Votes from the Colin Powell Republican middle is an open question. This depends on whether after she gets the nomination she can convince Wall Street that she is only about a level playing field, not Stalin. Here is my Warren wild card prediction. Trump voters treading water in poverty level jobs living paycheck to paycheck without health insurance — one illness away from bankruptcy — are the Warren wild card.

Michael Moore warned us that Trump would win because these voters were tired of being shit on and just wanted to throw a bomb at the system. My fantasy is that these folks might have buyer's remorse about having been bamboozled by a gold-plated sociopath and want to throw another bomb at the system by voting for someone who really is in their corner.

Bernie changed the landscape of American politics but America will not elect a 78 year-old angry Jewish man from Brooklyn. Plus his heart attack underscored what Fran Liebowitz told Bill Maher, "Biden and Sanders are not only too old to be President, they should have their car keys taken away."

Bernie is not the humble dropout type and will only secure his devoted army. Biden is looking worse by the day and can't seem to talk in full sentences that don't end with the word "malarkey." If he doesn't drop out it's all the Colin Powell Republican middle, a sprinkling from Black people and suburban women. Also even without even a shred of an allegation that Hunter Biden did anything wrong, the Burisma stinking dead fish gift to the Refoxicans was unforgivably clueless. Trump's, hopefully fatal, mistake was not to leave it alone.

Buttigieg is showing strong support in Iowa. He is a possible long shot with some serious brain power. Definitely the Colin Powell Republicans, but trouble with Black people and Bernie's army. And the problem of getting people to vote for a 16-year-old gay kid.

Harris would take votes from the Colin Powell Republicans, Black people and suburban women, but is too nauseatingly self-righteous with a sleazy record as a prosecutor where she was guided by political self-interest and not doing the right thing. Watching her try to be folksy when talking to crowds of people by droppin' the g at the end of words like thinkin', watchin', and hopin' makes me feel like pukin'.

Booker is a decent, unexciting guy and a likely pick for vice president.

Love, Uncle Bob

Bob Salzman is a retired lawyer and a past winner of the Funniest Lawyer in New York contest who blogs from his home in New York City. You can follow him on Medium and Facebook. His email is robert@salzmansalzman.com.

I LOST MY TWIN SISTER TO COVID
BY BUMMI NIYONU ANDERSON

On Friday, March 27, I had a close family friend call 911 because my twin sister, Femi, didn't sound like herself, and I was too much of a nervous wreck to call. I had spoken to Femi earlier in the morning, and she sounded fine. She hadn't been feeling well, but said she was feeling better. She had taken a COVID test and was waiting for the results. The wait would be at least five days, and those five days seemed like forever. Because of COVID, we were keeping our distance. It was the longest stretch of time we had been apart from each other. There was so much unknown about the virus, so we just stayed distant. The ambulance came and transported her as I stood outside her house. She didn't know me. She seemed confused, but even as they rode away, it never hit me that this was a serious situation. Death didn't enter my mind. At this time,

Albany, Georgia was a hotspot. Albany was on national news because so many people had contracted the virus, allegedly starting with two funerals that had taken place in the city.

My twin DID NOT attend either funeral, but she was a thriving entrepreneur in the city. She had reluctantly closed her art business because of COVID and went home. She was concerned about the future and the impact of the virus on her business. She was admitted to the hospital but transported to another hospital in the state. I felt the transport would be good for her. In the wee hours of Saturday, March 28, my twin sister passed after suffering cardiac arrest twice. I was devastated. I had to call our parents, and it was the hardest thing I had ever done. My life changed forever. For the first few months, I was afraid to leave my apartment. I suffered from anxiety and grief, and it was evident through constant vomiting and weight loss. I lost 50 lbs. because I had an almost non-existent appetite. Every day since, I've done my best to get through the terrible reality of losing my first best friend. Some days are tougher than others. My emotions run the gamut: I laugh and smile and cry and get angry. I always saw us growing old together, and now my vision is blurred. But I know, she's with me.

A native of Albany, Georgia, Bummi Anderson is a writer, teacher, and preacher, specializing in poetry and creative non-fiction. You can purchase her work on Amazon or any independent bookseller as well as find her on various social media platforms as Bummi Niyonu Anderson or on Twitter at @BummiNAnderson.

STACEY ABRAMS "AND THAT SAYS WHAT?" BY C. LIEGH MCINNIS

I can begin by reminding y'all that over 70 million people voted for President Agent Orange and that the election of noted and proud racist Cindy Hyde-Smith as Mississippi's Lieutenant over Mike Espy proves that the vast majority of White Mississippians would have never voted to "retire" the Confederate Flag as they resoundingly voted for Hyde-Smith who was one of the loudest critics of changing the state flag. Moreover, as it pertains to the national election, I never understood the logic of thinking that it would be a "liberal landslide." Maybe that was wishful thinking, but I simply consider it delusion. Or, maybe, I've merely accepted Mississippi and America for what they are. That does not change the things that I like about either, but it enables me to engage and strategize empirically rather than emotionally. Are all the White people in Mississippi and America racist? No. But, it seems that at least fifty-five percent are racist or are comfortable aligning themselves with racists. Yet, the same is true of people of color. Whether it is the model minorities (Asians and now some who identify as Latinos and Hispanics) who see African Americans as responsible for their own negative plight or whether it is some African Americans who have decided to roll with the oppressor in hopes of receiving scraps from the table, it is time for African Americans who do not define themselves in these ways to accept that they are the only people who can save themselves and begin the real work to do so. Doing anything less than this is tantamount to begging one's oppressor to be nice to them.

And, this is where the plot is twisted by the magnificent work of Stacey Abrams who, interestingly, is an award-winning author of several romantic suspense novels under the pen name Selena Montgomery. Abrams' work as a Georgia Representative, her 2019 gubernatorial campaign, and her founding Fair Fight Action is the reason that Georgia just voted for a Democrat presidential candidate since 1992. Yes, one can argue that Atlanta and its surrounding areas are booming with Black folks and other minorities. But, the sad truth is that the majority of Black folks don't vote as they should for various reasons. However,

Abrams was able to develop an infrastructure to inspire and mobilize Black folks, which is why President-Elect Joe Biden was clear in acknowledging that Black folks "showed up" at the polls for him. The history of America is the history of Black folks like Abrams who believe in the beauty, intellect, and power of Black folks enough to force this country to overcome its hypocrisy and achieve its fantasy ideals about itself as a democracy rooted in the land of the free and the home of the brave. As such, Abrams' work must be a lesson to African Americans from one end of this country to the other. Do African Americans continue to cry and beg White folks to see, hear, and help them? Or, do African Americans recognize the resources and power that they have and do for themselves? To be clear, Attorney and former State Representative Abrams is not a Black Nationalist as I am. Yet, her work proves that one does not have to be a Black Nationalist to understand and work for Black folks becoming self-determining. I don't care how Black folks get there. I just want us to get there. And, in the true fashion of Mavis Staples and the great Staples Singers song, "I'll Take You There," it was a Black woman leading the country on a spiritual journey to redeem its soul. I don't think that it is an overstatement to proclaim Abrams a political Harriet Tubman, leading Black Southerners on a path to freedom. Abrams got the South so shook that Mississippi Governor "Tater Tot" Reeves tweeted that "I will do everything in my power to make sure universal mail-in voting and no-excuse early voting are not allowed in Mississippi - not while I'm governor. Too much chaos." Talk about the plantation owner being worried about what the slaves are doing on his neighbor's plantation. Reeves and the other Southern governors are worried that their Black folks might become inspired by the work of Abrams and finally get organized enough to poke more holes in the Red Southern Wall. And while Mississippi's Black population is still not large enough to elect someone to a statewide office on its own, Abrams' work shows that there are many more battles that they can win if they simply recognize and utilize their own resources. Mississippi has long had more Black elected officials than most other states. But, Mississippi has lacked the type of consistent Black leadership that could inspire and lead Black folks to control their day and destiny. Afro-Mississippians constitute thirty-nine percent of the State, which makes it the largest percent of African Americans of any state in the country. While we can complain that White Mississippians are fifty-nine percent of the state and that ninety-five percent of them vote as a solid White block, the truth is that Afro-Mississippians don't vote their numbers and don't believe in themselves enough to create a unity that enables them to control their day and destiny. Thus, I'm hoping that Abrams' work inspires Afro-Mississippians in the same manner that it has scared and infuriated Governor Tater Tot and his Confederate Army. So, how Black folks get to a place where their day and destiny are in their hands is not the issue for me. That we do this and that more of us follow the lead of Abrams is most important to me. Other than that, a lot of folks must do some soul searching to decide what is the best way forward for themselves, their immediate community, and the country. To recap, ninety-five percent of White Mississippians voted for a woman who admitted that she would attend a public lynching, and close to fifty percent of Americans voted for Trump; yet, a Black woman raised in Gulfport, Mississippi, who relocated to Atlanta, Georgia, when her parents pursued graduate degrees, became the bulldozer to blast a hole in the Southern Red Wall, and that says what?

C. Liegh McInnis is a poet, short story writer, essayist, author of eight books, former editor of Black Magnolias Literary Journal, Prince scholar, and an English instructor at Jackson State University. He is also a former First Runner-Up of the Amiri Baraka/Sonia Sanchez Poetry Award sponsored by North Carolina State A&T.

"I AM SPEAKING" AND WHY BLACK AND BROWN VOICES MATTER
BY CLINNESHA D. SIBLEY

When my oldest daughter was four, she asked me why I was wearing a pamper. At that moment, I explained to her what a sanitary napkin was. We were in a gas station restroom and another Black mother just outside of the stall twinging with embarrassment for me interjected, "If my child would've asked me something like that, I would've slapped her in the mouth. Mamas these days will let their children ask them anything," she added. Her own daughter, silent and clearly fearful, was right there with her. The loud hand dryer muffled the closing of her speech, but she continued to reproach and judge.

"Mommy, why was that lady in the restroom so mad, Kaylee later asked me, her memory of the ordeal becoming more and more vague.

And with my pent-up anger I smiled and said, "Some people are just upset, sweetie."

As I continue to find my footing in parenthood, one thing I know is that it's important for children to have a voice. If they ask a question, I will honor it. If they have something to say, I will listen. I believe boundaries can and should be broken for the intellectual curiosity of an innocent child. Coaching them on how and when to use their voice is key.

Imagine if I told Kaylee to "shut up" that day. Her memory would be precise because it would've hinged on my embarrassment of or reaction to her question. She didn't know that I was being judged and demeaned by a stranger. She was four, and the lesson I chose to instill honed in on exemplary womanhood and taking the higher road.

Kamala Harris though? I believe she would've snapped back if she were having a conversation with her daughter and someone interrupted. I'm convinced and inspired that Kamala is a woman who doesn't let such intrusions slide. Imagine if Kamala were constantly told to shut up by her mother. Imagine if she were not allowed to express herself growing up. She may have never had the confidence to become a prosecutor or the first woman of color to become a vice-presidential candidate. Furthermore, the manner in which she was raised is what gave her the resolve to say to a White-man-terrupter, with power and authority: "I am speaking."

The odds are against Black and Brown children. They are more likely to be under greater home stress than White children and are more likely to experience humiliation, abuse, and oppression due to racial and social disparities. I often think that a dream gets deferred every time one of our children gets beaten, cursed out, overlooked, or discriminated against. The storm that's waiting out there for them is a tough one to weather. They desperately need our love, our umbrellas of affection.

Kamala's parents were immigrants. Her Indian mother, Shyamala Gopalan, is the central figure in Kamala's personal narrative–a story that is always linked to love, hard work, and resilience.

"My mother, who raised me and my sister, was a proud woman. She was a Brown woman. She was a woman with a heavy accent. She was a woman who, many times, people would overlook her or not take her seriously. Or because of her accent, assume things about her intelligence…every time my mother proved them wrong." - Kamala Harris

Kamala's hero is a Brown woman, academic, and activist who raised

two daughters on her own after divorcing their father. More than anything, Kamala's mom wanted her girls to be sure of themselves and valued in the world. According to Kamala, her mom was a woman who "never asked anyone permission to tell her what was possible." She recalls her mother saying, "Don't just sit around and complain about things. Do something." And we can't help but be inspired as we watch Kamala do her thing.

Essentially, it was Shyamala's daughter we saw debate Pence on October 7, 2020. For ninety minutes, we watched a woman become the hope and dream of her mother.

A healthy mother-daughter relationship matters. It can determine the self-esteem of a girl and the path she chooses on her journey into womanhood. Not every girl belongs in a corporate meeting or on a campaign trail; but every Black and Brown girl deserves her own unique road to greatness.

So many of our girls are silenced in their childhood because of mismanaged love. My Kaylee is nine now. I don't know for sure what she'll grow up to be–a performer, professor, politician, pharmacist, or president–whatever path she takes, I want her to be able to give and demand respect, express herself freely and responsibly, and take up space!

I want my children to speak up, speak out, and be a voice in the world. Because my babies more-than-matter. They are sacred and worthy.

I have to admit. Sometimes I regret not taking up for us in that restroom back then.

Previously published at TheWriteAddiction.com, Serenity Sunday

Clinnesha D. Sibley is a wife, mom, daughter/sister/auntie, literary artist, humanities scholar, and social entrepreneur. Her advocacy work is at the intersection of black/feminist thought, arts, culture, and community. Follow her on Instagram @clinneshawrites.

ON LOUISVILLE, BREONNA TAYLOR, AND MUHAMMAD ALI
BY DAVE ZIRIN
SEPT 25, 2020

I've been wrestling with the devastating miscarriage of justice that has taken place in Louisville, Kentucky, in the case of Breonna Taylor. I've been rocked not merely by this obscene decision to hold no one responsible for her death, but also the fact that Louisville is hallowed ground as the birthplace of Cassius Marcellus Clay Jr., also known as Muhammad Ali. One city is now marked by both glory and an act of unspeakable evil. In the same city that Muhammad Ali called home, Breonna Taylor was murdered by the police in her bed. The people of Louisville deserve so much better.

I went to Louisville in 2016 for Muhammad Ali's funeral. I saw airport tributes to him as soon as I stepped off the plane. I watched buses pass me by with flashing signs emblazoned with his face. I visited the modest home in which he was raised. I walked the street named after him. I spoke to a right-wing taxi driver, a White guy and Vietnam vet, who said to me—and I remember his words exactly—that he loved Ali because "I didn't agree with him, but dammit he had courage." I heard news anchors tell us that his funeral was only Louisville's second ever to have a city procession and day of mourning. The first, I kid you not, was Col. Sanders… as in the fried chicken. It was one hell of a sendoff for the son of a frustrated house painter and domestic worker who was raised on the segregated side of town.

I also walked Louisville for hours with those who lined the streets to pay their last tributes as Ali's hearse rode through the city. There were thousands of people. It was almost entirely Black. (I'm saying "almost" just because my pod producer Dan Bloom and I were also present.) Experiencing this overwhelming local outpouring of love, I was reminded of the fact that Muhammad Ali at the height of his fame would attend demonstrations in Louisville that were fighting redlining, segregated housing, and, yes, police brutality. He once said, speaking directly to the Black community of his hometown:

"In your struggle for freedom, justice and equality I am with you. I came to Louisville because I could not remain silent while my own people, many I grew up with, many I went to school with, many my blood relatives, were being beaten, stomped and kicked in the streets simply because they want freedom, and justice and equality in housing."

Spending the day speaking to Louisville's people—many too young to have ever seen Ali fight—about what "The Champ" meant to them, irrevocably changed me. So many had met him over the years, and Ali would make a point through a joke, a magic trick, or an impromptu sparring session, to make the experience forever memorable. It was a reminder about the ties that bind us to the past and the history that can sustain a community through a difficult present. There was deep poverty in Louisville. Legal segregation was gone, but that meant that the Black middle and professional classes had moved out of Ali's old neighborhood, creating more immiseration and social crisis for those on the bottom of the ladder. There was also a deep feeling that this was a place fighting to be heard. If struggle is truly the secret of joy, then I'll repeat: It felt like hallowed ground.

Daniel Cameron, the Kentucky Attorney General, has desecrated this hallowed ground. In his ambition to remain a Republican rising star, mentored by McConnell and beloved by Trump, he chose his career over justice and made the decision to use Breonna Taylor's body as a stepping stone to reach even greater heights. I know what people are saying about Daniel Cameron. I sure as hell know what Muhammad Ali would have said about Daniel Cameron. But to me this is less about the color of Cameron's skin than a naked and grotesque expression of what it takes to rise in GOP circles: You protect the cops, you blame the dead, and you assert, no matter the cost, that Black lives—particularly the lives of Black women—simply do not matter.

For the people of Louisville, Breonna Taylor's name will not be forgotten as surely as Muhammad Ali's. Maybe someday people will walk Breonna Taylor Boulevard in downtown Louisville and speak her name not merely as a tragedy but as a turning point towards true justice. Daniel Cameron's name, if remembered at all, will be thought of like the person who stole young Cassius Clay's bicycle, which inspired the 12-year-old Clay to take up boxing. He will be the anonymous, ignominious cudgel of immorality whose blows didn't put the people of Louisville down for the count, but propelled them to rise off the mat.

Previously published on thenationcom

Dave Zirin is the sports editor of The Nation *and the author of* Game Over: How Politics Has Turned the Sports World Upside Down.

E-NOTE
BY E. ETHELBERT MILLER

If the historians will not say it, then the poets must. Trump destroyed America by revealing what was in our nation's marrow. His embracing of White supremacy was simply an act of honesty. His claim that he was not a racist was just another lie. There are too many witnesses that can testify to this. Will his family members and former employees please step forward?

The destruction of America was made possible by the country's addiction to entertainment and the worship of Hollywood. Trump was a star turned comet, blazing across the 5O states and willing to watch California burn. His slogan "Make America Great Again" was simply snake oil turned into words and shaped into caps. It was a dress rehearsal for fascism and all that is "No" in the world.

Obama was America's first and last Black president. He was a sentinel elected to stand in front of a collapsing country. When our Towers were destroyed in New York, the nation sang our anthem as it echoed the deep and heavy blues. For a moment, we were one, but soon we turned into blue and red states. The rest is simply Babel.

So where are we? Biden is the "hyphen" between America and the New America. He is between and linked to Obama and Harris. Yes, Black people had his back and got him elected in 2020. His selection of Harris as VP is not a symbolic crack in a glass ceiling, but, instead, the lifting of the dark fog of racism and sexism. It's the ability of a New America to finally learn how to say "Kamala." Our tongues are ready to taste the sweet honey in the rock out of which America was built. Gone is the rooted bitterness of the past.

A New America is rising like a New Atlantis. It will require a new man and a new woman to govern it. Our new bones cannot wear an old flesh or hand-me-downs from Europe. Our past must now become our past. America was a great experiment that failed, thanks to Trump, the mad scientist. The lab exploded and our image was shattered. How we now see ourselves begins in our imagination. Hughes once attempted to dream of a new world. In 2020 we were given back our sight. We voted to see.

Welcome now, the "New America." This is not about reconstruction. It's the beginning of a new dawn, the lifting of fertile soil by hands of many colors, the planting of new flowers and trees. Oh, listen to your heart with your ears. Let us sing love into the air. Oh yes - this New America will BE.

E. Ethelbert Miller is a writer and literary activist living in Washington, D.C. His forthcoming book is When Your Wife Has Tommy John Surgery and Other Baseball Stories. *He can be reached at: emiller698@aol.com*

THE NFL AND TRUMP BOTH REEK OF HYPOCRISY AFTER GEORGE FLOYD MURDER
BY ETAN THOMAS

On one hand we have the person who currently occupies the White House Donald Trump urging governors to seek "retribution" and that they have to "dominate the protestors" and calls the protestors "terrorists"

https://www.theguardian.com/us-news/2020/jun/01/donald-trump-protests-george-floyd-dominate

while saying absolutely nothing about holding police officers accountable in any way shape or form when they act as terrorists in cases across the country on an everyday basis from Officer Daniel Panteleo (Eric Garner) to Officer Betty Shelby (Terence Crutcher) to Officer Darren Willson (Mike Brown) to Officer Blane Salamoni (Alton Sterling) Officer Jeronimo Janzez (Philando Castile) and now Officer Derek Chauvin who we watched heartlessly put his knee into the neck of George Floyd while casually putting his hands in his pockets for nine minutes as three other cops held him down.

On the other hand, we have seen an abundance of organizations, companies, and business entities feel led to issue public statements at the prevalent terrorism that runs rampant through police departments across America and proclaim that Black Lives do in fact matter despite the little to no value that has been displayed by the justice system by the mere fact that most of these police officers are rarely held accountable for their acts of terrorism.

Companies from around the country have issued statements expressing their disapproval of the vicious and evil killing of George Floyd that was caught on video for the world to see. These companies include Netflix, HBO, Starz, McDonald's, Target, Apple, Disney, Amazon, Microsoft, Twitter, Google, NHL teams, MLB teams, the Commissioner Adam Silver, the NBA and most of the NBA teams (except James Dolan and the New York Knicks but we'll save that for another article) https://www.si.com/nba/2020/06/02/james-dolan-defends-absence-statement-george-floyd-death

Which brings me to the NFL who also issued a statement which you can see in its entirety below

"The NFL family is greatly saddened by the tragic events across our country. The protesters' reactions to these incidents reflect the pain, anger and frustration that so many of us feel.

"Our deepest condolences go out to the family of Mr. George Floyd and to those who have lost loved ones, including the families of Ms. Breonna Taylor in Louisville, and Mr. Ahmaud Arbery, the cousin of Tracy Walker of the Detroit Lions.

"As current events dramatically underscore, there remains much more to do as a country and as a league. These tragedies inform the NFL's commitment and our ongoing efforts. There remains an urgent need for action. We recognize the power of our platform in communities and as part of the fabric of American society. We embrace that responsibility and are committed to continuing the important work to address these systemic issues together with our players, clubs and partners."

"We recognize the power of our platform in communities and as part of the fabric of American society."

Where was all of this when Colin Kaepernick took a knee?

I asked Eric Reid specifically why he and Kaepernick took a knee in my book "We Matter Athletes And Activism" and this is an excerpt of what he specifically told me.

"I just felt that people were losing their lives over traffic stops and nobody was being held accountable for that. The way things kept playing out was, you would have the initial report, they would say it was under investigation, and nothing would really happen. All of these families would be forced to deal with another loss of life, and nothing seemed to be changing. So, since my personal beliefs were in line with his (Kaepernick) on this subject, I wanted to show some solidarity and support for my teammate. He was getting a lot of backlash and I couldn't just not support him when I felt the same way he did"

And that backlash came directly from the NFL who has White-balled Kaepernick from the league since the 2016-2017 season when he began kneeling during the national anthem to protest police brutality and racial injustice. Kaepernick became an international symbol of resistance and nonviolent protest. He embodied everything that Roger Goodell just ironically stated that the NFL is striving to represent.

"We embrace that responsibility and are committed to continuing the important walk to address these systemic issues together with our players, clubs and partners?"

Who is advising Roger Goodell? You mean to tell me that nobody in their NFL office told him that this wouldn't go over well? That this statement wasn't dripping with hypocrisy? That neither Jay Z or any Inspire Change songs were going to mask the sanctimonious of everything he wrote in his statement?

https://theundefeated.com/features/nfl-partnership-an-open-letter-to-jay-z/

This would've been an opportune time for Roger Goodell to announce, not give a written statement (which let's be honest is starting to sound a little manufactured by the different companies and entities. Like they all have the same ghost writer preparing their statements) but this would've been well timed for Roger Goodell to call a press conference and actually verbalize something along the lines of...

We have seen the errors of our ways in our handling of the Colin Kaepernick situation and we as the NFL want to reach out to him to make amends for our caving into the pressure from the White House and our conservative fan base who purposely twisted Colin Kaepernick's message of peacefully protesting police brutality into being anti-police, anti veterans, and anti American. We know he was actually utilizing the example set by the great Dr. Martin Luther King Jr (since they love to bring Dr King into the discussion all the time when they want to talk about nonviolence which ultimately waters down and twists his message as well but I digress) We know that it is not Anti-American to speak out on the injustices of police brutality and we would like to not only give him a real opportunity to play in the NFL and not the sham of an opportunity that we created before

https://www.theguardian.com/sport/2019/nov/16/colin-kaepernick-nfl-workout-sham

We will come to terms with him and his agent on parameters for the tryout, we can make it all public if they like so that we are 100% transparent and regardless of that outcome, we want to work with him in particular and his Know Your Rights organization moving forward to bring about real change in our country because what happened to George Floyd cannot keep happening.

Then they can discuss how they recognize the power of their platform in communities and as a part of the fabric of American society etc etc. They don't even have to throw in Black Lives Matter like most companies have. They would've actually gone above and beyond all of the statements made by various companies because they would've given a distinct example of something they were specifically going to implement to put their words into action. A lot of companies are giving pretty words without any specifics which is a nice sentiment, but much more is needed.

Now, I know what I just described is completely far-fetched and wouldn't happen in a million years, but it would take something drastic and far-fetched to actually make amends for the White-balling of Kaepernick. And it's not just about one person, it's about what White-balling Kaepernick represents. The suppression of the powerful voices of NFL players out of a fear of being Kaepernick'ed out of the league if they dare to use their voices and platforms to speak out.

Statements like "The NFL family is greatly saddened by the tragic events across our country. The protesters' reactions to these incidents reflect the pain, anger and frustration that so many of us feel." are just as hypocritical as Donald Trump calling Violent White Supremacists Protestors who were actually Found guilty of first degree murder for killing paralegal Heather Hayer "very fine people" but calling protestors after the death of George Floyd "thugs." You both reek of hypocrisy.

Published originally on theguardian.com

Etan Thomas is a senior writer for basketballnews.com and is the host of the Rematch. He is a social justice advocate and mentor. His website is https://www.etanthomas.com/.

WE VOTED, SO NOW WHAT?
BY EVANGELINE LAWSON
October 29, 2020

After an intense summer of political brainwashing with campaigns, ads and debates, laced with a barrage of memes and social media commentary (Mike Pence's fly incident anyone?), we have survived one of the most intense presidential elections of our lifetime. If you exercised your right to vote, you either mailed in your ballot or stood in line to cast a vote for the new leader of the "free" world. Granted you've survived the logistical nightmare of casting your vote, you're now probably wondering, "What impact did that even have? How is my vote going to change this hectic and often unexpected life I am privileged to live?"

The world appears to be in utter chaos. There's a global pandemic that has sent us all into a frenzy. Do we just wash our hands with soap and water like we typically do, or reach for the hand sanitizer? Can we even find sanitizer? Now, in many cases, we are forced to wear masks in public spaces. We are also color-coordinating masks with our outfits. We're asking ourselves questions like: "Are trips that exist outside of the parameters of car travel canceled forever? Will I ever be able to comfortably spend time with my friends again? Will I ever experience that rush of standing in line for the latest sneaker release again? Can I return to campus or will I be forced to earn my degree online and lose the experiences of dorm living, campus parties, and sporting events?"

At the same time, we are being bombarded with the backlash of systemic racism. We are inundated with images and videos of Black people being murdered, and disproportionate numbers of Black people dying because of COVID-19. Being born Black is all it takes to fall victim to violence or COVID-19. We have witnessed the countless worldwide protests of people expressing fear and rage because of systemic racism. All of this leaves us to ask whether or not our lives will ever return to normal.

Now that the election is over and we've cast our ballots, we're trying to convince ourselves that the seventy-year-old White guy in office (whichever one is declared the winner) is going to deliver us from all of this. That somehow this grandpa-like figure will be able to either create or restore America to a country where pride, love, and confidence replace fear, distrust, and hate.

If you're like me, you probably have a lot of doubt. Is this man even capable of understanding the desires of the youth in this country? Youth aren't necessarily focused on social security, but they just want to be able to enjoy concerts and to travel again. Is this newly elected "savior" able to consider the concerns of women living in the country? While the emphasis may be placed on family planning and the right to choose, what about the fact that women are paid significantly less than their male counterparts? Can a White president truly embrace or understand the fears of a Black person living in America? Our dreams of thriving and capitalizing on all this country claims to offer is being dimmed by the reality of just wanting to survive. We want to feel safe in this world we live in, regardless of the skin we're wrapped in.

Most of all, none of us want to fear death from a virus that we don't truly understand, while being forced to permanently guess facial expressions through someone's forehead and eyes because the bottom half of their face is covered with fabric. What we want extends beyond empty promises. We want to feel like ourselves again. We want hope and the reassurance that this Democracy will actually be something that we can believe in, regardless of age, gender, or race.

No matter which older White man ends up winning this election, what the President can do is lead. Lead with actions, not just words. Demonstrating that he actually hears the people and cares enough to build and execute quality plans that will positively affect all of our lives-not just the lives of those that look like him, are the same age as he is, or have the same party affiliation. We want to live full lives. What we all hoped when we stood in that line or sealed that envelope was that whoever ended up winning would truly give a damn about us. We hoped that whoever occupied 1600 Pennsylvania Avenue would be just as determined and invested in getting us to the normal we have always desired though never quite reached as much as he was determined and invested in winning this election.

Evangeline Lawson is a Southern California-based writer, educator, literacy advocate and content creator. Her email is vangieluvsbooks@gmail.com and you can follow her on Instagram @vangieluvsbooks.

"BELINDA"
BY FELICIA S.W. THOMAS

"Belinda" is a 37 year-old struggling, single, Black mother. She works three jobs that keep her away from her children 18 hours out of a 24-hour day. She bathes and comforts the elderly, the disabled, and the injured. With the paychecks from these jobs, the sporadic child support she receives from her baby daddy, and the little sum'n sum'n her part-time man gives her when he's feeling magnanimous, she often finds that her monthly bills exceed her limited budget. Belinda has many problems similar to the countless other Americans who are trying to survive life at the bottom of the hill. She is earning too little to dig herself out of this rut and get ahead but earning too much to qualify for most government subsidy programs. While managing life between this rock and a hard place, Belinda will also be hit first and hardest by political decisions made at the top of Capitol Hill. She complains about her life, how unfair it is, and how she can never afford anything nice. Belinda curses the system that is responsible for the state of her life.

Yet, Belinda refuses to vote.

Upwards of hundreds of millions of people failed to vote in the 2016 election that installed the worst president in American history, and 55% of these nonvoters were Democrats and Democrat-leaning independents. Belinda was among those millions. Like many nonvoters of all backgrounds, she is the definition of the apathy, the nonvoter who can't comprehend that the decision not to vote is still a vote in favor of something and someone. Their inaction preserves the status quo and the life condition of the people at the top and bottom of the hill.

Black nonvoters like Belinda often stumble through lifelike political zombies in a comatose state, with unintelligible words dripping from their lips. A steady diet of toxic soundbites, nonsense, and misinformation caused her infection. Belinda fails to recognize she is consuming poison and is complicit in her own apathy and disenfranchisement. She happily shares it with her children, creating another generation of Black non-voters.

The telltale signs of having never read a history book or even understanding history makes her easy to spot. A fog encircles her head – the remnants of knowledge-repellent sprayed liberally to prevent intelligent ideas from penetrating her brain and locking in the fumes of polluted thoughts.

Voting is a responsibility that many consider the most powerful tool an American citizen possesses. A single mark in the voting booth can, and has changed the course of history. A history that has seen our forebears swim against the tide of hatred, bloodshed and murder, just to gain the right to enter that booth.

Try explaining this to Belinda. In slow motion, her eyes glaze over, her lips purse, and disinterest washes over her face. Belinda will exercise her lungs when she perceives she has been denied the right to get something for free. She will not exercise her right to vote when her basic rights to be free are eroded by a misogynist, racist, wealth-pandering president.

Despite these facts, she chooses to be cloaked in ignorance, somehow absolving herself of the obligation to vote.

Belinda is not unintelligent, yet it escapes her that voting affects her life. She struggles to articulate reasons why she doesn't. She is arrogant and loud as she exclaims:

"I'll be called for jury duty."

"The system is rigged."

"They don't need my vote."

The simple truth is Belinda can't articulate a valid reason. She doesn't have one. She could care less that scores of Black people died in pursuit of this right. She moans and whines in the dark about the state of her life. The state of her life is a direct result of her failure to vote. When shit hits the fan, the Black non-voter is the first to be splattered. Belinda wears her shit proudly.

To illustrate cause and effect, to encourage Belinda to vote in the 2020 election, I painstakingly explain that the coronavirus has proven more deadly than necessary because the wrong president was in office when the pandemic descended upon us. He did nothing and allowed it to spread unchecked for weeks. It's like giving a serial killer a four-week head-start before making any attempts to even identify him. So far, he's still four weeks ahead leaving carnage in his path. We're playing catch up in arresting this killer.

This president personally delivered a bomb to every American citizen – those who voted for him and those who voted against him. The millions of people who did not vote received the package, too. The right president would have been armed and prepared to vanquish this virus in its early stages – or at least, not ignore how dangerous it is.

Belinda contracted the coronavirus in September 2020. Her employer failed to provide her with personal protective equipment. She provided services to patients who were infected. Her body was visited by pain that rendered her immobile. She lost her sense of smell and taste. Fluid filled her lungs, causing her breathing to be labored. Her ability to earn a living was hindered for two weeks as she hovered between life and death. Thankfully, she recovered; however, between the period in which she was declared not contagious but had not yet tested negative, she was treated like a pariah. When she sought assistance for her economic hardships, she was required to disclose her diagnosis. People treated her rudely out of fear of being exposed to the virus. She will forever be traumatized by this experience.

Belinda has President Trump to thank for the illness and dire financial straits; the president who delivered that bomb to her. More accurately, she has herself to thank for that bomb.

Yet, Belinda still didn't vote in the 2020 election.

Felicia S.W. Thomas is a native of Quincy, Florida. She is an attorney and the author of 80 Proof Lives, *among other titles. Her email is feliciathomas917@hotmail.com. You can also follow her on Facebook at https://www.facebook.com/FeliciaSWThomasAuthor.*

50 YEARS AGO, GLORIA STEINEM WROTE AN ESSAY FOR TIME ABOUT HER HOPES FOR WOMEN'S FUTURES. HERE'S WHAT SHE'D ADD TODAY
BY GLORIA STEINEM

In the half-century since I wrote the essay below, as part of a cover story on "The Politics of Sex," there has been some definite progress. "Women's issues" are no longer in a silo but are understood as fundamental to everything. For instance, the single biggest determinant of whether a country is violent, or will use military violence against another country, is not poverty, natural resources, religion or even degree of democracy; it is violence against women. And since racial separation can't be perpetuated in the long run without controlling reproduction—and thus women's bodies—racism and sexism are intertwined and can only be uprooted together.

A belief in equality, without division by sex or race, is now held by a huge majority in public–opinion polls. But a stubborn minority of Americans feel deprived of the unearned privilege of that old hierarchy and are in revolt. The time of greatest danger comes after a victory, and that's where we are now. Many of the predictions of my 50-year-old essay about the future hold up, but there are a few lessons I've learned since then (including to negotiate a writing fee beforehand, since my agent later told me I was paid less than male contributors).

I won't be around when these words are read 50 years from now, but I have faith in you who will be.

What It Would Be Like If Women Win
By Gloria Steinem
Originally published: Aug. 31, 1970

Seldom do utopias pass from dream to reality, but it is often an illuminating exercise to predict what could happen if they did. The following very personal and partisan speculations on how the world might be different if Women's Lib had its way were written for TIME by Gloria Steinem, a contributing editor of New York Magazine, whose journalistic curiosity ranges from show business to Democratic politics. Miss Steinem admits to being not only a critical observer but a concerned advocate of the feminist revolt.

Any change is fearful, especially one affecting both politics and sex roles, so let me begin these utopian speculations with a fact. To break the ice.

Women don't want to exchange places with men. Male chauvinists, science-fiction writers and comedians may favor that idea for its shock value, but psychologists say it is a fantasy based on ruling-class ego and guilt. Men assume that women want to imitate them, which is just what White people assumed about Blacks. An assumption so strong that it may convince the second-class group of the need to imitate, but for both women and blacks that stage has passed. Guilt produces the question: What if they could treat us as we have treated them?

That is not our goal. But we do want to change the economic system to one more based on merit. In Women's Lib Utopia, there will be free access to good jobs — and decent pay for the bad ones women have been performing all along, including housework.*Increased skilled labor might lead to a four-hour workday, and higher wages would encourage further mechanization of repetitive jobs now kept alive by cheap labor.

*Gloria Steinem in 2020: As people look at screens more than at one another, the opposite has happened; the workday never ends.

*With women as half the country's elected representatives, and a woman President once in a while, the country's machismo problems would be greatly reduced. The old-fashioned idea that manhood depends on violence and victory is, after all, an important part of our troubles in the streets, and in Viet Nam. I'm not saying that women leaders would eliminate violence. We are not more moral than men; we are only uncorrupted by power so far. When we do acquire power, we might turn out to have an equal impulse toward aggression. Even now, Margaret Mead believes that women fight less often but more fiercely than men, because women are not taught the rules of the war game and fight only when cornered. But for the next 50 years or so, women in politics will be very valuable by tempering the idea of manhood into something less aggressive and better suited to this crowded, post-atomic planet. Consumer protection and children's rights, for instance, might get more legislative attention.

*Gloria Steinem in 2020: With Trump as a backlash to Obama, almost any woman President would be a relief.

Men will have to give up ruling-class privileges, but in return they will no longer be the only ones to support the family, get drafted, bear the strain of power and responsibility. Freud to the contrary, anatomy is not destiny, at least not for more than nine months at a time. In Israel, women are drafted, and some have gone to war. In England, more men type and run switchboards. In India and Israel, a woman rules. In Sweden, both parents take care of the children. In this country, come Utopia, men and women won't reverse roles; they will be free to choose according to individual talents and preferences.

If role reform sounds sexually unsettling, think how it will change the sexual hypocrisy we have now. No more sex arranged on the barter system, with women pretending interest, and men never sure whether they are loved for themselves or for the security few women can get any other way. (Married or not, for sexual reasons or social ones, most women still find it second nature to Uncle-Tom.) No more men who are encouraged to spend a lifetime living with inferiors; with housekeepers, or dependent creatures who are still children. No more domineering wives, emasculating women, and "Jewish mothers," all of whom are simply human beings with all their normal ambition and drive confined to the home.

No more unequal partnerships that eventually doom love and sex.

In order to produce that kind of confidence and individuality, child rearing will train according to talent. Little girls will no longer be surrounded by air-tight, self-fulfilling prophecies of natural passivity, lack of ambition and objectivity, inability to exercise power, and dexterity (so long as special aptitude for jobs requiring patience and dexterity is confined to poorly paid jobs; brain surgery is for males).

Schools and universities will help to break down traditional sex roles, even when parents will not. *Half the teachers will be men, a rarity now at preschool and elementary levels; girls will not necessarily serve cookies or boys hoist up the flag. Athletic teams will be picked only by strength and skill. Sexually segregated courses like auto mechanics and home economics will be taken by boys and girls together. New courses in sexual politics will explore female subjugation as the model for political oppression, and women's history will be an academic staple, along with Black history, at least until the white-male-oriented textbooks are integrated and rewritten.

*Gloria Steinem in 2020: Not until we start paying public-school teachers as much as every other democracy does

As for the American child's classic problem—too much mother, too little father—that would be cured by an equalization of parental responsibility. Free nurseries, school lunches, family cafeterias built into every housing complex, service companies that will do household cleaning chores in a regular, businesslike way, and more responsibility by the entire community for the children: all these will make it possible for both mother and father to work, and to have equal leisure time with the children at home. For parents of very young children, however, a special job category, created by Government and unions, would allow such parents a shorter work day.

The revolution would not take away the option of being a housewife. A woman who prefers to be her husband's housekeeper and/or hostess would receive a percentage of his pay determined by the domestic relations courts. If divorced, she might be eligible for a pension fund, and for a job-training allowance. *Or a divorce could be treated the same way that the dissolution of a business partnership is now.

*Gloria Steinem in 2020: Once domestic labor is accorded the same value as salaried work

If these proposals seem far-fetched, consider Sweden, where most of them are already in effect. Sweden is not yet a working Women's Lib model; most of the role-reform programs began less than a decade ago, and are just beginning to take hold. But that country is so far ahead of us in recognizing the problem that Swedish statements on sex and equality sound like bulletins from the moon.

Our marriage laws, for instance, are so reactionary that Women's Lib groups want couples to take a compulsory written exam on the law, as for a driver's license, before going through with the wedding. A man has alimony and wifely debts to worry about, but a woman may lose so many of her civil rights that in the U.S. now, in important legal ways, she becomes a child again. In some states, she cannot sign credit agreements, use her maiden name, incorporate a business, or establish a legal residence of her own. Being a wife, according to most social and legal definitions, is still a 19th century thing.

Assuming, however, that these blatantly sexist laws are abolished or reformed, that job discrimination is forbidden, that parents share financial responsibility for each other and the children, and that sexual relationships become partnerships of equal adults (some pretty big assumptions), then marriage will probably go right on. Men and women are, after all, physically complementary. When society stops encouraging men to be exploiters and women to be parasites, they may turn out to be more complementary in emotion as well. Women's Lib is not trying to destroy the American family. A look at the statistics on divorce—plus the way in which old people are farmed out with strangers and young people flee the home—shows the destruction that has already been done. Liberated women are just trying to point out the disaster, and build compassionate and practical alternatives from the ruins.

What will exist is a variety of alternative life-styles. Since the population explosion dictates that childbearing be kept to a minimum, parents-and-children will be only one of many "families": couples, age groups, working groups, mixed communes, blood-related clans, class groups, creative groups. Single women will have the right to stay single without ridicule, without the attitudes now betrayed by "spinster" and "bachelor." Lesbians or homosexuals will no longer be denied legally binding marriages, complete with mutual-support agreements and inheritance rights. ~~Paradoxically, the number of homosexuals may get smaller. With fewer overpossessive mothers and fewer fathers who hold up an impossibly cruel or perfectionist idea of manhood, boys will be less likely to be denied or reject their identity as males.~~

*Gloria Steinem in 2020: I would cut this line, since it's now more clear that we are born whoever we are.

Changes that now seem small may get bigger:

MEN'S LIB. Men now suffer from more diseases due to stress, heart attacks, ulcers, a higher suicide rate, greater difficulty living alone, less adaptability to change and, in general, a shorter life span than women. There is some scientific evidence that what produces physical problems is not work itself, but the inability to choose which work, and how much. With women bearing half the financial responsibility, and with the idea of "masculine" jobs gone, men might well feel freer and live longer.

RELIGION. Protestant women are already becoming ordained ministers; radical nuns are carrying out liturgical functions that were once the exclusive property of priests; Jewish women are rewriting prayers—particularly those that Orthodox Jews recite every morning thanking God they are not female. In the future, the church will become an area of equal participation by women. This means, of course, that organized religion will have to give up one of its great historical weapons: sexual repression. In most structured faiths, from Hinduism through Roman Catholicism, the status of women went down as the position of priests ascended. Male clergy implied, if they did not teach, that women were unclean, unworthy and sources of ungodly temptation, in order to remove them as rivals for the emotional forces of men. Full participation of women in ecclesiastical life might involve certain changes in theology, such as, for instance, a radical redefinition of sin.

LITERARY PROBLEMS. Revised sex roles will outdate more children's books than civil rights ever did. Only a few children had the problem of a Little Black Sambo, but most have the male-female stereotypes of "Dick and Jane." A boomlet of children's books about mothers who work has already begun, and liberated parents and editors are beginning to pressure for change in the textbook industry. Fiction writing will change more gradually, but romantic novels with wilting heroines and swashbuckling heroes will be reduced to historical value. Or perhaps to the sadomasochist trade. (Marjorie Morningstar, a romantic novel that took the '50s by storm, has already begun to seem as unreal as its '20s predecessor, The Sheik.) As for the literary plots that turn on forced marriages or horrific abortions, they will seem as dated as Prohibition stories. Free legal abortions and free birth control will force writers to give up pregnancy as the deus ex machina.

MANNERS AND FASHION. Dress will be more androgynous, with class symbols becoming more important than sexual ones. Pro-or anti-Establishment styles may already be more vital than who is wearing them. Hardhats are just as likely to rough up antiwar girls as antiwar men in the street, and police understand that women are just as likely to be pushers or bombers. Dances haven't required that one partner lead the other for years, anyway. Chivalry will transfer itself to those who need it, or deserve respect: old people, admired people, anyone with an armload of packages. Women with normal work identities will be less likely to attach their whole sense of self to youth and appearance; thus there will be fewer nervous breakdowns when the first wrinkles appear. Lighting cigarettes and other treasured niceties will become gestures of mutual affection. "I like to be helped on with my coat," says one Women's Lib worker, "but not if it costs me $2,000 a year in salary."

For those with nostalgia for a simpler past, here is a word of comfort. Anthropologist Geoffrey Gorer studied the few peaceful human tribes and discovered one common characteristic: sex roles were not polarized. Differences of dress and occupation were at a minimum. Society, in other words, was not using sexual blackmail as a way of getting women to do cheap labor, or men to be aggressive.

*Thus Women's Lib may achieve a more peaceful society on the way toward its other goals. That is why the Swedish government considers reform to bring about greater equality in the sex roles one of its most important concerns. As Prime Minister Olof Palme explained in a widely ignored speech delivered in Washington this spring: "It is human beings we shall emancipate. In Sweden today, if a politician should declare that the woman ought to have a different role from man's, he would be regarded as something from the Stone Age." In other words, the most radical goal of the movement is egalitarianism.

If Women's Lib wins, perhaps we all do.

*Gloria Steinem in 2020: The relationship between violence against females and all violence other than self-defense should inform our foreign policy.

Previously published in TIME.

Gloria Steinem is a writer, lecturer, political activist, and feminist organizer.

CHILDREN OF REVOLUTION – BIDEN AND HARRIS WON'T BE SAVIORS (BUT WE'LL TAKE 'EM)
BY HAYDÉE CUZA, ED.D.

To the folx who were children born into revolutionary households, the ones whose parents stayed up late to host community meetings to create a better world...to those who attended rallies to dismantle capitalism, hunger and lack; our childhoods were sacrificed for the possibilities of something better, for the hope of revolution. We marched, sat on picket lines and sold revolutionary newspapers to strangers on the steep walkway of the Griffith Park. The knowledge of what is possible and the demonization of authoritarian greed was embedded in our worldview.

The election of Trump was not a moment of surprise but inevitable as we saw the spotlight put on U.S. cultural apathy. He cheated to become president and the media response was "give him a chance." It verified a willingness to minimize our democracy and accept deplorable traits of White bigoted politicians with toxic ideologies. He's not the only one by far – just the most publicly influential at this time.

We know that Biden and Harris won't be saviors – they are a reset back to a normal that was never acceptable and is no longer tolerable. (Side note: they may not be the revolutionary ticket but I must say that seeing a Black and Indian woman as VP feels amazing.) Having an empathetic president will be refreshing, unfortunately, it won't change the system that created Trump.

Trump's presidency lifted the cloak of the abusive manipulation strategies in our politics. The blatant and extreme disrespect for life over the last four years unveiled were the flaws in the U.S. democracy and economic structures.

These past four years have amplified the oppressive application of 'trickle down' economic practices, 'broken windows' policies, lack of economic and personal reparations for centuries of systemic racism that stole and segregated resources, undermining of feminine attributes, denying of natural expressions of love and gender, and the poisoning of our air, ground, water, and food for mass production with the goal to hoard at the expense of the majority. Those who benefit from our division are hell-bent against our bodies being our own and our labor benefiting our communities.

This will continue into the next presidency.

The difference today is that we are witnessing a brutal and necessary reawakening, if we are to live in the spirit of what we were taught and are worthy. Gaslighting with 'public opinion' rhetoric is not sustainable when our human experience reveals the truth.

Through our personal experiences and the political analysis of Assata Shakur, Malcolm X, Amanda Seales, and many more, we know White toxicity and class division are long-standing flaws within our democracy that have obstructed our collective innovation and the quality of daily life.

From the invasion of White immigrants, political structures were built on diminishing our expressions of humanity and exploiting people and land for the benefit of supremacist ideology and practices. The culture that has been cultivated expects us to obediently compromise our well-being and very existence at the expense of our families and communities.

When political gains for human dignity are made, the backlash we experience is relentless. Our government is structured to favor accumulation and power over people and lives through racist corporate politics.

Movement builders fight and live in fear of destruction, prison, starvation, and ultimately death. There is no wonder how we became weary and distracted as communities deteriorated and education limited the knowledge of our full stories.

And when exhaustion set in I saw my parents assimilate to a certain extent. Now, I observe a similar assimilation in adulthood stemming from my own exhaustion.

We are busy 'producing' profit and working for the purpose of survival, for basic needs. And for the honor of doing that work we're forced to go against our values and pay taxes allocated to preserving violence, control, chaos, and division at the expense of our ancestral knowledge, joy, and collective power.

Many of us experience the oppressive freedom sold to us in the U.S. We are educated to believe that we are free.

We are free to die of a curable illness because healthcare is inaccessible, free to live on a sidewalk because vacant buildings are more valuable than housing people, free to be without reward for hard work, free to be in debt to get an education and career, free to live in fear of racism and its toxic influences on our well-being.

Although there are many structures to dismantle and rebuild in the image of humanity, I am witnessing a greater acceptance of folx expressing their truths.

I dare to hope in these truths because I know something different is possible. I dare to carry on so we can all be liberated from the sharecropper mentality of capitalism. Liberated to dream of a society built on love where food, shelter, creativity and community resources are abundantly accessible.

The realities of capitalism's brutality and inequities, taxation without representation, racism and corporate influence on our democracy, and the toxic entitlement of imperialism and colonialism are being discussed openly. The Black Lives Matter Movement is a part of mainstream dialogue. Who would have thought? These are dreams children of revolutionaries have heard since birth but with the fear of phones being tapped and dangers of violence for talking about alternative economic possibilities and human rights.

I hold tremendous gratitude for the work and efforts that went into re-enfranchising and uplifting individuals to express their priorities. It is a nostalgic validation of our parents' fight.

This upcoming administration may not transform the U.S. but I'm hopeful this administration will restore some of the broken pieces. The foundation for liberation will continue to be strengthened. The voter turnout, community organizing, and our collective visioning laid the groundwork for holding them accountable. I hope we will continue to focus on systemic transformation and move away from the false responsibility of individuals to be complicit in their own oppression and depression.

Haydée Cuza, EdD is a sensitive, queer, multi-cultural/racial womyn, wife, mom, abuelita, daughter, sister, and friend with decades of experience in nonprofit, finance, research, and writing. She is a lifetime believer in the fundamental worthiness of everyone to be fed, housed, clothed, loved, and with the means to thrive. Read more of her work at haydeecuza.com

RED WINE, CHICKEN NUGGETS AND ZOOM: A WORKING MOM'S PANDEMIC TALE
BY HEIDI M. BARKER

May 2020

I'm a ballerina… gracefully twirling between rooms… arms outstretched to charge this laptop or reboot that one. Hush. I absorb a dramatic stillness when I think my boss says my name through my earbuds.

I effortlessly resume my dance when I realize he didn't. Trotting through the hall to quietly curl up next to my 10-year-old, a single finger reaches toward the computer mouse and gently clicks to start the video for his distance learning. I rise like a flower blowing in the wind, bending out of view from his teacher and classmates, backing away slowly into the hall. I turn my gaze toward the other room to see my 8-year-old online as well.

He says, "Mommy, stay with me."

I bring my finger to my lips to signal quiet, point to my earbuds and retreat as the dance ends, still listening for my name.

My personal cell rings. This is not part of the routine. I silently pray that my turn on the work call will not come.

"Hello?"

"Yes, is this Miss Barker?" a man asks.

"Yes."

"This is your second grader's Spanish teacher. He's not logging into the app correctly. I don't see his work. Please write down these instructions to get into the app."

"Sir, I can't. I'm on a work call. Can I please call you back?"

"Ma'am, I have 100 students. I cannot accept incoming calls. Just remember to use his first initial and last name, click on his homeroom teacher's name, then use the code I'll send through the Class Dojo app, okay?"

"Um… okay, thank you."

First initial, last name, homeroom teacher, code, First initial, last name, homeroom teacher, code.

Wait, where do I get the code again?

"OK- now… Heidi, any update on communications?" my boss asks.

"Yep, so we're working on messaging for Tuesday's announcement, and recommending that department heads…"

"Heidi, Heidi? If you're speaking, you must be on mute. Unmute yourself."

I pull the phone out of my pocket and click.

"Ok, now can you hear me?"

"Yep, go ahead."

"MOM! THE ZOOM STOPPED WORKING! I CAN'T SEE MY CLASS ANYMORE!"

Which kid is yelling?

My colleagues laugh, empathetically, as each has also starred in this situation comedy.

"Stand by, guys… I'm moonlighting as an A-V tech. Ok … rejoin… no, don't touch it! See? OK, it's back. Sorry, guys."

Focus! Graceful. Ballerina.

"So, we're working on messaging for Tuesday's announcement…"

This dance is not sustainable. I'm a working single mother trying to balance virtual work with virtual school, while fortifying a household-turned-bunker against a global pandemic.

The doorbell rings with a grocery delivery. I slip on plastic gloves, which tear pretty easily, but somehow make me feel safer. I wipe down everything. What's for dinner tonight? What's for lunch now? Damn, did I not order ketchup?!

First initial, last name, homeroom teacher, code. First initial, last name, homeroom teacher, code. DOJO! He's putting the code on Class Dojo!!

I'm not cooking tonight. Whatever delight I found in culinary exploration dissipated early in the shutdown. Screw it, we're just having chicken nuggets. All of us. I silently dare anyone to judge me for not having a proper adult meal. As I pour my favorite pinot noir, I again tell myself I'll stop drinking wine on weeknights... starting next week.

Red wine, chicken nuggets and Zoom. What has my life come to??

***

Now, I'm facing the probability that I'll have to lace up my ballerina slippers again this fall. As medical experts, educators and politicians debate whether to open schools, hold virtual classes, or a combination, I feel anxious and uncertain. I relive that moment when year-end report cards came out, and I took each grade personally. *Just a "B" in Reading? What the hell (WTH)? I uploaded all of those blasted worksheets on time.* I find that mantra of "what doesn't kill you makes you stronger" to be highly questionable. Thankfully, it didn't kill me to juggle it all and keep my family safe, but I'm the sole adult here. I pretended to be a ballerina, handling everything with grace. In reality, it physically and mentally exhausted me.

I'm not ashamed to say that. Too often, women don't vocalize or acknowledge our stresses for fear someone will recognize us for what we are: human. Breaking news: we don't always don a Superwoman cape. And when we do, it often needs ironing and we're too busy or too tired to do it. I know I'm not alone in sometimes wanting to wave a white flag of surrender. *I give up! I'm not Zooming anything for anyone today, period.*

We will do whatever it takes to protect our children. And if that means jumping back into the never-ending virtual vortex this fall, we will do it. But I urge my fellow ballerinas to forgive yourselves for feeling overwhelmed at times.

Do not suffocate. Breathe. Pray. Keep moving with exercise. Mask up and go for a walk each day. Talk with friends, spiritual advisors or professional therapists. Create breaks by asking others to virtually hang out with your kids.

My ex-husband, a health and wellness enthusiast, lives in another state. When I began caving from the 24/7 lockdown pressure with our sons, I asked him to lead them in virtual yoga three times a week. My sister pitches in as well, playing an online "Jeopardy"-type game with them weekly for an hour, sometimes more. Their support gives me a chance to relax. But here's the key: I asked for their help. No one can read your mind. Tell others how you're feeling.

And when you start running on empty this fall- and you will- don't feel guilty. Kick the ballerina slippers under the bed. Hang up the Superwoman cape. Take a break with that perfectly-paired match of red wine and chicken nuggets, and know that you're not alone. We're dancing together through this crazy ballet known as 2020.

Heidi M. Barker is a child of God, devoted mom, communications expert, writer and speaker. She is based in Miami and Chicago (you can guess which seasons she spends in each.) Follow her on Twitter and Instagram @heidibmedia.

WHY BLACK TRANS WOMEN ARE ESSENTIAL TO OUR FUTURE
BY IMARA JONES

Trans people are not new. We have always been here. As long as there's been recorded human history, we have always existed. But we have been written out of the human story—and when you come from a community that is without a full range of possibility models, it raises the question, in yourself as well as others, of whether or not you deserve rights or a place in society. Because everything generally in society fails Black trans women, that's how we get to epidemic levels of violence, mass levels of unemployment and a lack of education for us.

For years, trans people have been marginalized within movements because of the idea that anything not accessible to mainstream society is damaging to the prospect of Black liberation. But we've learned from history that this incremental approach has been a failure—because when not everyone has the same rights, the rights of everyone are actually incredibly fragile. In the words of Martin Luther King: "No one is free until we are all free."

So there cannot be Black Lives Matter without the centering of Black trans women. Because if we're able to secure the rights for the most marginalized, then everyone is going to have rights. What we're proposing in this latest BLM moment is a reimagination and an expansion of Blackness—and a fundamental understanding that we're all going, or none of us is.

Black trans women are essential to creating the future, because when everything fails you, you're more clearly able to reimagine what it would look like if things worked. This is why Black trans women are, in many cases, the most visionary and progressive leaders within social justice movements. As a leader of the Stonewall uprising, Marsha P. Johnson understood the link between Black civil rights, women's rights, gay rights and trans rights, and was crucial in the struggle for liberation for all of them.

Now Black trans women are leaders of radical efforts, including Toni-Michelle Williams in Atlanta, who is helping to reimagine how we imagine a world without incarceration; Ianne Fields Stewart who is fighting food insecurity; and Micky B at the Transgender Law Center, who is coordinating a project reimagining Black trans liberation and life across every spectrum. And there are countless others doing the same across the country in every way that you can think of.

The future is trans because the ways we've gone about organizing human life have changed in really fundamental ways. Trans people, just through our existence, show the power and the resilience of change, and possibility of how we can do things differently. We are creating a future less defined by gender roles, and defined more by what we can create than what we can destroy. And because we've already had to do this work, we are essential to building this future.

The events of the past couple months have created new space for us. But the key thing to remember is that in the long fight for civil rights in the U.S., no one moment is ever definitive. As important as this shift and recognition of Black trans women that's started to take place has been, we have an incredibly long way to go.

Previously published in TIME.

Imara Jones is a journalist and the creator of the multimedia platform TransLash media.

WHAT DONALD TRUMP UNDERSTANDS ABOUT AMERICAN MEN
BY JACKSON KATZ

Trump understands something fundamental about manhood in a patriarchal culture: A lot of men fear being 'unmanned' more than they value democracy.

Donald Trump's many shortcomings of character, empathy and intellectual depth are well known. But he has one quality—aside from his inherited wealth—that has gotten him very far in life, most recently in politics.

He possesses an intuitive grasp of the deep-seated desires, frustrated dreams, and seething resentments of millions of American men, especially White men.

He might not identify with most of them: He admires rich tycoons and sports heroes and regards most working and middle-class men as losers.

But he knows why these men identify with him, and throughout his long career as a bombastic real estate developer and reality TV star, he found ways to monetize their affections. With his turn to electoral politics in 2015, it was only natural he would seek to alchemize their fascination with him into political support.

Trump's unexpected victory in the presidential election of 2016 was the result of a constellation of historic cultural and political forces. But practically speaking, he won because he was able to win the votes of an overwhelming majority of the White male vote.

Just look at the numbers. Among college-educated White men, Trump beat Hillary Clinton 51 percent to 36 percent. For White men with a high school education, he won by a stunning 71 to 23 percent margin— the largest among any candidate in exit polls since 1980.

The only way he can win this time is by preserving and expanding this dramatic level of support. In fact, one of the most striking features of the 2020 election is the enormous gender gap. In a recent ABC/Washington Post poll, Joe Biden led by 23 points among women, while the candidates were tied among men.

Most analyses of this gap focus on Trump's tanking support among women, especially suburban White women. Trump's standing among men—especially White men, his biggest supporters—is treated as a given and is rarely discussed in any depth.

Political scientists and media commentators have long noted that Trumpism as a political movement is not as much about issues as it is about identity. This point was driven home during the Republican National Convention, which was such an unapologetic vehicle for Trump's cult of personality that the GOP didn't even bother to offer a party platform.

The conventional wisdom about Trumpism is that it's driven by White racial resentment, whether in the form of opposition to immigration from south of the border, or old-fashioned anti-Black racism that sadly —more than half a century since passage of the Civil Rights Act—has never really gone away.

But, as a just-released documentary called "The Man Card" that I helped produce makes crystal clear, Trumpism is not just a White identity movement; it is a White male identity movement.

Donald Trump knows this. He figured out a long time ago that by presenting himself in the media as a kind of throwback playboy and tough-guy businessman, he could appeal to millions of White men—and a much lesser but still notable number of White women—who respond positively to that retro performance.

There is little evidence that Donald Trump cares even a little about the lives and daily struggles of White working and middle-class men. But he instinctually understands that countless men—in an era of feminism and increasing gender fluidity—crave respect as men and long for the return of old-fashioned patriarchal authority.

Unlike the former Hollywood actor Ronald Reagan, who in the late 1970s tapped into the all-American cowboy archetype and fashioned himself as a John Wayne-like character who would restore national greatness by riding into town to rescue the culture from the feminizing forces of weak-kneed liberalism, Trump knew when he got into politics that he was more believable as a kind of anti-hero.

As New York Times television critic James Poniewozik put it, in order for Trump to have been elected in the first place, a large enough portion of America had to "accept the sales pitch" that the president did not need to be "morally admirable, or trustworthy, or empathetic, or self-sacrificing, or curious, or self-reflective, or capable of acting as though other people's interests were as important as his own—as long as they believed he could do the job they wanted done."

That job was reclaiming White men's cultural centrality at the end of a dying era. As Poniewozik notes, "From his earliest days in the tabloids, the character of Donald Trump was a performance of hyperbolic maleness."

In the 2016 campaign he implicitly and sometimes explicitly ran on masculinity "as an idea, a Strangelovian value, a vital essence to be preserved." He marketed himself as "a political Viagra pill for a following anxious about its potency."

Trump's White male voter base had already been primed for his arrival by the rapid growth of conservative media over the past generation, starting with the meteoric rise of right-wing talk radio host Rush Limbaugh in the late 1980s, and the creation of the Fox News Channel under the leadership of Roger Ailes in 1996.

From the very beginning of his thirty-year run as the undisputed king of talk radio, Limbaugh, an exceptionally talented vaudevillian showman, made the denigration of feminists and an unapologetic celebration of old-fashioned White male authority central features of his bloviating and boorish stage persona. Not surprisingly, his large audience consisted mainly (but not exclusively) of White men, especially those over fifty years of age.

This was the same demographic that Roger Ailes targeted with Fox News, which became a vehicle for Ailes's brand of angry and paranoid conservatism, in which White men were the victims of condescension and contempt from sneering elites whose liberalism, multiculturalism and feminism were "wussifying" a once-great country.

These media-savvy entrepreneurs understood that millions of White men felt disrespected and adrift in a changing country and were ready to fight back—if only they could find the right political champion to channel their resentments.

Donald Trump was that champion. For a time, his relentlessly aggressive attacks against his opponents and constant rhetorical bullying effectively silenced most opposition on the right, or in the Republican Party. No one wanted to be the next "Low-energy Jeb," or "Little Marco"—2016 GOP rivals who Trump not only defeated, but emasculated.

Trump might not be a sophisticated political thinker or student of history, but he understands something fundamental about manhood in a patriarchal culture: The system remains in place because a majority of men fear being "unmanned" and losing the respect of other men more than they value abstract concepts like commitment to scientific reason, equal justice under law or even democracy itself.

It takes a great deal of self-confidence and even courage for men to withstand attacks on their good standing in the brotherhood. And as the former Republican congressman and TV host Joe Scarborough says, "We have learned all too often during the Trump presidency that there are few courageous leaders within the Republican congressional caucus or behind the pulpits of the evangelical community's most powerful churches."

But the popularity of a bully is fragile because it is based on others' perceptions of his strength, not the real thing. And so the tide began to turn against Trump once he started to show signs of electoral vulnerability.

After a chaotic term marked by deep corruption and perpetual scandal, and above all by his egregiously incompetent leadership in response to the coronavirus pandemic, the voices of his critics began to grow louder.

Long before his foray into electoral politics, the bombastic real estate developer and reality TV star had been the object of ridicule and derision among progressives and especially among feminists, who were more contemptuous than impressed by his deep misogyny and cartoonish displays of masculine bravado. But something shifted when they were joined by a growing number of White men, including those with traditional "masculine" credentials.

When retired military leaders began to publicly criticize the president, including some who had worked directly with him in the White House, they provided cover for other White men to do so. They could now oppose Trump and not have to worry that doing so would make them appear soft and "unmanly"; their criticisms of him could instead be understood as stemming from differences with him on policy, and disapproval of his temperament and style of leadership.

If Donald Trump loses to Joe Biden on November 3, as most polls say is likely to happen, it will be because tens of millions of women and people of color turned out to reject his misogyny and racism, his scapegoating of immigrants, and his sowing of conflict and division—as well as his general managerial ineptitude.

But it will also be because they were joined by a critical mass of White men, who were able to resist the pressures imposed on them by the forces of White male identity politics in order to vote for the greater interest of the country and its people.

Previously published at http://msmagazine.com/.

Jackson Katz, Ph.D., is an educator, author, lecturer, and expert on masculinities, politics, violence, and culture. He is the creator and co-producer of the recently released video The Man Card: White Male Identity Politics from Nixon to Trump, *available at themancardmovie.com. His personal website is jacksonkatz.com*

A BRIEF CELEBRATION
BY JAMES PHOENIX

On a Saturday afternoon, I see people flooding the streets across American cities after the networks projected Joe Biden as the victor of the 2020 presidential election. I feel a sense of optimism and relief knowing the election is over. It is a moment to celebrate because the former reality show host and failed businessman will no longer be president. These last four years were uncomfortable and brought much uncertainty leading up to the election.

Yet, I know that having Trump out of the White House is not the solution, but a step toward a different direction. I voted for the Biden-Harris ticket because Trump had to leave. I did not support either candidate during the Democratic primaries. I know Biden is a centrist Democrat who is friendly with Wall Street and is fundamentally not a candidate focused on pushing an agenda with significant changes. I have similar feelings about Kamala Harris. During her candidacy, she did not appear confident in her political positions, and I found her prosecutorial record in California problematic. What I want to see are candidates across all political positions who support progressive policies such as universal healthcare, a Green New Deal, real legislation addressing systemic racism, and significant taxation on the wealthiest Americans. To expect President Biden and Vice President Harris to support such an agenda is not a given.

It was utterly disgusting to see more than seventy-four million people vote for Trump though. I knew his supporters were motivated especially after seeing them attend large rallies during a pandemic and disregarding safety protocols. Even though the polling was in favor of Biden in numerous states, it did not seem there was significant enthusiasm to vote for Biden. If anything, it was enthusiasm to vote out Trump. Regardless, the results looked too similar to the 2016 election. That was a learning moment.

What I learned from this election is that Trump's support is stronger than I thought. This country is deeply divided politically, and millions of Republicans will stick with supporting him or a similar candidate regardless of how such a candidate acts or says. His racist statements, xenophobic remarks, consistent lying, separation of families - I can go on and on. This was not enough for Republican voters to quit supporting him. How can we expect policies that bring significant change when 48 percent of Americans decided to reelect a former reality show host?

Who is completely fine with the GOP holding power in Congress? It is even reaching a point where basic caring for people is being challenged with our current political environment. I cannot be surprised, but I had hoped that more than enough people would have broken away from Trump. It did not happen.

Although Biden won the election, the celebration was short. Democrats lost seats in the House of Representatives, and did not win enough seats to take a majority in the Senate. They might be fortunate if they win two seats in Georgia in January 2021, but I am not expecting that to happen. This means it will be more difficult for progressive, or even watered-down progressive version legislation to pass through Congress. It will require Republican support to pass anything of significance that Democratic voters would want. We also are stuck with a solid conservative majority on the Supreme Court without Senate control.

What does this mean for me? I am one person with mixed feelings about this election, and feel uncertain about what is to come in the near future. I know our future is based on what Americans want. Hoping for politicians to do the right thing is not a sustainable strategy. The same energy Americans had against Donald Trump must persist under a

Biden presidency. What I fear is such energy dissipating these next four years and it results in a more empowered Republican base. If we want anything, it requires consistent pressure on those elected to political offices at all levels and not only during a presidential election. Nothing I am saying here is new, but it requires holding the people we vote for accountable.

This is about more than a president. We must look at ourselves to determine what really matters. Too many voters were content with a second term of Trump and gridlock in Congress. Too many wanted a future orchestrated by White supremacy and big business. Too many wanted lying politicians. This pattern cannot continue if we are to be a country that cares for its people, and can be respected by nations across the world. There is much fighting and work ahead. Any change that occurs will be gradual and will not happen overnight. We are at a crossroads. We will determine the direction this country takes.

James Phoenix is currently a high school history teacher in Memphis, TN, and has interests in writing on topics related to politics and American society. You can contact him by email at jamesrphoenix@gmail.com, or follow him on Facebook.

2020: A LOSS OF BALANCE AND INNOCENCE
BY JEANNINE ETTER

2020 for me began with a traditional New Year's Eve house party. It's become a ritual to meet with friends on NYE and create elaborate vision boards for what we'd like to manifest in the coming year, all while playing chess, cards, and dominoes, listening to good music and enjoying Black cultural New Year's food -black eyed peas, collard greens, and cornbread. For those who are unaware, a vision board is made by cutting out pictures from magazines that depict what you'd like to see in your life, and pasting them creatively on a large piece of cardstock paper. The idea is to look at this board every day and take steps to make your dreams a reality.

My vision board was wildly optimistic this year. In addition to my standard inclusions of increases of income, increases in good health, and increases in love prospects, this year also included an increase in multiple travel destinations. I've only traveled outside the U.S. once - to Cuba a gazillion years ago. And this was the year to change all of that. It was 2020. Just the number alone seemed magical. Mystical. 2020. The year of balance. 2020 turned out to be like 2012 was predicted to be according to the Mayan calendar that suggested an ending of sorts. And this year was actually 2012, until September, according to the Ethiopian calendar. But I didn't know any of that yet... France, Spain, the UK, Mexico, and Bali were first up on my list.

A mandatory statewide stay-at-home order in California was issued on the first day of spring on March 19 and changed all that. My passport issued at the end of 2019 is still stampless and empty. While I do have friends who are traveling internationally undeterred by a little thing like a pandemic, I'm not prepared to take the extra precautions like quarantining for weeks, nor am I prepared to take that extra time off, as many of them are able to work remotely, quarantined or not. I work in media. I am an essential worker. Since I work for a daily newscast, I must go into a relatively empty building. I have not had the luxury of adding extra drama to a travel itinerary. And although my spirits have remained relatively high through most of this, it has not been high enough to desire to travel before I see a light at the end of the COVID tunnel that is sunlight, and not an oncoming train.

In the meantime, I've satiated my need for travel by going on long road trips, camping, and finding new hiking trails throughout the Bay Area. Those hikes were temporarily halted by poor air quality from historic, unprecedented wildfires in California due to climate change. One morning, the sky was apocalyptic orange from the fires raging across the state. After yet another COVID detour, I shifted gears and ordered a pair of roller skates and joined the resurgence of a skating community reminiscent of the 70s. We skate on weekends around Lake Merritt and on Saturday nights at basketball courts where the hoops have been removed due to COVID restrictions...all while wearing masks, of course.

In my spiritual practice, I understand the concept of rolling with the punches when necessary, staying grateful for every gracious gift and trying to see the bigger picture beyond what my human senses can understand. So I watched 2020 unfold, somewhat detached, as if looking at a science fiction movie. Fires. Locusts. Plagues. Mandatory masks. A narcissist in the White House who could arguably rival any villain, real or fictional. Everything was surreal with a dream-like quality. The Matrix. Inception. Star Wars. Planet of the Apes. And watching the unfolding events of COVID 19 spiraling out of control and a Republican party growing more psychotic by the day.

The murders of George Floyd, Breonna Taylor, and Ahmaud Arbery were flashpoints for racial reckoning in America. Protests broke out worldwide, and it was good to see the powers that be being brought to task. Police officers were being fired. And yet, peaceful protests were met with police violence. Rebellion was called rioting. Property was deemed more valuable than human life. And far right extremists were traveling to protests against police brutality "helping" to maintain "law and order," sometimes fatally so. Hope was met with new examples of new lows. And the days rolled on...

This was also a presidential election year and, in late August, the Republican National Convention. The Democratic National Convention was a disappointment for me as no progressives had a seat at the table; however, the RNC was a circus like nothing I'd ever witnessed. I remember thinking that this was how the beginning of every dystopian movie I'd ever seen must have started. A Handmaid's Tale. The Hunger Games. V for Vendetta. 1984. And while the election results in November, with Biden winning the presidency, provided a glimmer of hope for many, it was not a New Hope for the rebels (or for the progressives either) as referenced in the Star Wars movie franchise. And it seemed that in the end, many in the rebel forces did not want to topple the Empire. They wanted to join it. And be validated by it.

And so now, nearing the end of a historic year like no other, it seems as if a portal is closing and a new day is on the horizon. As we move into the dark winter, things seem to be shifting toward the light, eagerly awaiting January 1, 2021. Not ecstatic hope. But soberingly cautious optimism. An end. A beginning. Now when I look back on how

BY JEROME HURT

Hi Jazzmine. My Princess. I know it has been a stressful four years. Hearing all of the things coming from the current occupant of the White House pointed toward women, particularly Black women. The disrespect towards White House press correspondent, April Ryan, bothered me because of the way she was treated and not backed and supported by her colleagues. I wondered if it was because she is a Black Woman. Omarosa, a former aide to the current occupant was called a dog. So many other stories and cases showed us exactly what a pig he is, but worse, what others will say and do in support of him.

Then at about 11:00 am last Saturday, it was announced that former Vice President Joe Biden and Senator Kamala Harris had won the election. Jazz, I screamed. I yelled out the window that it was finally over. The reign of terror and tyranny heaped upon us was going to end. Now please understand, I know our work is not done, not by a long shot. But just as I hoped that first time you were old enough to vote in an election for Barack Obama, I'm full of hope that a Black woman making it to

Vice President is empowering.

Seeing Kamala Harris on stage gave me pride and the ability to show you better than I can tell you. Baby Girl you can do anything. There is space for you as a Black woman. All of the hopes and dreams I had for you the day you entered this world, is backed by you seeing representation in places and spaces where when I was your age, I could have never conceived.

Kamala Harris's parents came here from other countries just as your Mom did. When you were born, I was so determined to make this world a better place for you and other women as well. It hasn't been easy, but having a Black, Indian, woman as the Vice President is a move in the right direction. I desire to push forward in my work to make this planet a better place for you, for all women, but particularly, Black women. Things will not get better quickly, but your Dad, the first man to say "I Love You", is working tirelessly to make it better. I know you know that.

Jazzy Girl, I am proud of you. I know how hard you have worked to be where you are at this time in your life. You have overcome so much and I am here for all of the greatness that is still to come. As your father, I want to say, believe in your dreams. There is not a thing on this planet that you cannot do. You still have the softer side of my heart and I Love you unconditionally. Be encouraged that your voice will be represented. There are many more #BlackGirlMagic opportunities for you to come.

Love You

Dad

Jerome Hurt is a writer who is also a Financial Professional and Founder and CEO of BuyBlack4Life. Jerome is an activist, organizer, and passionate about fighting for equal treatment and rights for Black and Brown Communities. You can follow him on IG @BuyBlack4Life

WHAT IS YOUR FINAL ANSWER?
BY JOHN AGNELLI

I see this world through a video camera that could define the man I am and not today. I see the world using my video camera but need you to hold it to video tape what I am about to say. I see the world using this video camera and realize I cannot edit what I don't want to face or am in denial of. I see the world through this video camera in hopes of catching just a glimpse of Superman saving the day.

I look at this world as a movie that keeps being rewound over, and over and over again with just different cast of characters wearing different styles that meet the current fad. I see this world on a Hulu and wonder when that too will seem a bit outdated and or of poor quality. We are the people of this United States looking so hard to see Superman, and in the meantime we just wait for her to arrive while kryptonite is being thrown at our children in what should be their very own Avatar.

We look at people as we do actors and actresses ranking them in classes of A-list, B-list or less. We move around this planet following some yellow brick road in hopes that we don't Crash into each other in search for the American Dream or is it the American Tale. These days seem to be about Wall Street, forget about Little House on the Prairie, Sesame Street and 21 Jump Street and don't even think about Mr. Rogers Neighborhood, it foreclosed months ago before they figured out that there was a need to freeze eviction while COVID-19 assaulted Maslow's Hierarchy of Needs. This is why I am waiting for my Superman, where is she and when will he come.

Just look at what we have done to the elderly, we seem to think that what we are doing simulates that of Driving Ms. Daisy when in reality if you walk through a nursing home it is more like the Titanic except they can't jump as Rose did. This is why I am waiting for my Superman, where is he and when will she come.

When we examine the financial disparity between races, we can see with great ease the color of the Lion King as well as what color most movements in American History X are and it's not The Color Purple. While the environmental sustainability movement is a predominantly White movement our globe continues to soar through the levels of Fahrenheit 9/11 in talk and rhetoric instead of creating communities that live in peace and harmony. This is why I am waiting for my Superman, where is she and when will he come.

When we see the poor on the streets we are shocked and impressed by the stories portrayed as acts of kindness when they should be seen as acts of obligation to our fellow brothers and sisters. What we can't debate is that we are a country that really believes in the Fields of Dreams, but we simply do not know how to make this field accessible for all people, even the ones that have flown Over the Cuckoo's Nest. This is why I am waiting for my Superman, where is she and when will he come.

If we truly believe as a people that there are Six Degrees of Separation, then why are we not trying to know more people, genuinely without an agenda or judgment as witnessed by the assumptions you will make when you see Three Men and a Baby strolling through Greenwich Village? This is why I am waiting for my Superman, where is he and when will she come.

In 2020 we are reminded daily through failed but honest politicians and children committing suicide of our journey to Brokeback Mountain because it's still broke and we can't simply just Rent this special interest group while we are In The Heights of a political season. November cannot be the only Season Of Love for a community that is under attack. If the amount of young children that committed suicide for being gay, had caught COVID19 we would call it an outbreak tittering towards the level of an epidemic. This is why I am waiting for my superman when will he come.

When we truly examine marriage in America, we simply can't assume we are having a reunion with Madea. We can't just expect that at my Best Friend's Wedding, A Big Fat Greek Wedding or even if I attend my Big Fat Gay Italian Wedding that this will be the light to illuminate the path for others to follow through some Footloose of Dirty Dancing through the very biblical interpretation robbed from Notorious RBG. It is clear that the conservative spectrum would only embrace folks coming together in the name of love through the images of Ghost or is that a Figment of my Imagination. We must see All In The Family as equals through bad times and Good Times as it clearly can be at minimum understood through Liberty and Justice for all that it is Diff'rent Strokes for different folks. The Brady Bunch can be the facade seen in a Small Wonder with robotic children and Michael Brady, but we still must hold those accountable those who commit and embrace domestic violence even if we are Silenced By The Lambs while they feel forced to be Sleeping With The Enemy. This is why I am waiting for my Superman, where is he and when will she come.

Why am I here today writing before you? This is my 13 trillion dollar COVID Cares question! I didn't really know at first. I didn't really have an idea until I reflected on the movie Waiting for Superman. I cried copiously at the end (Guilt) and renewed my commitment to education and society. I realized at that defining moment that I can no longer wait for Superman, I have to believe in her or him before and in me. It occurred to me that I can no longer stand on the sidelines with my cape thinking can alone fix the problems of the world. I can no longer assume that I am on Gilligan's Island playing a high stake game of Apprentice with the future of democracy in my hands knowing that at any point since I am older I can say, your fired and you can't phone a friend or even use a lifeline but attempt to overturn an election in theory through toxic rhetoric decisively used to slaughter Americans seeking hope and change. This is why I am looking for my Superman man, where is he and when will she come.

You trust me as an adult and I don't even deserve this level of trust based on history and her story. I am the same adult that was to protect you from Star Wars in the Reagan years, yet voted or not which is voting on this war that your children will be forced to pay for in yet another sequel which one may call the Empire Strikes Back but it internally is feeling like Armageddon. I am the same adult that told you it will be ok, and that hole in the ozone continues to open sucking up life of rainforest, killing species to extinction that no human can clone or knows how to bring back from the endangered species list that this generation future has now been added to but again this is why I am so desperately waiting for my Superman where is she and when will he come.

I am the same adult that demanded respect, sharing, and peace, yet fund war through taxes, keep and waste food for myself and still allow my ego to form opinions and policy to insure that of the 2.1 million incarcerated people in the united states of America 85% Black and Latino, yet I think I am Superman looking for Lois Lane, who am I kidding. I am forced to watch this movie with a critical eye. An eye that knows and benefited from 34k a year tax dollars pay for per inmate in our system equating to 136,000.00 in 4 years, in comparison imagine what we could do in 4 years if each of us were given that money specifically for higher education and the long term impact this investment could have, the Price is Right and it could turn into a Wheel of Fortune but as I noted, I am waiting for my Superman where is she and when will he come.

This movie will continue to play and will have a sequel sadly maybe two or three. With each generation before me, we are guaranteed very little so we roll the dice, we pick a number and we dictate who should be educated in the top schools and who should not. Even though we understand that knowledge is power and no one can take that away from you! Do you have what it takes to be Superman or superwoman in a world in need of compassion, even those living with Tom Hanks in Philadelphia?

This is the question we ask our young people in hopes that they will take the torch and run like Forrest Gump, this is the question that was asked of us when we were children growing up around the icons of John Lennon thinking he was a part of E.T. but had not yet phoned home. Even then many were passing judgment because he was a dreamer, but guess what, he is not the only one, and I really know someday you will join us and this world could potentially live as one.

This is the true Sound of Music being echoed from the Sands of Iwo Jima to Montana, from Pearl Harbor to a Miracle on 34th Street. Are you the Superman I have been waiting for? Are you her? Are you the one that will save us? I thought so and Alex, that is my final answer.

John Agnelli originally from Pawling, NY, is an educator and pioneer in the social justice movement, developing and teaching the course "Men and Masculinity" at Pace University, and "Social Issues" at SUNY New Paltz. After a three year bout with addiction to opioids from a doctor's order and looking up at rock bottom, John's painful yet transformative journey through recovery, and leading an addiction facility in West Palm Beach, returned him to serving young people as the Director of the Boys & Girls Club on the Palmetto Campus. John has celebrated his sobriety through all parts of life and can be reached at JohnF.agnelli@bgcmanatee.org

JOE WHO
BY JORJINA KOFFI

It was a beautiful, sunny Saturday afternoon and I was still in bed on yet another Zoom call. Topic of discussion: current emotional climate in this country—a debilitating pandemic, social injustice and the lack of indictments for the killers of Breonna Taylor, a drama-filled election—the Zoom where it happens was heavy.

On screen, in the middle of discussion, one of my co-workers stopped speaking as she checked her phone. She said,
"Joe Biden won!" Well—

I hear my phone buzz. Text from my Brooklyn home girl…

WE GOT A NEW PRESIDENT!

Yeah right! I thought—not because I didn't want that abomination out of office—I definitely did. I just thought about some of my former classmates in Indiana having no problem throwing support to one of the worst governors in Hoosier history. I thought about how long it really takes to count and audit those ballots. Yeah right!

"OH MY GOSH!" Another co-worker shouted. "Joe Biden won!" In a sea of vanilla and spice, there were seven chocolate Sistahs on this call. We managed to look at each other on screen. Our thoughts…

JOE WHO?!

We weren't thinking about Joe (glad he won, though). We were thinking of Kamala! Senator Harris, now Vice President-elect Kamala Harris, is the physical embodiment of historic firsts:

*First female VP

*First Black VP (after having the first Black POTUS)

*First Asian-American VP

*First biracial VP

On screen, seven chocolate Sistahs started crying, tears flowing like the River Jordan as we basked in this moment of greatness.

Then reality hits.

I text my best friend—she still lives in Indiana. I told her the good news, then I told her to be careful...

Jorjina Koffi is a Brooklyn-based actress, writer, and educator. Follow her on Instagram @JinaKaye.

LOVE THY CHRISTIAN NEIGHBOR
BY JUDITH MALVEAUX-ELLERBE

This year's election season provided many Christians of color, like myself, with moments of perplexity – and clarity – extending beyond those from the abnormalities experienced in the COVID-19 "new normal." Not only are we collecting disinfectant cleaner and toilet paper while isolating, we're also openly questioning who is the Jesus that many self-proclaimed Christians reference to defend their discriminatory dogma.

Christians of color are not ignorant of Christianity's institutional inconsistencies. We know our melanin-enhanced relationship with the teachings of Christ doesn't always align with some of our cross-wearing,

Christ-professing, faithful fellows. I mean, so-called "Christians" used the Bible to justify forcibly enslaving Africans more than a thousand years after Christ commanded us to "Love thy neighbor as thyself." I guess Jesus meant any neighbor not from the Motherland, though I haven't found that assertion in any translation so far.

But, because we love Christ, we accept the misapplication, misinterpretation, outright bastardization of His teachings, and the Old Testament application to cover the failings of men. We accept it because we know they do not speak for all of us. They especially don't speak for many Christians of color. Jesus' teachings, we know, don't justify racism or radical hatred. Bigots justify those things.

Then came the end-of-days, the apocalyptic year that is 2020.

Killer hornets. Check.

Wildfires. Check.

Hurricanes. Check.

An actual plague complete with makeshift morgues, medical supply shortages, and statewide quarantines. Check. Check. Check.

It was like each month looked at its predecessor's perils and said, "Hold my beer."

As many of us studied The Book of Revelation to determine if we really are in the last days, we witnessed Christian leaders hijacking scripture to justify words and deeds that would have made Jesus turn over a table or two. And, with this 2020 election, we've seen claimants to the Kingdom overtly laud the leaders who fit into the "right" intersection of the Venn Diagram of beliefs they use to determine endorsement. "Pro-life" as long as they aren't born yet. "Pro-America" as long as you never contest the greatness of America's history or structural systems.

It's not really about a person's faith, life, or character. It's about their political positions. The hyperbole offered in religious justification of racially prejudiced, polarizing politics has berthed unbridled backing for some – and condemnation and admonition for others – and it all seems to fall along lines abandoning Christian principles. We've seen this script before, but social and cable media make it feel like the Amplified translation, not the typical King James.

The pathological liar? "He jokes a lot."

The Adulterer? "He's just terribly friendly."

Idol worship? "We don't worship you, but could you autograph our Bible?"

Many so-called "Christian Influencers" condemn world leaders for humanitarian words and actions. They then quote scripture to embrace or undergird actions of leaders espousing hatred and violence because, after all, "God ordained them to lead." If God ordained someone because they were democratically elected, then why demonize those who were also democratically elected? Did their ordination get stuck in transit? Maybe that's part of the new New Testament.

It's an insult to instruct Black Christians to embrace the racism and xenophobia embedded in the evangelism and propaganda spewed from the pulpits of many Christian mega – and minor – churches to the community. We're not so saved that we don't see hypocrisy. We have the wisdom to discern opinion from scripture.

We can no longer pretend to be comfortable with microaggressions masquerading as "message" and bigotry buoyed by Bible verses stitched together with threads of self-superiority and nationalism. If faith fuels their actions, then where exactly does their faith lie? We ask because the "Jesus in us" doesn't recognize the "Jesus in them," and it's not so easy to love. A loving savior doesn't ridicule and threaten. A servant leader sets an example of selfless excellence in service to others – not inhumanity.

So, where do we go from here? What scripture can be referenced to urge us to unlearn or overlook what we've seen and know? Only God knows that. And maybe one day, these people of faith will know God, too.

Judith Malveaux-Ellerbe is a Charlotte, North Carolina based writer, communications professional and educator. She has worked as a newspaper reporter and public relations professional in North Carolina, Virginia, Florida and her home-state, Louisiana. Her email is judithamalveauxpr@gmail.com.

NOT TODAY!
BY KAYINDE HARRIS

My sacred breath, I own. It belongs to me, no one else. Just like I own my mind, the way that I communicate, and the way that I think, my air is my ceremonial space, an elemental gift that I am in control of. That I am capable of chiseling into new thought forms and ideas. My free will and ability to exhale any stress, on my terms, inhaling ease and peace, is my superpower. However, this year, 2020, I found myself in a conflict that I never anticipated. A conflict that would test my power and endurance, and my faith.

On March 19, my family and I were diagnosed with COVID-19, a disease that seemed so foreign in nature one month prior to becoming a space invader that infiltrated my home, and my body. A disease that I watched nightly, from a distance, with an empathetic heart as I witnessed the escalating numbers of lives that were fading away overseas, never considering that within one month, this virus would become a tangible reality, finding its way to me and mine. I was humbled and paralyzed with a fear that I desperately tried to conceal from my family. The media often highlights the effects that COVID-19 has on the elderly, and though both my parents are relatively active and youthful seniors, the news that they too were exposed to the disease terrified me. One evening in February, before our diagnoses, I recall watching a segment on the horrors of this disease on a small community in Italy. I cried as the reporter went through pages and pages of obituaries of all the lives lost, while daily numbers were creeping up into the thousands. Even still, the virus was thousands of miles away.

Initially, I was never afraid for my own well being, but the well being of my immediate family members. My parents both have minor pre-existing conditions, and my sister suffers from asthma. When I learned that we were exposed to COVID, I distinctly remember sharing with the nurse practitioner how worried I was about my parents. Her advice to me? Pray, and remember that 85% of those infected experience a mild case with a full recovery. Okay, so there is some hope here.

COVID-19 is misleading. Initially, you feel like you are battling a cold or the beginning of the flu. Not too bad, right? Nah! This ain't like the flu! It's an insidious entity that challenges your entire temple - mind, body, and spirit - simultaneously, and the game that is played is the most dangerous one of all; it's a role playing game featuring a virus that tests your wit and will power. How do you try to win? You have to outsmart the opponent. You can't give in!

We survived the weekend in good spirits with mild symptoms, but four days after diagnoses, the battle began with my sister ending up in the ER and my mother developing a fever that would waiver between 100-101 for nearly nine days. All senses of smell and taste vanished for everyone. I am an educator, and the day that my symptoms intensified, I logged in to greet my students. It was the first day of remote learning, and the last thing that I wanted to do was vanish for a few days while battling this beast. In fact, teaching brought me solace, it delivered consistency and hope, during a moment where hope seemed to be fleeting, at times. I say that this virus is both a physical and mental challenge because as your body is fighting this foreign entity in what feels like an army gone rogue, you are constantly working towards preserving your mind and your sanity. So, being present in my classroom, although virtual, brought me peace and provided comfort in my familiar, in my sacred space, and those were moments that I needed to sustain my spirit. I recall countless nights of slipping into deep depression and anxiety, two symptoms connected to this viral outlaw, while glaring at the television and wondering why the media felt it necessary to share the rising death toll ticker, an ominous reminder of the fate of anyone who comes into contact with the virus, with subliminal undertones reminding all that this could be you. My soundtrack came courtesy of the numerous sirens that would race down the street, my house is twelve blocks away from a public hospital. I felt as if I were transported into that scene from Orfeu

Negro, when Eurydice's lifeless body is carried away in the ambulance as the sirens fade into the depths of the Underworld. The sounds and scenarios were repetitive, paralyzing, and overwhelming, but again, you have to remain two steps ahead of this opponent.

Two steps ahead and conscious of fear. Fear is all about perception. There is the school that acknowledges fear as the notion of failing to have faith. While I, in this moment, acknowledged a greater truth about fear. Fear can also be the fuel that inspires survival. I met fear face forward, at the crossroads, somewhere between day seven and ten, feeling its eeriness and its manipulative nature in trying to capture my mind in this weakened state, in a house full of achy bones and stuffy heads, with chests heavy like lead, legs listless, and minds entangled in dreams incredibly surreal that you are constantly trying to decipher the difference between reality and surrealism. So, It was here, standing in that crossroad, standing in my kitchen over pots of hot chicken broth and thyme tea, thinking about my sister in ER having her breathing monitored, thinking of my mom who had a consistent fever and who could barely walk to the bathroom. Thinking of my cats who began to experience symptoms, yes, just like us, with waning appetites and heavy breathing, it was then that I summoned my Arya Stark warrior alter ego and jokingly, yet assuredly uttered the words aloud to myself in that kitchen - "Not today!". There I stood, just me and fear, and God. And then came the warmth, then came the reminder, the assurance, that no matter what, you always have the power. When you grow weak and you begin to feel defeated, Spirit intervenes sending messengers and messages of reassurance, pouring into your soul. It's the little things that you believe in fighting for. You fight for hugs, for smiles, you fight for love. You fight for your family, and you change the game plan. And just like that, with your Arya Stark on, you remember that everything that you have lived for and that has molded your spirit and that has brought you joy in the face of family, is worth fighting for. The goal, change the game and play it better. Mind over matter is real! It's a life jacket that appears out of nowhere sustaining you and reeling you back to hope and purpose. And so that day forward, the purpose was not about me, but about doing everything that I could to lift up my family. We turned off the news and only watched for one hour adopting comedy and Hallmark movies as our new source of entertainment. We weren't avoiding or escaping the crisis, but riding the tide and finding love and laughter and cleansing the mind to visualize some semblance of peace and positivity.

Nine months later, and I am still humbled with an even more profound respect for the Creator, faith, and the importance of staying in the moment (literally, one moment at a time). My heart flows in an abundance of love and gratitude for all of the family and friends who consistently checked in, sent a smiley face here or there, sent words of encouragement, music, remedies and recipes, virtual hugs and love, and overall support when warm hellos felt like timely magical healing antidotes that could feed the soul with enough fuel to get to that next moment. The isolation is deep, especially when you are trying to combat this. Folks, check in on your people just to make sure that they are okay. Fortunately, I was around family, but there are so many people dealing with this solo. My family and I survived, and as of 11/3, we still have our antibodies. I didn't feel well today or yesterday. This is the frustration with COVID. Sometimes you feel the same original symptoms like the coughs, the lethargy, the chest aggravation, and the dry eyes. It can be frustrating because you always lift a side eye like, what the hell is this? It's interesting how the mind works like a sponge, absorbing everything that we feel and harboring those emotions. However, in times of crisis, our strength comes in remembering that we are all alchemist, built with an internal knowing, an intuitiveness that allows us to shape-shift into our true "beingness", tapping into our purpose and our want and need to survive, our want and need to... live!

Kayinde Harris, a Brooklyn native, is a NYC public school teacher and documentarian who enjoys writing and reading in her spare time. She is currently developing a lifestyle and wellness blog for teens due for release in 2021.

2020 IS A WAITING ROOM
BY KENDRA STOLL

When asked about what the year 2020 is to me, on reflection, 2020 is a waiting room.

I reflect upon my birth, where family members would wait in a hospital waiting room filled with fluorescent lights, chairs not too comfortable to make you want to stay awhile, and the smells of disinfectant in anticipation, excitement, and joy of the birth of a new life with the promise of a future and faith in what transpires. Much like the start of a new year.

As time progresses, life brings other waiting rooms, those in airports, bus and train stations. These waiting areas are hives of activity, places to marvel and designed for maximum efficiency. The planes, buses, and trains are moving monuments to man's inventiveness to conquer the physical limitations of one's environment. The people around are paying specific attention, are driven, and interested to get to their destination. When the system is working well, the mechanics of the system are invisible. Much like a virus, like COVID-19.

However, when the system fails, is delayed, or stopped, the cracks show. The cracks reveal the distress of those passengers whose lives are disrupted, the delays that must be made to fix the problem, and the need to find alternatives to get to their destination. Due to the virus, there are endless adaptations, some small, some large, in the lives around us. School, work, and social gatherings are now conducted via Zoom. Our daily public place has shrunk to a Wi-Fi connection with a screen. Are we liberated by this technology, or are we prisoners visiting the world behind glass?

Others found in the airport, bus, and train stations are not there because it's their first choice, but it is their place of the last shelter. When the stations are full and bustling, these folks are easy to pass by or to look the other way. As the systems stopped, these folks became visible. They are like wildlife, such as coyotes, who had been invisible, but now in the daylight we cannot ignore.

Another waiting room is the doctor's office. Like the hospital waiting room, it now looks so familiar yet behaves so differently. Doctors, nurses, and office staff who have jobs that, in non-COVID-19 days, would lay hands on patients. Now, everyone is wearing masks, gowned, and trying to keep a respectful distance when possible. People say these essential workers are heroes. Like soldiers, sailors, marines, and airmen, they would say, "I am not a hero." They wish instead that people would listen to the messages of preventing the spread of disease so that they can receive some rest.

Rest stops off the highway are not true waiting rooms, but often act like ones. They are areas to eat a snack, go to the bathroom, and stretch one's legs during a long car ride. In California, they are named after natural landmarks or well-connected people. In this time of COVID-19, there are those of us who are so stressed, anxious, and so frazzled that real rest seems like an illusion. Then there are the obituaries that will often lead with "so-and-so has gone to eternal rest." This eternal rest brings a sense of loss and sadness for days to come.

Then the election of 2020 came. My waiting room, like other Americans, was my living room. A space filled with things that I like and am familiar with. The election proceeded in ways that were expected. The behavior of the candidates and their supporters did not. I am still hopeful about the peaceful transition of power, but unlike elections, the past does not take it for granted.

So, as this year ends, 2020 is like a waiting room. I wait to see what 2021 will bring.

Kendra Stoll, MLIS, is a Librarian who specializes in History, Public Health, and Engineering. She is currently working as a Contact Tracer for the Los Angeles County Department of Public Health.

THE PRINCIPLES I STAND FOR
BY KIMBERLY MILTON

As I tiptoe into November, I do so full of reluctance and lack of fervor.

Some of my despondency rests upon the state of complete chaos of our nation and the other portion is due in part to the outcome of the last election.

For some, the last election four years ago is in the distant past; however, for me lately, I have been having a plethora of flashbacks where old feelings resurface from that presidential race. What I remember most is afterwards, there was a sting. The sting was not because the person I chose did not win, but it was something more, indescribable no less. It hurt! It felt like a gut punch, not even like a toe stubbed in the middle of the night, but something deeper and memorable. A punch that would take some time to process and heal from. That kind of sting. Like seeing your ex with a new bae, and to add insult to injury, the ex is wearing a shirt that you bought. Yes, that kind of sting, not life threatening, of course, but a serious ass blow!

Needless to say, I slept very little the night of the last election. There was a lot of tossing and turning, thinking, and rethinking of what was to come. Before rolling out of bed the next morning and attempting to start the day, I remember giving myself a pep talk and even tried to mentally find a happy place. While trying to secure that happy place, I realized that there would be a need for many more pep talks to get me through the next four years of unexpectancy and uncertainty. Although that talk with myself didn't make me feel any better, it was the reality check that I needed to give me the push to get out of bed, make coffee, and grab the morning paper from the front lawn.

Truthfully, I wasn't expecting to see anyone, but I heard my name as soon as I stepped outside. Surprisingly, it was my neighbor from across the street. He waved and I waved back. He and I talked politics a time or two and although we were on opposite ends of the spectrum, we were cordial. He came to the edge of the driveway with a serious look and offered an apology "about last night," election night. He proceeded to add that he voted the way he did because of his loyalty to his party. Admittedly, I was floored by his candor. I assured him that he owed me no apology and that it was not my duty to vote-shame. What I wanted to say to my neighbor was that we were all in it together. Good or bad we would have to endure and see it through. He looked relieved at my response, he waved, and our conversation ended.

Honestly, I replayed that conversation multiple times recently because here we are again on the precipice of another pivotal election. I'm concerned about the day after the election and how things will all play out. It's even crossed my mind if this will pan out like Groundhog's Day, reliving the election, and me interfacing with the neighbor again as I retrieve the paper. What if the ticket I voted for doesn't win again? What does that mean for me mentally and the people I care about? What will it mean to have to endure four more years of the continued rhetoric of negativity & blame, and no regard for human life. Not to mention bigotry, racism, stereotypes and unequal treatment of marginalized groups and no immediate plans for the containment of the coronavirus. WHAT WILL IT ALL MEAN AND WHAT'S TO COME?

As I have confessed, November has me shook! And as a historian, knowing and teaching history limits my optimism. But what I will say is history has shown that we've been here before, and in many cases, the same issues that I mentioned earlier have occurred under some past administration. My concern, as a country, is we should always strive to progress and not regress back to what America was, but move to what America can and should become. I do know that change does not happen overnight. It is a slow, slow process in which the overall challenge is having conversations that encourage critical thinking. This is what is most needed for us to evolve and grow and become better.

I tap into the strength of the universe so that the results this time will be favorable for the ticket that I supported. And most of all, if this does happen, I do hope the opportunity will present itself and I run into my neighbor. There will be no apology on my end just a few simple words to readdress the conversation he initiated four years ago, the day after the election. I would relay that I am not loyal to a party; however, I would let him know that I am loyal to human life, and I choose the party that best aligns with what I stand for and that encompasses the needs of the people that I care about most. That being my immediate family, parents and aunts, cousins and friends, that have preexisting conditions and comorbidities and are Black, Indigenous, and people of color (BIPOC) which makes them vulnerable to the virus. And lastly, I even care about him and his wife who are baby boomers and susceptible just the same, but who I happen to consider my fellow man. That's the America that I want to be a part of. One that sees a human first and could give a shit about a party, but has a strong concern for humanity over party. That is what's most important to me regardless of who wins or loses. These are the principals that I will stand on for the next four years and thereafter.

Kimberly Milton resides in Houston, Texas, and is originally from Florida. She is an educator, thought leader, writer, and fashion and style enthusiast. Her website is: http://www.kimberlymilton.com/ You can follow her on: Twitter & IG @kimberlyjmilton; FB- @kimberlymilton; LinkedIn- kimberlymilton ; Email: kimberly@kimberlymilton

EXPLORING THE RELATIONSHIP BETWEEN IMAGINATIVE LANGUAGE AND BELONGING
BY LUIS J. RODRIGUEZ

How does one belong in a time of not belonging? Or find a language for this? Wars, poverty, and climate disasters have forced increasing numbers of people across the globe from their land-based homes. Being uprooted —a refugee—is endemic to our times. And even if one has a home, the alienations linked to survival, or lack thereof, continue to intensify. Most people feel like exiles in their own land. The underlying basis for wars, poverty, and climate disasters—contributed by industrial and post-industrial development—are human action or inaction. In other words, these are "monsters" of our own making.

From time immemorial, human beings had stories, poems, teachings, and such to steer them along any road of development, even when the paths were not carved out. We had long-standing truths and lessons to draw on —including ancestral knowledge and mythic imaginations. For example, human beings throughout history have honored the four key connections that have kept us whole and on common ground— regardless of nation or territory. They are 1) the connection to nature, its laws, rhythms, patterns that have allowed for critical human growth across millennia; 2) the connection to one's own nature, the internal gifts, geniuses, and "story" to be lived out; 3) the connection to others as "we are all related" or "you are the other me," or as the Golden Rule summarizes, "treat others as you want to be treated"; 4) and the connection—however this may be best expressed for time and place—to the Divine. The ties or separations from these, and the ordeals this may engender, have been integral to our collective stories. Today being disconnected is contributing to a fear-based, hate-filled, and tumultuous world. To be modern is to be lost.

Capitalism, which has governed our societies for at least 500 years (from pre-capitalist formations to the shifts from agriculture to mechanical industry to digital technology) has one fundamental concern: the drive for maximum profits. This drive, which is counter to all major texts, scriptures, and stories, oral or written, is now our norm.

While more wealth has been created under capitalism than in any other economic/political system, it has also produced deep poverty, climate change, war economies, and social injustices within countries and across borders. This includes a widening wealth gap between a smaller number of people and the vast majority.

For "maximum profits" to make sense, a fabricated sense of scarcity had to be established. Under scarcity, the main mode of exchange and interaction is competition, not cooperation. The healthy and safe wellbeing of everyone and the earth is sacrificed for "the strong will survive," "I'll get mine before you get yours "or "kill or be killed." Competition is society's fetish.

It's a world of winners and losers. Not only that but the wealth and wellness of a few is dependent on most people barely scraping by. Winners win because losers lose.

In recent months, 25 million people filled the streets in protests for Black Lives Matter following the police murder of George Floyd in Minneapolis. The call to end mass incarceration and to defund police stirred local, state, and national governments to their cores. The idea stems from two-tiered policing, one for Black and Brown people, and another for White people (except the poorest). But the counter to this is there can't be complete justice for Blacks without taking away from everybody else. Somehow, strangely, this response is based on our supposed limits—instead of what's immensely possible. There continues to be those who say being pro-Black, pro-social justice, is just not "American." Again, restricting what imaginations and capacities exist to extend and strengthen the US Constitution and beyond.

Think also about the Mexicans and Central Americans, among others, stuck on the U.S.-Mexico border. They are in cages, refugee camps, or like ghosts floating on the impoverished Mexican side or as low-wage workers on the U.S. side. In the past four decades, many of these migrants included Mayans from southern Mexico or Guatemala; Mixtecos or Zapotecos from Oaxaca; Nahuas from central Mexico or El Salvador; and other Indigenous peoples throughout the continent that still maintain language and cultural ties to their tribe or nation.

They have roots to this land that go back tens of thousands of years. Yet these Brown people—color of the earth they walk on—are now the "strangers," "foreigners," the "aliens." They no longer belong because of made-up borders, a complicated documentation process, and arguments there are not enough jobs or social resources to go around. These arguments don't have to be true. They just have to fit the well-spun scarcity narrative.

On top of this, the majority of Mexicans and Central Americans are de-"Indianized." Over 500 years of conquest and colonialism in what is called Meso-America has forced them to "forget" who they are. They are now labeled "Hispanics" or "Latinos" based on European/colonial trappings. Many are called mestizos, mixed-blood, which stems from the Spanish hierarchal casta system that determined people's worth based on how much of this "blood" or that "blood" they may have had.

What a rotten way to classify people! Yet our society clings to these fictions of identity, of superiority and inferiority. Belonging has become less meaningful, except in how class and race are used to divide and disaffect.

In this climate, we have a revival of "America First." The rise of nationalism, often called White nationalism (as if "White" were a nation), demand the most expansive interests succumb to the most narrow. Yet, this does not guarantee the United States will do better. The only guarantee of that is to make sure all nations have the means to do well—especially with the organic abundance abounding in properly adhering to the four key connections.

It's okay to love your country. But you have to love the world more. If humanity across the globe were on an equitable footing, again with collective and healthy wellbeing enshrined for all, that includes the United States.

The naked and unregulated competition between nations, classes, belief systems, and races only make life precarious for everyone. There are circumstances where competition is appropriate. But the guiding principle should be to strive for overall balance and harmony. This means governing and working aligned with nature, deriving healthy sustenance from earth, sun, water, and air, and relating meaningfully to oneself, each other, and spirit.

Regardless of the real and wondrous cultural/language/religious differences between us, this is how, in the end, we all belong.

Exploring the relationship between imaginative language and belonging originally appeared on 1508, the University of Arizona Poetry Center Blog

Luis J. Rodriguez has 16 books in poetry, fiction, nonfiction, and children's books, including the bestselling memoir Always Running, La Vida Loca, Gang Days in L.A., *and served as Los Angeles's Poet Laureate from 2014-2016. He's founding editor of Tia Chucha Press and co-founder of Tia Chucha's Centro Cultural & Bookstore. His website is www.luisjrodriguez.com.*

TEACHING IN AN AGE OF CORONA
BY DR. MARK NAISON
Friday, August 14, 2020

During the Spring Semester of 2020, I was teaching two of my favorite classes- From Rock and Roll to Hip Hop, which had nearly 40 students, and my research seminar in African American and Urban Studies, where I was supervising 10 students writing their Senior theses. When the Pandemic hit, classes moved online, and everyone had to leave campus, my students and I were fearful and in some cases traumatized by the COVID-19's impact on their families and their futures, A few had family members who were essential workers and feared catching the virus; some faced sudden impoverishment because their parents lost jobs; many mourned the loss of an opportunity to experience a live graduation, and two students, both Bronx residents, had parents who had caught the virus and were deathly ill.

Given the emotional distress my students were in, I decided that my primary goal was to lift my student's spirits and give them an opportunity to express how they felt about what was happening to them, I did this in several ways; first I tried to cheer them up with humorous short rap videos I made for them, secondly I changed course requirements so all exams were take home and students had ample time to complete their work, third, I gave my thesis students the opportunity of writing Coronavirus diaries if it was impossible to complete the research they had initially undertaken, fourth, I scheduled Friday afternoon Happy Hours where students could unwind and share their feelings, and fifth I allowed students to post songs which made them feel better during all our online class sessions.

By the middle of April, I started to see the results of these strategies. Students began submitting work of superior quality, given an opportunity to choose essay subjects that meant something to them, students started class projects of their own which got their classmates excited, one of which a Bronx COVID-19 Oral History Project which is still going strong this summer, and most gratifying, student after student thanked me for not pretending this was a normal academic experience, for showing that I cared about their well being and mental health, and for giving them the opportunity to write about subjects they cared about.

I am taking their energy and enthusiasm into my approach to the Fall Semester. At age 74, I don't feel safe going into an indoor classroom so I applied to teach remotely. That is what I will do every Friday, but on Tuesdays, I will be meeting my classes outdoors on Edwards Parade where we will be wearing masks, maintaining social distance, and bringing our sound systems so we can play some music! My students are excited about this opportunity and so am I. And I expect to get some great work on written assignments which I will tailor to students' feelings as much as to the course material we will be covering.

Mark Naison is Professor of History and African American Studies at Fordham University and is the Founder and Director of the Bronx African American History Project, one of the largest community based oral history projects in the nation.

CRIMES AGAINST HUMANITY, OR THE CHANGING SAME
BY MICHELE L. SIMMS-BURTON, PHD

If a difference exists between 2016 and 2020, the chasm lies in my inability to predict that Donald J. Trump's method for committing genocide against Black, Brown, and Indigenous people would be his willful neglect or incompetence, or both, in handling the COVID-19 pandemic. He is a racist and a eugenicist. I knew extermination of non-White people was his tacit agenda item. I just did not know how he would accomplish genocide. I never doubted that he was dangerous. I never doubted he would commit crimes against humanity.

On June 16, 2015, when Trump and his wife, Melania Trump, descended the escalator at Trump Tower in New York City, my body cringed. Having never been a Trump fan, having never gotten curried into seeing him as anything less than a New York City thug despite his attempt to rebrand himself through his television show "The Apprentice," I watched his 2016 campaign with horror. I suspected he could win the election. I also believed that Russian oligarchs financed his businesses and campaign. And as I watched Republican members of Congress fold and one-by-one become Trump's sycophants I told my partner, Michael Poole, "if I had any power, I would order an audit of every Republican member of Congress right now. They are all receiving oligarch money."

See a few years ago, I engaged in a deep dive into Russian history to write a guide for Callisto media. To the best of my knowledge, Callisto never published the guide but what I learned about the rise of the Russian oligarch class mesmerized me. While conducting my research, echoes of conversations with a friend, who is a Paris-based artist, resounded as I heard him say, "the Russians have all the money." Indeed, they do. Money means power in the world. The Russian oligarchs solely answer to Vladimir Putin and they maintain their money, status, business, and lives by furthering Putin's global agenda.

On November 9, 2016, the day after Trump won or stole the election, I recall sitting in the Starbucks on Alki Beach in West Seattle devouring Noam Chomsky. It was Chomsky who argued that the Republican Party was the "most dangerous organization in human history." In Chomsky's writings, I sought not answers but simply a way to drop my rudder and stay the course. The goal was not to panic but to acknowledge that non-White people in America were about to enter the most dangerous epoch in the United States since the post-Second World War civil rights movement. But, I did not have to remain in America.

Fleeing the country was an option. Fleeing the country without my family, particularly my son, stopped me cold in my tracks as each family member, except my nephew, told me that they weren't leaving the U.S. As my father, Charles Simms said to me, "we built this damn country, I'm not going anywhere."

Here we are four years later. Trump has lost the 2020 election for president. Yet, as of this writing, he refuses to concede. His overt disregard for the norms that define the office of the presidency, his flagrant violation of laws, and his Mafia-like behavior make the U.S. a much more dangerous country than it has ever been in my lifetime. As

Sarah Kendzior, the author of the book Hiding in Plain Sight: The Invention of Donald Trump and the Erosion of America, says: the Trump family is a "transnational crime syndicate masquerading as a government." When Kendzior sounded the alarm about Trump in 2016, the media disregarded her, branded her as hyperbolic and reactionary, and assured her that the U.S. system of government had checks and balances and could stop Trump from collapsing our democracy. The media ignored Kendzior's experience studying autocratic regimes and her doctorate degree. Now she warns us that if President-elect Joe Biden and his administration do not charge and prosecute Trump, Ivanka Trump, Jared Kushner, Stephen Miller, and anyone else who aided and abetted the Trump administration's criminality, Ivanka or another person with autocratic aspirations will emerge and potentially win the 2024 presidential election. But next time the candidate will be smarter and more organized than Trump. Trump tested our system of democracy and he unveiled all its holes. He has laid the groundwork for an autocratic regime to take over the U.S. and sell it off for parts.

I sit here in my home across the Potomac River from Washington, DC wondering how it is that so many Americans either are naïve or selfish. Or how their quest for White supremacy permitted them to stand silently by while an egomaniac destroyed the country. What they do not realize about autocratic leaders is that everyone is expendable. An autocratic leader with narcissistic tendencies only cares about himself. People's Whiteness will not protect them forever when democracy dies under autocracy, authoritarianism, or fascism.

I doubt that the incoming Biden administration will prosecute Trump and his international crime syndicate without public pressure. White people, especially White men, in government have a history of committing crimes and going unpunished or summarily admonished and allowed to walk. I just hope that as the population in the U.S. becomes browner that we use whatever power we have to hold criminals in government accountable. If not, a fascist apartheid-like rule in this country will only worsen as people who identify as White become a minority in the population and exercise draconian control.
I am hopeful but only because I have a son and younger family members who I know will not vacate the U.S. I am hopeful that the desire for equity, to abolish the police, institute a basic universal income, forgive

student loans, provide universal healthcare, make affordable housing accessible, and end racism will prevail. I know that change comes in increments. This democracy is a great American experiment. It ebbs and flows. We have lost so much during the Trump administration. We must not let this happen again.

Michele L. Simms-Burton is a DC and Seattle-based journalist, public speaker, scholar, and author of essays, poetry, and fiction appearing in national and international publications. Her email is michelelsimms@gmail.com and you can follow her on Instagram @michelelsimms and at abriartandculture.wordpress.com.

BUILD BACK BETTER
BY MONA J. ESKRIDGE
New York City

Well my loves, for those of Abba's Mona Girl Blog Family in the US, we are exactly thirteen days from our November 3rd, 2020 General Election, the most important, life changing election in our nation's history. And for those of our world-wide family who follow the political drama that is the United States of America, we the people are to save the soul and lives of Abba's America.

I feel deep in my soul that the last four years of enduring the horrors of the current administration was Abba giving us a big wake up call to who we are as a nation and to exposing the shocking and evil underbelly of what has become of Abba's America. The last four years was our wake up call, to see with our own eyes, the true state of our union. And Lord have mercy, what we've witnessed is not pretty, not unity, and definitely not God.

But all is not lost. We are thirteen days away from the biggest turning point in our nation's history. As of today, more than 35 million

Americans voted via mail-in ballots and early voting at the polls. Folks are not playing y'all.

Because of the last four years, we've had enough of the drama, lies, cruelty, corruption, disrespect, bullying, evil, hate, hypocrisy, and the reckless disregard for human life.

And folks are continuing to show up and show out in record breaking numbers to vote them all out. They are voting out those in our White House's Oval Office and candidates up and down the ballot. It's been a powerful, inspiring, and unifying thing to watch in real time.

We are done with business as usual and step into a new era of powerful leadership. Leadership that is about honesty, respect, compassion, kindness, peace, humility, godly character, love, justice, integrity, trust, democracy, and the rule of law.

We're blessedly moving into a "Matthew 22:39" season of leadership. One of the mantras our president-elect and his campaign use is "Build Back Better." I am so in love with what this mantra means. The vision I see in my heart when I hear it, read it, or speak it is "Oh Hallelujah. Build back better."

My family, these three powerful words make my soul leap for joy in excitement and anticipation. Honestly, these three words now carry a deeper meaning to me than just being part of our president-elect's mighty mantra. These words represent a personal rallying cry, an individual confirmation that no matter what I've been through, no matter my circumstance, no matter the difficult lessons learned, no matter the heartbreaking losses, no matter what, no matter who, I can rise, we can rise. Rise up and step out and "Build Back Better."

Oh yeah, to my tenacious resilient ones, it's become personal. It's part of our DNA. It's in us and now it's our time as individuals and as a nation to courageously BUILD BACK BETTER.

So as I close out our time together, I encourage us to spend some "be still and know" time with Abba to reflect on and soak in what it means to, "Build Back Better." Because in order to step into all Abba has for us to do and be as His bright lights in America and the World, we must first get our own souls and hearts right. We can't pour out and share what we don't have. It's gotta be in us in order for us to give out. "Build Back Better" is something we must first do with Abba for ourselves and then we can do it for Abba's America!!!

"The vote is precious. It is the most powerful non-violent tool we have in a democratic society, and we must use it." - Representative John Lewis

Previously published on monagirlnyc.wordpress.com

Mona J. Eskridge is based in New York City and is a Writer, Author, Blogger and Public Speaker for ADONAI Global Ministries. You can reach her via email at Wincty@aol.com, follow her on Twitter @MonaGirlNYC and Subscribe to Mona Girl Blog at https://monagirlnyc.wordpress.com.

HOUSEGUEST
BY PADMINI PERSAUD-OBASI

"And God said 'Love Your Enemy,'and I obeyed him and loved myself." -Khalil Gibran

My phone rang. It was my supervisor. I had already been working from home for two weeks when COVID landed in New York City and shut down the office. A conference call wasn't on my calendar and sales were down. I braced myself for the inevitable blow. All I heard was "bad news" and "entire team furloughed." Furloughed, not laid off. Ok, I thought, I still have a chance to keep my job. I was told to collect unemployment. But weeks later, the ultimate decision came. We were all let go.

The stable life I built for 19 years with that one corporate job was instantly snatched away. After hearing the news, the eyes of my 14 year old son, who relied solely on me for food and shelter, conveyed the question his mouth couldn't form, "Are we going to be homeless?" Eyes that once housed joy now sheltered fear and asked if we will have enough.

Opting for remote learning for my high schooler, I watched him get up everyday with the purpose of continuing his daily curriculum without teacher supervision. The change of routine didn't appear to affect him or disrupt his life. But as he watched me wake up later and later each day, "You need to get up" became his early afternoon greeting. He was witnessing the slow unraveling of who I was into what I have yet to become. After just two interviews that produced zero results, the pity party began. The strong head of his household was reduced to a pathetic ball buried in layers of covers. Wasn't rest supposed to be an act of resistance? It affected him.

Apart from shutting down major organs, I was told anxiety, mild depression, and losing a sense of purpose, were common symptoms of COVID and I shouldn't worry. While I lost two family friends from my childhood neighborhood, other friends lost parents and grandparents to this silent killer.

Losing my job with the threat of being food and home insecure in the distant future put me on top of the lucky list. I didn't die or lose immediate family members, and still had severance to fall back on. But the pervasive effects of COVID slowly took hold of me. It picked at my insecurities. It highlighted all my broken parts while eviscerating the work I considered essential and turned it into meaningless fodder. It stuck by me and kept me up at night to remind me of what awaited me the next morning - not having a job or the means to take care of my family.

Its unwanted glances appeared in every mirror as I wandered mindlessly from bedroom to kitchen to living-room; exposing my disheveled appearance and sapped ambition. It replaced my morning ritual of getting dressed for work and listening to music while reading during my subway commute with - long weekly social-distance walks to Target, my new secret hang out. What it didn't know was that during these isolated walks on beloved Brooklyn streets, away from the constant barrage of media COVID-coverage and the distraction of a job, I was able to face my self-doubts, gather my thoughts and work toward living a more mindful life, one moment at a time.

It is a constant struggle, but I made a conscious effort to replace defeatist thoughts that attempt to take up permanent residence in my mind with positive affirmations. In an attempt to unlearn all that no longer served my higher purpose, I began to release myself from being the victim of past choices tied to generational trauma; trauma that kept me silent and led me to place the needs of family before my own well-being. While I can identify and label this for what it is, it takes an extreme amount of willpower to counteract the inherited notions of self-pity and lack mentality I was conditioned to watch and imitate from an early age.

It is a painful process complete with revisiting the past and releasing it through late night solitude-cries while seeking strength and guidance from a higher power. It is through this unfolding that I'm able to muster the courage to invest in my future at age 51 and choose to love myself enough to get out of my own way; to replace blame with forgiveness.

As I sit and write after being home for nine months due to COVID, "I'm proud of you" fills the space of our home. It comes from my son as he watches me write, study for the MAT, and practice mindful breathing. In this moment, I realize self-love truly is a radical act capable of ending generational trauma and transforming the formula of a family to a new one built on a foundation of progress and abundance.

My work here is not yet done. As I reset myself with the rest of the world during this global pandemic, I look forward to opening myself to all the infinite possibilities life has in store for me. My phone rings with opportunity but I let it ring while I dance to my favorite songs in the comfort of my living-room. I'll call them back - when I am done.

Padmini Persaud-Obasi is a mom, writer, student at Bank Street College and owner of @BrooklynLotusCreations - an Etsy shop featuring her one-of-a-kind handmade creations. She is dedicated to using her voice to share her wealth of knowledge on everything from Inclusive education to leading a life of purpose.

MY RANT ON CONTROL (OR THE LACK OF) DURING 2020
BY QUENTIN WALCOTT (CHEY'S SON)

2020. It has been the longest, shortest year, in the almost 50 years I've experienced. It was simply to be a rebound year from 2019 when I suffered a separated shoulder in an accident, and a pivotal year for me because I was reaching a milestone age. The actual pivots were beyond what I could have imagined. COVID-19 and 2020 became interchangeable in this period of challenge.

My work as a national and international anti-violence activist/educator is about individuals, relationships, communities, and the roots of health, safety, justice, equity and love, in the intimate, social, spiritual and political locations where people thrive. My work is most importantly about preventing and interrupting the violence that is caused between and because of people. At its core, my work is about gaining and maintaining power and control. What you do with power and control is also an essential part of my work for the last 25 years.

One of my mantras I tell people in their most frustrating and overwhelming moments is, "you can only control what you can control, and that is YOU." I found that to be true in my life as well. I often need to be reminded of this mantra in moments of loss and failure, a reminder of accountability. Early 2020 made that mantra become a resonating echo and rallying cry. The lack of control from who will get the virus, to who will survive it, to who will lose their job, to who will be furloughed, to who will face joblessness or homelessness, to where will the next healthy plate of food come from, reminds me of my mantra.

CONNECT, my organization, provided spaces for people to come together via virtual reality, Zoom, and social media during COVID quarantining and New York City lockdowns. We've pivoted our work from face-to-face in-office or in the community to face-by-face, lined up neatly in a grid on our laptops or phones. We've expanded our work virtually to meet the needs of the people from all walks of life who are struggling with not being able to control the things they can't control and who are also struggling to control the things they usually can control, themselves.

In the Men's Roundtables I led twice a week primarily with African American and Brazilian men, we talked about this lack of control in the context of how we were socialized to be men in places where systemic racism controls our movements. The major theme of the roundtables and circles is that who we are forever changed. Who we are as men, partners, parents, and leaders in our communities has changed. The great and mighty United States via its leadership's lack of response to a virus has led to not only death, but also to isolation and disconnection from our loved ones and friends. We've been exposed to some of the realities of what so-called "developing countries" endure in the face of pandemic and economic turmoil.

So as men, particularly Black and Latino men, the ways we've been socialized from boys into men have been challenged. The ways we inherit the idea of controlling our partners and families in toxic ways have been challenged to its core. The ways we were taught to lead and provide for our families have been challenged due to COVID-19's impact on the workplace and home. The ways we parents have been challenged due to shelter-in-place. Now, schooling several children from home and sometimes using one computer is a challenge. Or just simply engaging in conversation with your partner or spouse…or earning the respect of a child when you are not usually home engaging with them throughout the day is a challenge. Or even the more precarious situation of sheltering at home when there is violence in the home is a challenge. These things have changed us all. Those directly impacted to those of who are bystanders are challenged with the added obstacle of watching from a screen while trying to maintain control.

These are just some of the ways we are challenged and changed, hopefully for the better, because of 2020. It's one thing to facilitate these conversations about 2020, COVID-19, systemic racism, health disparities, masculinity, allies, and etc. For me, I've always talked about holding hope in one hand while holding a heavy dose of despair in the other. I've been challenged by including hope in my conversations about 2020. Now, after a crowning loss, hope challenges me.

I'll describe myself as one of two Black boys born and raised in NYC by a Black woman from Harlem. She was a starving artist and photographer. Chey is my mother's name. She fit the description of the type of person who COVID-19 would impact mostly: Black, 70 years old, and diabetic with other health disparities. Together, we made the decision that she would shelter-in place, at home, by herself for several months in the midst of the pandemic in NYC, a city that experienced some of the highest cases and deaths at the time. I am still distressed about this decision.

My mother survived the worst of days of COVID-19 at home but suffered greatly as a result of isolation. Frequent phone, video calls, and food deliveries didn't help with the isolation. It impacted her emotionally, mentally, physically, and medically. She survived COVID-19, but not the conditions created because of it. COVID-19 led her to the place where she transitioned, just weeks ago, in a rehabilitation center, without the ability to see or touch her family in her last moments. My struggle is between lack of control and the notion of hope. I couldn't control if she would continue on.

Hope will prevail. It has to. It must. For her, for me, and for all of us. Hope is not absent of despair, and now loss, for me. We can feel more than just one way. We must be different on the other side of 2020 and on the other side of COVID-19. I hope.

Quentin Walcott, known as "Q," is a leading national and international anti-violence activist and educator. Quentin's work over years engaging men and boys as allies and activists in the movement to prevent intimate and gender-based violence, has a focus on the intersections of violence—race, class and gender—and its impact on marginalized communities.

PATRIARCHY'S POST ELECTION END DAYS
BY ROB OKUN

Now that the presidential race has been decided, it is imperative for the U.S. to begin holding a series of national town hall conversations; high on the list must be one about rejecting patriarchy. Male supremacy continues to play an outsized role in aggravating the divide that afflicts us.

Which representation of manhood we choose going forward will in part contribute to determining what kind of a nation we will be: Proud Boys' country or a land-promoting compassionate men; a Handmaid's Tale world of subjugation or a nation empowering women and girls.

Even with President Joe Biden in office, Trumpism will still be with us, as will the aforementioned Proud Boys, the faux militia Wolverine Watchmen, the civil war-promoting Boogaloo Boys, and the ex-military/police Oath Keepers. Not to mention the misfits shooting up schools, nightclubs, houses of worship and movie theaters—even threatening sitting governors. White male supremacists one and all.

By the end of 2020 it was impossible to ignore a national flashing caution light: unless we acknowledge the connection between those groups' brutish expression of patriarchy and its White collar counterpart, represented by the likes of, say, Mitch McConnell and Brett Kavanaugh, rather than hearing patriarchy's last gasp, we'll be supplying it with fresh oxygen.

"The culture is changing and becoming in some ways more like [President Joe] Biden," Jackson Katz, creator of a new documentary, The Man Card: Presidential Masculinity from Nixon to Trump, told the Washington Post. But is it changing quickly enough?

"Trump still clearly has a large appeal to men who understand the more traditional appeal of aggression, physical strength, the willingness to authorize violence," Katz says.

While Trumpists at best reflect Archie Bunker's 20th-century masculinity, Biden offers "a more complex 21st-century version ..." Katz believes. "It's compassion and empathy and care and a personal narrative of loss."

As a White man in his seventies, Biden may seem like an odd choice to be the poster boy for a kinder, gentler expression of manhood; nevertheless he is. He now has a national platform to promote it. And pro-feminist men must seize every opportunity to urge him to use it. Donald Trump secreted poisonous masculinity; Joe Biden must actively advance healthy masculinity.

Hopefully, with the coronavirus pandemic now being responsibly managed, there will be time for a different kind of healing, beginning with young people, especially boys and young men.

Often, males of all ages do not readily acknowledge how much courage it takes to embody compassion and empathy, and conversely how cowardly it is to rely on callousness and indifference. It's on us to teach them, bringing into focus a new boyhood, a transformed manhood. We'll have to demand that parents, educators, coaches and other mentors develop programs that nurture young men's emotional growth and wellbeing.

I've long advocated that the CDC pilot a program at Head Start for preschool teachers to cultivate boys' emotional intelligence. Perhaps now, with the contrast between the presidential candidates' brands of masculinity still fresh in our minds, Congress will draft such legislation.

None of this will be easy. Nevertheless, there are bright spots. Even within the narrow world of electoral politics, the number of women winning elective office is a powerful antidote to patriarchy's poison. Strong women—from Stacey Abrams of Fair Fight Action to Michigan Gov. Gretchen Whitmer—are a corrective to the misogynous rants we've endured for four years. They represent a model of womanhood more men may be willing to embrace now that we've finished "rounding the corner" on the orangeman-demic.

Unfortunately, the notion of empowered womanhood is still suspect in some circles, branded as "feminist." While feminism simply denotes believing in the political, economic, and social equality of the sexes, over the last four years Trump et al. have sought to destroy it at every turn. With Kamala Harris as vice president, and Joe Biden's compassionate masculinity an antidote to Donald Trump's White male supremacy, conditions are ripe for males to begin to reconsider feminism. Men must now be willing to reach out and talk honestly with other men about how feminism benefits everyone.

Finally, to bridge the political and cultural chasm that has split open the U.S., we'll need to acknowledge that patriarchy's grip—if not its final gasp—and the assault on feminism are two sides of the same coin. We may have begun to acknowledge that racism has its knee on the necks of Black people, but to fully heal America we'll have to admit patriarchy has its other knee on the necks of women. In 2021 and beyond it will be imperative we do so. Are you in? I hope so.

Rob Okun is an activist, writer, and editor whose books include THE ROSENBERGS: Collected Visions of Artists and Writers, *and* VOICE MALE: The Untold Story of the Profeminist Men's Movement. *Syndicated by PeaceVoice, his commentaries appear in a range of digital publications and in newspapers across the country. He is editor-publisher of* VOICE MALE *magazine (voicemailmagazine.org). His email is rob@voicemalemagazine.org*

50 YEARS AGO, POLICE FIRED ON STUDENTS AT A HISTORICALLY BLACK COLLEGE
BY DR. ROBERT LUCKETT

May 13, 2020, 1:58 p.m. ET

JACKSON, Miss. — In the 1960s, White motorists driving along John R. Lynch Street, which cut through the middle of the historically Black campus of what was then called Jackson State College, would often taunt students along the way with racist epithets, throw objects at them and threaten to hit anyone in the crosswalk. On Feb. 3, 1964, a White driver slammed into a Jackson State student named Mamie Ballard, sending her to the hospital. This incident began a years-long push to close Lynch Street to traffic, which in turn helped drive the already potent local civil rights movement.

Jackson State may have been majority Black, but it was located in the capital of a state dominated by White supremacists, who in turn governed the college. Informed by the modern civil rights and Black

Power movements, students naturally saw the fight over Lynch Street as a cornerstone of their broader push for justice and equality. With an increasingly aggressive tenor, the ensuing student demonstrations, which peaked each spring, demanded justice for Ms. Ballard, who survived, and that Lynch Street be closed.

On May 14, 1970, someone set fire to a dump truck parked in the middle of Lynch Street, a few blocks from campus. While there was no evidence to suggest that student demonstrators had been involved, White authorities took the vandalism as a green light to crack down on the movement, criminalizing the victims of White supremacy and legitimizing the use of force.

Late that evening the Jackson Police and members of the Mississippi Highway Patrol marched onto campus, accompanied by the so-called Thompson's Tank, an armored personnel carrier that Allen Thompson, the city's segregationist mayor, purchased ahead of what he termed the civil rights "invasion" of Freedom Summer in 1964. That same year the Mississippi state Legislature had passed a bill that gave the Highway Patrol broad authority to intervene in protests, even if local authorities hadn't requested them. They still held that power in 1970.

The phalanx of officers proceeded to Alexander Hall, a women's dormitory, arriving close to midnight. But instead of facing a mass of angry protesters, they found scores of students relaxing outdoors, enjoying a Thursday evening as graduation neared. Later asserting that a sniper had shot at them from a window in Alexander Hall — an absurd claim with no evidence — the police fired more than 400 rounds of ammunition over 28 seconds in every direction. In the chaos that spilled into the early morning hours of May 15, two men, Phillip Lafayette Gibbs and James Earl Green, were left dead; a dozen other young people were wounded in the gunfire. Hundreds of others bear physical and psychological scars to this day. Gibbs was a junior political science major at Jackson State.

He had married his high school sweetheart, and they had one son. Unbeknownst to Phillip and his wife, Dale, she was pregnant at the time with their second son.

Green was a senior at nearby Jim Hill High School. He had been walking home from his after-school job on the opposite side of the street from Alexander Hall, which meant the police had turned to fire in the other direction from the supposed sniper.

Graduation was cancelled at Jackson State, and the members of the Class of 1970 received their diplomas in the mail. A number of injured students, and the families of Gibbs and Green, sued the city and state, represented by the renowned civil rights attorney Constance Slaughter. The plaintiffs lost their case, and no one was ever charged in the police murders. Lynch Street was finally closed through campus, and the Gibbs-Green Memorial Plaza now stands in front of Alexander Hall. But, those concessions were not victories, and did nothing to lessen the trauma for those who survived.

The 50th anniversary of the police attack at Jackson State comes at a moment when America is struggling with a pandemic, the impacts of which have weighed heavily, and unjustly, on Black bodies. When considering the insufficient and belated response of state and national leaders that has inflamed the pandemic, the news is clear, especially in Mississippi: People of color are disproportionately represented among COVID-19 cases, and they bear the brunt of the government's aggressive enforcement of quarantine rules.

Then came the news that Ahmaud Arbery, an unarmed Black man out for a jog, was murdered in Georgia in February. Activists took to the streets to demand that his assailants face trial, but, as the protesters at Jackson State, the survivors of the May 1970 attack and modern proponents of Black Lives Matter understand, justice remains elusive.

Through it all, we must be reminded that state-sanctioned violence aimed at the marginalized remains a systemic part of America. That ever-present threat continues to prop up White supremacy in this country.

This spring, Jackson State's class of 2020 was supposed to graduate in a special ceremony: The Class of 1970 was prepared to walk across the stage for its 50th reunion and officially receive their diplomas for the first time, while relatives of Phillip Gibbs and James Green were set to accept honorary doctorates on behalf of their murdered family members. While the administration at Jackson State and our community hold out hope that we will be able to safely gather for these events at some unknown date, there is a real prospect that this modern catastrophe, 50 years later, will prevent us from doing so.

Whatever happens, the moment must not go unrecognized. The students, alumni and community at Jackson State must demand an honest dialogue around our White-supremacist history and its present-day manifestations. As the civil-rights demonstrators in Jackson demanded a half century ago, White Americans in particular must be willing to take responsibility and action if our society is to begin rooting out racist power and all its implications.

50 Years Ago, Police Fired on Students at a Historically Black College originally appeared in the New York Times.

Robert Luckett is an associate professor of history and the director of the Margaret Walker Center at Jackson State University.

CLEAN, CREATE AND EDUCATE: A COVID-19 SURVIVAL GUIDE!
BY SADIA JAMES

The title pretty much explains it all. Clean, create, and educate, and in this article, I hope will do just that. I got inspired to write this blog because I know right now everyone's a little stir crazy, and although some of us are just fine, I felt the need to put something together that we can all appreciate. "Each one, teach one." I've been researching a lot of information on the whole coronavirus pandemic and although the media and a lot of new sources are making this seem super scary and super unavoidable, that is not 100% the truth. So, first I want to start with "clean".

CLEAN: From hygiene, to food, to soul food. It is very important to make sure that you were not only washing your hands consistently and avoiding touching your face when you're traveling or just in general, but that you're also making sure that the spaces that you were in are thoroughly cleaned, especially if these are spaces such as a workspace because not all of us have the opportunity to work from home. Seeing that you are not carrying outside germs into your sanctuary. Mainly making sure that you are in fact doing the best to keep your hygiene in tiptop shape. But it's not just all about the outside but also it goes inside of us *pause* with what we consume on a daily basis, what we eat, what we expose our psyche to, and how it's benefiting us and our bodies. WASH UP! WASH YOUR HANDS! DRINK YOUR WATER! AND EAT YOUR VEGGIES! No, but seriously, do it. Your body will thank you for it and those around you would do the same (from 6 feet away of course). I'm going to list below in the "educate" section all of the things that boost your immune system and what it helps with...for the most part. I will certainly give you the seeds, you just have to plant them.

CREATE: I already have a feeling that this is going to be my favorite section to write since I am a creative. Creating in general and having the ability to do so is a blessing. I think during this coronavirus lockdown not only are the introverts extremely happy and ambiverts halfway happy (sorry to the extroverts), but some creatives are taking the time to hit their "to-do" list the best they can and are definitely going to town putting their talents to work, and I'm loving what I'm seeing on my socials! However, keep in mind and be very mindful that creatives, at least a lot of us, are empaths and anxiety and confusion isn't always the best recipe for quality output and quality content! So, even though downtime is a great time to tackle things we've been meaning to do, it's not always the greatest time to create something of quality. And I just want to say to my creative's that may be reading this (and all who are used to being busy), take it easy… Take your time. It's OK to rest. It's OK to take breaks. It's OK to be still because you cannot be your best if you don't take care of yourself and create a healthy space overall for you to execute. So, yes for those who feel it, CREATE! 2020 is still our year! But for those who don't right now, that is ok too. Unwind and everything will happen in due time.

EDUCATE: OK, so this part is where all the gems and jewels get dropped. Health is wealth and it is very important in this time, like I mentioned earlier, to pay attention to what you're consuming. So, I came up with the idea to make a list of herbs and supplements that you can get that help boost your immune system and help with a variety of other things when it comes to your overall health. So, this part will be easy and most of this you can order on Amazon.

Some of these you would probably have to do some research and find sites that sell it! Do your own research! I am not a licensed doctor. Also, shout out to Rizza Islam because I've been paying very close attention to the knowledge that he's been dropping which also helped me create this list! But before I make the list, one more thing, try to drink natural spring water... thank me later. Also, if you need to stock up during the pandemic and you're afraid that you'll run out of food, make sure to get glass canned foods, beans, wild rice, a water filter, vitamin C, and have a first aid kit and solar powered chargers ready and available.

IMMUNE SYSTEM BOOSTERS ETC

- Elderberry -Used for its antioxidant activity to lower cholesterol, improve vision, boost the immune system, improve heart health, and for coughs, colds, flu, bacterial and viral infections, and tonsillitis. Elderberry juice was used to treat a flu epidemic in Panama in 1995.

- Bladderwrack-is also used for obesity, arthritis, joint pain, "hardening of the arteries" (arteriosclerosis), digestive disorders, heartburn, "blood cleansing," constipation, bronchitis, emphysema, urinary tract disorders, and anxiety. Other uses include boosting the immune system and increasing energy.

- Black seed oil- the black seed is used for treating digestive tract conditions including gas, colic, diarrhea, dysentery, constipation, and hemorrhoids. It is also used for respiratory conditions including asthma, allergies, cough, bronchitis, emphysema, flu, swine flu, and congestion.

- Sea Moss- Sea Moss is a source of potassium chloride, a nutrient which helps to dissolve catarrhs (inflammation and phlegm in the mucous membranes), which cause congestion. It also contains compounds that act as natural antimicrobial and antiviral agents, helping to get rid of infections.

- Ginger

- Turmeric

- Echinacea

- Colloidal silver

- Oregano oil

- Super Lysine

- Chlorella

- Garlic

- Astragalus

- Chlorophyll

- CARDIO!

That's all folks. I hope you have gracefully made it to the end and were inspired to take out a pen and paper and got busy making a new grocery list. Or even if you knew about most of these things, pass along the article to those you'd feel needed a reminder to re-order or purchase some. But I hope that everyone is doing very well in these weird times and hopefully we can all turn up this summer and put this behind us. Be lovely live chaotically! XO -Sadia J.

Previously published on muselovelychaos.com

Sadia James is a West Indian American Born New York City-based Writer, Poet, Blogger, Content creator and independent business owner. Her email is sadiajames@gmail.com and you can follow her on Instagram and Twitter @SadiaJamesNY.

MOTHERHOOD, JOURNALISM, AND STORYTELLING IN THE AGE OF COVID-19 AND RACIAL UNREST
BY TAIGI SMITH

As a mother and a journalist, I am always expected to have the answers, but lately it seems there is just one question that stumps me every time: How much trauma and unrest can a child be expected to process at one time? After months of sheltering in place and disconnecting from friends, schools, churches, loved ones-- am I now expected to talk to my child about police brutality? Am I supposed to tell her about the senseless killing of a Black man, George Floyd, on a Minneapolis city street? It was the brazenness of Derek Chauvin that hit me, the way a stream of liquid, urine I imagine, slowly crept towards the curb as George Floyd lost breath, and then life, beneath Derek Chauvin's knee. I cannot imagine a more terrible way to die.

From the images we saw on social media, it was clear that thousands of people, Black and White, were angry beyond belief; frustrated, devastated, and unsure of what to do or where to go for the help and healing. Out of answers and seemingly tired of prolonged police brutality that has stalked African-Americans for far too many years, ordinary citizens from all walks of life took to the streets--protesting, breaking windows, destroying businesses, defacing structures, and straight-up tearing cities down. As a journalist, that moment in time felt surreal, as I had been there before. It felt like just yesterday America had exploded when Philando Castile was gunned down by a police officer while a little girl sat in the back seat of his car, and witnessed the attack on Mr. Castile's life. His girlfriend captured the deadly episode on her cellphone. While the images of Philando Castile's death were similar in their utter disregard for human life, there is a different feeling in the air this time, one that tells me that enough may finally be enough.

As a human, I had been stewing about the death of George Floyd for days, I could not stop scrolling through Facebook and my newsfeed, watching the world as I knew it, literally go up in flames. I had received a call from my mother in San Francisco telling me that there were riots going down in Oakland and she was afraid of what was about to happen in her city. I was hearing from friends in Brooklyn, who sent me pictures of protesters shouting for justice on Flatbush Avenue, eerily close to where I used to live. Many of my White friends reached out, asking how I was doing, and wondering if there was anything they could do to help. They all asked my daughter and were genuinely concerned about her well-being. "What are you telling S," they wanted to know. "How are you explaining all of this," they wondered.

It was around 1pm on Monday afternoon when I received an email from my boss, saying we were launching a network special that would examine the death of George Floyd. I had become obsessed with George Floyd's story after watching that tragic video, and now I was assigned, along with a network wide team, to cover the protests that by now were now raging across the world--Washington, DC, Atlanta, Brooklyn, Los Angeles, even Japan. It was at this moment that I turned to my husband and said, "I need to focus for 24 hours. I cannot be disturbed." I then went downstairs to my basement and began to tackle the story at hand. Upstairs, I could hear my daughter, oblivious to world's events, asking my husband for lunch. My husband is a Black man, a retired federal agent, and when he saw the images of George Floyd dying underneath Derek Chauvin's knee, he went quietly inside himself, to process what he'd seen. All weekend, he had been asking, "Are you working on a story? Have you been assigned? Is the network going to do a special." Finally, I was able to tell him, that yes, people at the top believed this story mattered, and that we were going on air with a breaking news special. "Go downstairs and do your work. This is why you became a journalist." And downstairs I went.

Producing these types of stories requires razor sharp focus and unyielding support. It requires the understanding and respect of loved ones. It requires a journalist to go deep inside her own bubble and work passionately and quickly, while managing the emotions of herself and those around her. During times like this, I always tell my daughter, "Mommy is working on a big project. You understand, right? This is how we eat. This is how I pay for summer camp. This is how we can pay for food. This is an important story. Mommy loves her work" It is a very basic way of explaining my work and she understands WHY I am working so hard when I explain it this way. She has never known a day when I haven't worked as a journalist, telling the stories that I love to tell.

Fast Forward---it's now 8:56pm on Tuesday night. Mama has been downstairs working the basement for 12 hours straight. I even slept in the basement so I could maintain my focus. My daughter brought down a snack, and my husband brought down dinner. At 8:56pm, I hear my daughter opening the basement door and then I hear footsteps. "Mommy. Is your show about to come on?" "No, Baby," I tell her. "It's not airing tonight." My husband is listening from the top of the stairs, and for a moment, he is confused. "Your piece isn't coming on tonight???" And then I say it again, this time, the pitch in my voice is different. "No. NOT TONIGHT. Maybe another night." I have just lied to my child--my 8 year old innocent Brown girl--and told her that what mommy has just produced will NOT be airing because I am not strong enough or spiritually equipped to tell her that the world as she knows it is in complete and utter chaos.

In the safe cocoon that I managed to create in the age of COVID-19, I have been able to shield her from the ills of the world. We don't go outside, don't socialize, she won't hear about the death of George Floyd in school, there are no playdates right now, and so she won't hear about it from her friends. I made the conscious decision to leave Brooklyn when my daughter was 8 months old because I did not want her to grow up surrounded by sirens and decay and the occasional waterbug. Nor did I want her to struggle to find her place in a rapidly gentrifying section of Brooklyn, so we moved to a bucolic part of New Jersey, filled with journalists like me, many of whom are working diligently to shield and protect their children from the dirty, nasty reality that we as journalists, have come to cover day after day after day. Back at home, within the safety of my four walls, I nervously tell my friends, "We are not discussing these issues with S. It's all unicorns and rainbows over here." And that it is. We are talking about Harry Potter books, the highs and lows of remote learning, flower bulbs, gears on bikes, and how to bake red velvet cakes. We are in constant conversation with God, praying for those who have lost loved ones to COVID-19 and praying for those on the front lines. We pray for our communities, our co-workers, our friends, our teachers, our family. Over here, we are not talking about the list of casualties that continues to grow each time an officer's bullet hits another Black body, but we are talking about what is good in life. We talk about graphic novels, and telling the truth (God, forgive me), and whether or not to remove the bird's nest from our deck. We are feeding the birds and chasing off the squirrels. We are truly living in the age of innocence around my way.

There is an irony in all of this. I am able to tell the world the cold bitter truth on TV, to create and shape the narrative of what it means for a community to watch a Black body lose breath right before our very eyes, but I am unable to tell the truth to my own flesh and blood. For more than 20 years, I have worked in the true-crime genre, reporting and writing about murderous wives, conniving children who kill their own parents, serial killers, school shootings; I've produced stories about best friends who plot murders of the men they call their husbands. My daughter has always known mommy to tell these types of stories and for better or worse, when those stories air, I allow her to watch them. She loves crime podcasts, she knows a good tease when she hears one, she's even critiqued my rough cuts. She'll tell me when a story gets boring or loses steam. She is my biggest fan and my greatest critic. This is a child who has grown up amidst true crime and truly appreciates the genre. So even I was confused when I lied, on the fly, and told her, "Nope. My story is NOT airing tonight." My husband quickly caught onto the ruse and cautiously went along with my narrative. He put our child in the tub and fed her a very late dinner. I sat downstairs, alone, and watched the network special with pride as I listened to my colleagues tell this painful story in their own words. I was so proud of us, of our entire multiracial, cross generational team. We had pulled together an amazing special in one day.

Fast-forward. Now it's Wednesday, June 3, 2020 and my daughter is no fool. She is demanding to watch the story that kept me on lockdown in the basement. She wants to know when it will air. And so, after dinner, I hand her my phone and tell her to watch the piece so brilliantly written and reported by our correspondent. I still cannot allow her to watch the entire special, especially when she is still processing the trauma of being ripped away from her school, friends, classmates, babysitter, playdates, birthday parties, church, and day-to-day pre-COVID regularities. So, she watches the piece on my cell phone and 5 minutes 12 seconds later, her life is changed.

She looks at her father and I and she doesn't know what to say. "I don't like that story. I don't feel so good right now." Innocence shattered just like that. "What is it that you don't like? How did that story make you feel?" She tells me that her heart is beating fast and she just doesn't understand. And then her father chimes in. "There will always be haters, but there are more good people in this world than bad. But there are haters out there." Haters isn't even a word we use in our home, but he's doing his best to explain something I have neither the words or courage to unpack with my 8 year old. And then there is a brief silence. She is about to say something. "What is it, baby? What do you want to say?" And I wait.

"Can I have some strawberries for dessert?" Crisis averted, I think to myself as I get up and fill a cup with strawberries. And then I Thank God, that tonight, once again, I have managed to avoid unpacking the ugliness of this world for one more day.

Taigi Smith is an award-winning broadcast journalist from San Francisco. Her essays on race and gentrification have been published extensively. She is a proud mother and die-hard true-crime producer. Follow her on Twitter @cgmTaigi or email her at taigismith@gmail.com

ON ELECTION DAY, THERE ARE A FEW THINGS WE KNOW FOR CERTAIN
BY TIM WISE

Forget the polls for a minute. Forget the punditry. Forget the campaign hype that seeks to tell us what we want to hear or what the other side wishes to believe. The fact is, we don't know for sure how this is going to turn out.

I can sketch out very plausible scenarios by which Joe Biden wins in a rout, but also a few, only slightly less convincing, where Donald Trump squeezes out another victory in the electoral college, while, of course, losing the popular vote handily. Such is the lasting force of an institution created by those who sought to maximize the power of smaller states dependent on human bondage and trafficking. And such is the way in which that force continues to empower precisely the kinds of people it was designed to empower, all these years later.

But for today, I won't discuss either of these two possibilities: a Biden victory or a Trump re-election. Nothing I say on that score will matter at this point. If you're reading this, you've already voted or will within the next several hours. Frankly, I can't imagine that any prognostication on my part as to the likely outcome would be the thing that sent you scurrying to the polls if you hadn't already been there or mailed in a ballot. Instead, let's focus on what we know for sure.

First, if all who wanted to vote were able to do so, and if every vote were counted — so there were enough machines in each precinct (meaning no crazy lines), enough early voting stations, no suppression efforts, no courts tossing ballots, and no Postal Service slowdown — Trump gets crushed. Most Americans reject him and the message of his movement and party, and have from the beginning.

The Republicans — the torchbearers of conservatism, in whatever guise — have only won the popular vote for president one time in the last three decades. And the Senators with Rs beside their names represent many millions fewer people than those with Ds. If voting is the ultimate popularity contest, conservatism is decidedly unpopular with the majority of the country's people, even as it wields outsized political influence because of the way the machinery was constructed by kidnappers and their enablers 230-plus years ago.

The only way these forces can believe they have the country behind them is to say that "if you exclude California and New York, we win in a landslide." In short, by saying that certain people aren't Americans — they don't count. The whole of Trumpism is a politic of division and exclusion. And so if a disproportionate number of Democratic voters reside in a handful of states, they'll say it's the acreage that matters. "Look at all that red in the middle of the map," they bellow. "Those are the 'real' Americans."

Actually, those are cornfields, but I digress.

Likewise, only by presuming that Black and Brown folk are lesser Americans can they believe they have the majority behind them. Essentially, they govern as if White support is all they need. It should not be lost on us that this is precisely what David Duke said in 1990 and 1991, too, after losing the U.S. Senate race in Louisiana and the race for Governor, while still carrying between 55 and 60 percent of the White vote. "Well,' Duke intoned, 'I carried my base." Birds of a feather, indeed.

But know this too: in a nation where the share of White folks is dwindling — and not because of immigration (so walls won't stop it), but because White folks' median age is 42, and that means less baby-makin' — the future does not belong to the Trumpsters. What we're seeing is the ugly, audible death rattle of a particular America, long past its expiration date — the death of White hegemony. What is waiting to be born is a multicultural, pluralistic democracy. It cannot be stopped, ultimately, through electoral means, without cheating.

All they really have left is violence. Terrorism. Intimidation. There will be some very troubling days and weeks and years ahead, no matter the outcome today. If Trump wins, they will feel encouraged to do maximum harm to their dear leader's enemies. So be prepared to defend yourself, whatever you take that to mean.

If Trump loses, they will begin to realize, slowly perhaps but eventually, that what they stand for has been rejected. And a cult built on grievance and victimhood does not react well to rejection. More than that, they will do what Carol Anderson has reminded us they have done throughout history. Deploy White rage. It is not speculation. It is documented over and over again.

Every time Whites have seen people of color, especially Black folk, moving forward in some way or "winning" over them (however limited the victory), they have lashed out. This time will be no exception. Even though it might seem absurd to think Joe Biden is symbolic of a victory for Black people, given his decidedly mixed record on several vital issues, it will be seen as such by the MAGA crowd. Kamala Harris ensures it. Restoration of the Obama legacy ensures it. The mere fact that Trumpsters associate the whole of the Democratic Party with Black and Brown "others" ensures it most of all. The GOP is a White identity gang, and if they lose, they will see it as a loss for team Mayo, not just a loss for their favorite candidate.

So once again, be prepared. And arm yourself...

...with knowledge.

The knowledge that every time White rage has reared its awful head, Black and Brown folk survived. And they are still here, reminding us of who we are, but also attempting to show us who we could be as a nation.

What Justice Taney and the Confederate army and the Klan and the Black Codes and the Lynch mob and the White Citizen's Council and Bull Connor and Jim Clark and George Wallace could not defeat, will not be laid low by the likes of the fucking Proud Boys.

Those who survived the march to the sea, the middle passage, the whip, families being torn apart and sold, the rope, the blowtorch, and more, will not be laid low by the denizens of Breitbart. They will not be knocked off stride by cos-playing, toy soldier militia goons sporting beer bellies, camo, and truck nuts.

Those who survived having half their country stolen and then expulsion from the U.S. in the 1930s (even those who were citizens) to open jobs for Whites will not be deterred in their quest for dignity by QAnon loons. Those who survived the death squads we backed in their countries in the 1980s will not be defeated by some pissant glue-eating Kapo from Santa Monica High School with a Joseph Goebbels fashion jones.

Those who survived campaigns of extermination and forced removal by men like Andrew Jackson — whose Crow's Nest sits a twenty-minute drive from where I am typing these words — won't be erased by a failed game show host and his vaseline-foreheaded son in law.

My point is simple but worth repeating: those whom the MAGA faithful seek to put in their place have faced tougher and worse than this. And look who's still standing. Look who is still here. Look who is standing in line for 10 hours in Georgia to vote.

So remember, every time you are afraid, every time you find your faith in humanity flagging, think of Ella Baker. Think of Fannie Lou Hamer. Amzie Moore. Unita Blackwell. John Lewis. Bernard Lafayette. C.T. Vivian. And regardless of what happens today, always, always…

Bet on Black.

Tim Wise is an antiracism educator and author of nine books on race and racism, including White Like Me: Reflections on Race from a Privileged Son *(Soft Skull/Counterpoint), and the latest,* Dispatches from the Race War *(City Lights).*

THE BREATH OF BLACK FOLK AND THE CARCERAL STATE
BY TONYA LOVELACE

Breath, for Black people, is historically imperiled. Chains, ropes, ocean and river water, bullets, elbows, feet, knees, legal mandates, executive orders, many devices are employed to choke us out.

Before COVID-19, Black people have known that they have the highest rate of asthma, high blood pressure, and heart disease due to structural and medical inequities. The struggle to breathe, no matter the income or locality is a daily occurrence for many Black folk.

Amid COVID-19, at a time where the entire globe is at risk for illness and death, Black folk are panting, gasping, and dying at higher rates due to state and systemic entrapments of essential service jobs and close living conditions, and others are just now noticing.

Amid COVID-19, the spirit of the carceral state is alive and well, swirling out to Brooklyn, where the majority of people arrested for nonadherence to social distancing are Black.

The carceral spirit swirled over to Central Park, stoking the theatrics of a White woman to threaten the breath of Christian Cooper by calling the police, so moved by her very own performance that she repeatedly strangled the breath out of her dog to do so.

The carceral spirit located to Louisville to the home of Breonna Taylor, an EMT, an essential worker, who worked to protect the breath of the community, had her own breath snuffed out when a no-knock warrant allowed police to barge in and shoot her in her sleep.

The carceral spirit traveled to White men with shotguns claiming to attempt a citizen's arrest based on suspicion and took the breath of Ahmaud Arbery while out jogging.

The carceral spirit lilted to three police who kneeled on the body and neck of George Floyd while he choked out the words, "I can't breathe," six years after Eric Garner met the same fate.

The carceral spirit is out trolling protesters at this moment, inhibiting breath with tear gas, mace, batter rams, clubs, and guns.

I posit that breath is political. Black people are fighting for their very right to breathe. Those with the privilege of respiration without trepidation do not understand the daily struggle to simply breathe.

Non-Black people join me in this brief, Unrest Meditation.

Inhale deeply, 1, 2, 3.

Exhale, 1, 2, 3.

Repeat. Repeat. Repeat.

As you continue to breathe deeply, allow yourself to reflect on your privilege to breathe. Notice how breath expands your lungs, oxygen flows through your veins, through your limbs.

Allow your thoughts to float to continuous, unrelenting, public, high profile, bold, desperate acts upon Black bodies, squeezing out our breath. Limbs limp, non-oxygenated, still.

Envision your well-oxygenated hands picking up the phone to call the Minneapolis District Attorney to bring more charges to the arrested officer and to charge the other officers who all pressed the life out of George Floyd. Imagine your fingers typing messages about the privilege of breath to your friends and family on Instagram, Facebook, and Twitter.

Wiggle your toes and see them slipping into shoes to walk out and stand in peaceful protest with your loved ones you invited to stand with you, in your living room or the street.

Feel your lips moving to tell Karen and Becky that they do not have to call the police. They do not need displays of proximity to power for validation. They already hold unearned privilege and do not have to employ this power grab. Encourage them to resist their history in doing so.

Finally, wrap your arms around yourself and visualize hugging the mothers, fathers, sons, daughters, brothers, sisters, aunties, uncles, nieces, nephews, cousins, friends, and people of the Black men and women who lost their breath to the carceral state and COVID-19.

Slowly bring yourself back. Promise that you will continue to do these actions and more.

So Black people can breathe.

Tonya Lovelace is a visionary leader, global citizen, and movement maker, organizing Black people & women of color on DV, SV, community, & state violence for nearly 35 years.

TOUCH SAVED ME FROM LONELINESS. WHAT WILL WE BECOME WITHOUT IT?
BY V (FORMERLY EVE ENSLER)

I am afraid of what I will become without touch. Already the frayed edges are beginning to show. So much of my life and the lives of so many women is found through touch. We touch our babies, we hold them to our breasts and bellies, we wash our ageing mothers' bodies and comb and braid our daughters' hair. We massage and we pet and we soothe and we tickle. We do this with each other.

I have been blessed to feel and embrace and be embraced by women all over the world. To hold their stories and their hands, weep with them in my arms. We know how to do this, women. We know how to express loss and grief with our shuddering bodies and tears, transform our rage into medicine with the simplest caress. We know how the body is filled with microaggressions and macro ones. We know how to loosen ourselves into grieving and tighten ourselves into rage. And many of us are practised in that particular hug that shelters, that relieves, that confirms. Hugging is how we know we are here. How we feel each others' existence and meaning and value and substance. How we transmit our love, our empathy, our care.

I am sure that so much of what we women do – so much of our so-called beauty routines – have as much to do with touch as they do with appearance. I cannot wait to have my hair washed at my hairdresser. There is one particular woman; I will call her Nina. Her hands are delicious and confident and kind, equally firm and gentle. When she digs her long, waltzing fingers into my scalp, mixed with the warm soapy water, I know salvation. The same with the woman who does my nails, the little hand massages, her fingers pressing deep into the stress of my palm, the flesh-to-flesh contact and energetic exchange. I need that. We need that. Particularly those of us who live alone, who don't live with partners or spouses. Particularly those of us most likely to perish from the virus – the older ones. Touch is how we go on.

I think of women hairdressers, manicurists, masseuses, nurses, caregivers, nannies, yoga teachers, acupuncturists, physical therapists. Who will they touch again and when?

The other night, the man I live with, James, a magical being, was playing and suddenly threw himself on top of me. His body was perfectly heavy and it felt unbelievably good to feel human weight, muscle flesh pressing down on me. It had nothing to do with sex, but everything to do with life, connection and vitality. He smushed me good. The imprint has lasted. These are desperate times.

We all know the significance of touch. We know babies who experience physical contact show increased mental capabilities in the first six months of life. Touch makes your brain grow. And we know that those seriously deprived become aggressive and develop behavioural problems. Touch is how we become part of this human community.

So here we are in the middle of this pandemic, knowing our cough can potentially kill; our body could be a lethal weapon. How do we make sense of this? How do we live with this unbearable skin hunger?

Part of the agony of this crisis is that even in death we are denied the possibility of touching the body. By four o'clock each afternoon, I can feel the disintegration begin. After a day of disembodied voices, blurred and frozen faces, loud news. After a day of ever-increasing numbers of the invisible dead, the bodies piling up in unseen warehouses, the back of huge trucks and cold-storage rooms. After a day of aerial shots of mass graves, wooden coffins stacked on top of each other like boxes of invisible pain. After a day of wanting to reach through the screen, the void, the isolation, to feel a heart beating, take someone's hand, breathe with another's breath, I can feel myself begin to disappear.

The body cannot and does not exist now. Not in life. Not in death. Thousands are disappearing without fanfare or acknowledgment, without family or ritual.

I want to make each body a person, each person real. I want to know their story and who they loved and what they were most proud of and where they first discovered beauty and what horizon they looked out on for most of their days. But death is moving so fast. You go to the hospital. You leave your loved ones. You don't return. No touch, no closure, no body. Nobody. Nothing. No longer here.

I think of Claude Rains in The Invisible Man unwrapping the bandages around his head only to reveal there is absolutely nothing there. Nothing. No flesh, no face. No person. Nothing. I was 10 years old the first time I saw that movie. I remember vomiting and staying up the whole night in terror and being afraid of the dark after that. But it wasn't the dark I was afraid of, it was the disintegration of the body, becoming meaningless, becoming nothing.

I discovered early the best defence against this horrifying dissolution was touch, kissing, massive amounts of physical contact, otherwise known as sex. I salvaged the world through my hands, body, mouth and skin. As a young woman, I needed to press my flesh against almost everything and everyone. Of course, misogynists interpreted this as promiscuous, loose. They called me a slut. But mine was an existential crisis. I needed touch. I needed physical connection. It saved me from unbearable loneliness. It allowed me to feel my impact on the world. It gave me pleasure and agency. It let me know that I existed, that I was here. It allowed me to fulfil my desire and heal the deepest physical wounds. It taught me trust might be possible and gave me undeniable moments of comfort.

A friend reported that a venture capitalist recently told her he saw a "touchless" future. I fear this is what the technocrats and AI people and fascists are dreaming of – a touchless future. The body has always been that lowly human thing that got in the way – messy desire and rage and passion and sex. I come from the land of the 60s. My consciousness was fashioned there in that ecstatic river of sex, drugs and rock'n'roll. There I learned that the body is the loci of revolution and change. So here, now, where our bodies are locked behind masks and gloves and screens and filters, where will the centre of our revolution lie? The quarantine is necessary. But we must ask ourselves: what kind of mutiny is possible in a quarantine?

I light a candle every night for those who have left the world that day. I imagine their faces. I sometimes am able to find their names. I touch the candle and feel the warmth of the flame on my body. I try to make them real. I allow myself to grieve their loss.

My act of resistance is simple. I will have a healthy respect and fear of the virus. I will maintain physical distancing for now. But I will not be afraid of your body.

I will not kill off my yearning to touch you. I will let it guide me. I will fantasise about it. I will write about it. I will draw it. I will remember us cuddling in January, mad dancing in the protest last July. I will feel the soft skin of your precious hand in mine. I will embrace you as you cry and cherish the wetness of your tears on my blouse. I will feel the fire of rage in my belly and the impossible sorrow in my throat. And I will learn over time how to translate this hunger for your body, for your burning skin, into the making of this most necessary new world.

Previously published on theguardian.com.

V (Formerly Eve Ensler) is the Tony and Obie award-winning, New York Times best-selling playwright, author, and activist with plays and books published in over 48 languages and performed in over 140 countries. She is the founder of V-Day and One Billion Rising and a co-founder of City of Joy.

AN ELEGY FOR BETTER TIMES
BY VICKI MEEK

We done been through some stuff. We nervously waited for the 2020 elections to roll around so we could possibly right this backward course we were traveling. It's hard to pinpoint exactly when I started feeling a sense of dread about the 2020 election outcome. Like many hopeful Americans, I woke up on Wednesday, November 4th breathing a little less haltingly than I have for the past 3 ¾ years. But I wasn't quite breathing a sigh of relief. I knew if the Biden/Harris ticket didn't win by a landslide, the current occupant of the White House was definitely going to cry "Stolen election!"

Boy, oh boy, has that proven to be true in spades.

My greatest fear throughout this guy's presidency has been that he would manage to undermine the integrity of all our national institutions and indeed he has. His Republican enablers, who have given up any pretense of putting country above party, continue to prop him up as he carries out their draconian social policies, while raping the national coffers as they enrich their already obscenely rich donors. This latest attack on our democracy shouldn't be viewed as something new. This country has suppressed the Black vote since Reconstruction, but what is new is the response by young White voters. Many of them refuse to follow their parents' lead in desperate moves to hold on to White supremacy with everything they can muster.

We always had White allies throughout our liberation struggle, but the numbers never reached what we're seeing today. This is why I have not totally given up on America, despite its sordid, twisted relationship to Black people. In 2020, with the results of this election, we see a coming together of most Black people with other communities of color and young White people who reject their parents' ideology. Granted, much of this camaraderie is steeped in the moment, when the country has finally chosen to take notice of the dispensability of Black bodies at the hands of police. I know something different is in the air in 2020, because violence against Black bodies is not new.

So, what do I see as the path forward from the 2020 election? I see more strategic organizing, like we saw in the taking of Georgia by the Biden/Harris team and other states that went Republican in 2016. I see a renewed commitment to local politics being a focus of some of these organizers, as more and more new, young voters begin to recognize how our political system works. My hope is that this election will restore the idea in our political strategizing, that one vote can make the critical difference so everyone must get engaged.

I also hope that communities of color begin to realize that unity and solidarity around common issues gives us more political clout than blindly supporting any one political party. Nothing Black people have gained in this country has come without organizing. So in addition to my other hopes for 2021, I hope we renew our commitment to unifying through grassroots organizing. It's been the worst of times, but we can turn this into the best of times if we simply keep our eye on the prize.

Vicki Meek is a nationally recognized artist, curator, educator and activist living in Dallas. Her email is msart0822@gmail.com and you can read her blog Art & Racenotes at https://art-racenotes.blogspot.com/.

JUST ME. 2020 THE YEAR THAT TRIED TO DRAG ME, BUT I'M STILL HERE!
BY WANDA ELIZABETH GREEN

It is without one doubt that I can surely exist right here and tell you all that this has indeed been my "Annus Horribilis." I haven't been solely selected, others have faced this wielding dragon just as I have. It is every bit of me that stands face to face with this demon and declares victory over my life. From birth to today, every step, every lesson and every word of love, every encouragement, and every experience keeps me standing. I'm still here. The year 2020 has been my Hannibal moment and I'm not slain. I am still standing!

My perfume will make you swoon, Egyptian Musk with Sweet Almond Oil, Patchouli and whatever else I can grab. You know when I'm coming and you know when I've been there. Lasting Sensory Memories.

I'm a dissenter, a rebel. I speak up and I'm not afraid to challenge that which needs to be addressed. I call it as I see it, and I see it exactly how it is. I have the ability to discern, that's from being around folks: church folks, school folks, work folks and being around elders that point out everything for our own good. Being around grand natured and weathered hand seniors, often pointing out (quietly of course) with a whisper and a nudge: Watch this, Watch out for that, Did you see that? Did you hear what they just said? Did you see how he just looked back? Don't do it like that, but like this. Many times telling me to just sit, be still, and observe. Gray hair and violet candied breath, assuring that it will all be revealed by and by and that no matter the ruckus or battle or challenge, I can get through it. The challenges have indeed come.

Our culture is everything to me. The Culture First! We are beautiful and lovely, bright and valiant, creative and savvy, thinkers and doers, sowers and givers. We are makers and soil entrenched. Black people are moon touched and sky readers, we are sun kissed and different. We are sweet, because if we weren't sweet, well, you know! We are that denied and hidden gift that rings of love and power, no matter the trampling, our bell still rings.

I am a fixer for others, but often shy, and handicapped to move for myself. I promise, I'm working on it. This has been that year. I've been forced to love on me and to hold my own hand, not to faint and to keep on walking. I love to watch television, remember roller derby (remember those ladies helmets?) What about the ladies themselves? Their strength and tenacity and not one of them Negro, but we didn't miss that message. Persevere. I love the beach and to travel (My name is Wanda. The Wanderer. It's Hellenic and I'm part of the Vandals tribe. When I first read that, I was like "Oh Hell Yeah"). I don't know how mommy got that so right. My name...How could she know? I guess that's why she is my mommy...her task.

She has Alzheimer's now.

I'm a Maker, one who loves beads and colors and fabric and thread. I love pretty cakes and lovely buttons. I love dangling earrings and incense.

I imagine myself in the Motherland again...Brooklyn has a hold on me. I belong there, indeed the city of champions: snowy winters and unbearable circumstances...for many. The sweetest hugs and safe shelter. Nanny's ever warm breath and lovely hugs. Her trust of a little girl to walk around the corner to Anna's to get the paper and to make sure my change was on point. That trust is my invisible staff, my walking stick, used to hold on tight when my road is rocky and mired.

I adore to sit and be still. My faith in the Creator is overwhelming. I trust in his power completely. One of my favorite songs says it best "Who taught the sun where to stand in the morning? And who told the ocean you can only come this far? And who showed the moon where to hide 'til evening? Whose words alone can catch a falling star?"

I am a Christian with Muslim tendencies! I'm a believer! Gotta be for this year!

I am in love with the whole idea of The Black Man! C'mon now, still here, still standing, still beautiful, still the epitome of the universe. Black men exude Creation, no matter where they stand: The Mountains, The Jailhouse, The Nursery, The Car Wash, The Kitchen, The Farm, The Chain Gang, The Pulpit, In his drunkenness, With a broken and withered heart, In his loss, In the Cross Hairs. In their weakness and tiredness, In his tears...ain't nothin' like a Black Man. Black men give me strength!

Word is Born!!!!!

My kid died in January, his name was Haji. Haji was named after the little Brown boy from Johnny Quest. What a sweet spirit and gentle soul. I picked up his ashes last Wednesday, the day after election day. It was time for my continued boldness. I worked the election all week and had some challenges (shoot, there were a lot of challenges and so much on my mind, but I knew my steps and met great people who were out there on the move, making sure that they made it in time to cast their vote. Some spoke English and some not, but they kept coming) I was courageous that day.

I picked up Haji's ashes. That ring is wrenching and vicious and weakening...it makes me shy away from how it all changed. I won't question The Creator's path for him, but my mind will forever rewind picking up my kid's ashes. I picked up Haji's ashes on November 4, 2020. Mommy picked up Haji's ashes!

2020 tried her best, but I'm still standing!

Wanda Elizabeth Green is a Los Angeles based writer and actor, as well as a practicing tax resolution specialist, and marriage officiant. Her email address is afrocubanmommi@yahoo.com and you can follow her on Instagram @Uigei.

WHITE AMERICA IS EATING ITS OWN TAIL
BY ZENZILE GREENE-DANIEL

We thought that we had hit rock bottom and then we heard a knock from below.

The host of one of my favorite podcasts repeated this quote in the introduction of an episode to give context to a conversation with an artist about her theatrical piece on the Constitution. And I thought, what a perfect analogy for the way I feel about this election and about this entire administration. Immediately after 9/11, I began to sense this consciously. Hatred and xenophobia emerged and concentrated in groups and chat board discussions that scared me in ways it never had before. I tried to escape by surrounding myself with what I believe to be common sense people, discourse, informative op-eds, essays and lectures. However, no amount of immersion in common sense and facts will ever change how a large majority of White America feels about Black and Brown people in this country, not to mention humanity in general.

It's not lost on me that racism has been alive and well in America long before I was born. What does shock me is the lack of concern reflected in a vote for 45 by people who espouse values and morals.

A large majority of women in this country voted for a man who is on record joking about assaulting women on an Access Hollywood bus. Just let that sit for a moment.

Women with daughters.

I did not know self-hatred could run this deep and in such staggering numbers.

And, I don't think it's necessary to look two steps ahead of what was said on that bus to begin to understand how far a racist White majority will go to maintain their privileges while still daring to uphold some perverse pretense of decency, morality and humanity, none of which they actually appear to understand or practice. A democratic process, it seems, only works fairly when it works to their advantage.

As Professor Eddie Glaude stated so eloquently on MSNBC recently, we cannot place the blame primarily on 45's shoulders. He is a manifestation of the sick, ugly, pathological truth about what this country has been built on. It is a crumbling foundation of theft, lies, genocide, rape, lynching, false narratives, stereotypes and standards of acceptability tailored toward advancing White mediocrity in ways that have taken ages to disengage from through varying levels of awareness.

But the process of disengagement has never stopped. The fight for injustice has never stopped. The seeking of truth has never stopped. The call to serve all versus some has never stopped. The strength to confront the darkness without allowing it to contaminate the soul has never stopped. In the lives of those who are committed to the struggle for human rights, it doesn't stop. In the spirit of our ancestors, it doesn't stop.

So I try not to spend too much time frozen like a deer in headlights, gaping down the barrel of the bottomless, fathomless, danger that is Whiteness and listening to the knocking from below. So many of us have tried for so long to be what they said we needed to be in order to not die, to not be tortured, to not be murdered, to not be raped, to not be decapitated, to not be humiliated, to not be kicked and spat upon, to not be turned away. But you can't make deals with madness without becoming mad yourself.

Instead, I choose to proceed to play my part to reveal the light of truth in this world. I do so with the knowledge that I am worthy without even trying. Yes. Worthy without having to struggle. That I am a divine manifestation of the love I choose to accept within me. And that the nature of struggle we are most familiar with exists in a system bent on constructed illusions of measurement, comparison and selection based on superficial identifiers that define not one of us as human beings. Not one. I'm not saying struggle isn't necessary. But all we have ever really known of struggle is what oppression, unfairly leveraged opposition, deception, and a lack of self-acceptance have forced upon us.

Who would choose that kind of struggle to define oneself? And who would choose to normalize and accept it?

You may say that struggle is rarely chosen. Well, you're not likely to be in the 1 percent if you do.

Even the poorest White Americans are being held hostage by the bottomless greed of an idea conceived decades ago to make slaves of us all. Meanwhile, crumbs of distraction are tossed down to us from ministries that master in the design of "power," another falsely constructed cage.

I think in his statement, Glaude was clearly indicting Whiteness as a device that was not only conceived explicitly to motivate through hatred, fear, racism and division, but which has also unraveled, undone and inflicted nameless damage even on those who have wielded it.

There are those participating in Whiteness that want to be rescued or forgiven by those whom it still attempts to enslave without ever taking responsibility for the assault. There are those who are so ignorant, dangerous and irredeemable, that they will continuously support a structure which is also killing them, which is also keeping them poor, jobless and sick as long as they can carry the mantle of a manifest destiny they never deserved.

It is a cycle of violence with no end if White America continues to refuse, as Glaude states, to acknowledge its sins; to stop the bullshit and look itself in the eye so that humanity at large, and generations to come, might one day be able to choose to struggle for reasons far more unifying than surviving Whiteness.

Originally from Brooklyn, New York, Zenzile Greene is a poet, writer, photographer and editor. Her websites are urbeve.com and zlay72.wixsite.com/zanography7 Her email is zlay7@hotmail.com. You can follow her on IG @urbneve and @fotogemini and find her on Facebook at Zenzile Greene-Daniel.

PART II: POETRY

WHILE BLACK
BY AALIYAH C. DANIELS

White men spray spit in cops' faces while marching through city hall. In riot gear, cops hold their composure telling a crowd, 'we want you to express your freedom of speech.'

A Black man rots in jail for thirty years for the murder of some Georgia children. A documentary says the KKK killed them, but the FBI destroyed the evidence, 'You could say they prevented a race war.'

White man with an AK-47 propped on his right shoulder screams, 'You are supposed to protect the people. You are not doing your job,' to a cop during quarantine. I think he wanted a haircut, or apple pie from his local diner.

Black man runs down a dark street, hunted like an animal and killed. White America has another hero vigilante. Black America has another dead body to use as a martyr with no permission.

Terrance Hayes was right. There was no black male hysteria, no black hysteria, but I think there will be one soon. Yesterday, I read a post about the AK-47 white man threatening a composed cop. A Black woman said, 'Just like that Blue lives don't matter anymore.'

Aaliyah C. Daniels is a Bronx-born and raised poet and community activist. She was a member of the 2019 Urban Word NYC National Slam Team, a two-year NYC Youth Poet Laureate Ambassador, and the first-place winner of the No Tokens Journal Young Poets' Prize. She currently attends Kenyon College. Follow her on Instagram @insertblackgirlname

STAR LIGHT
BY AARON "SPAZECRAFT" LAZANSKY-OLIVAS

Star light, star bright, first star I saw that night.

I wish I may, I wish I might,

    continue to see that star shine bright.

Even through the hurt and fight,

    this fire we share can still ignite.

I wish I may, I wish I might,

    some time soon stay warm from your light.

Create is what I'd like to do,

like pollen from plant, plant seeds with you.

Do you see me in my truth?

Can we both express our truth?

Will we continue to pollute

or clean our air to deeply breathe....?

To listen and try to believe.

    To look to the stars instead of grieve?

To grow our own brand of love,

instead of tossing off a glove,

feel connected below and above,

    to make our dream reality and fly like dove.

To gently encourage instead of shove?

To embrace our problems and help see through,

    like good friends would and always do.

Star light, my love for you will never die,

    my tears birth worlds now when I cry.

Sew up these holes in our fabric of now,

    let's find a way, some way, some how.

Aaron "SpazeCraft" Lazansky-Olivas is a New York City-born and based Pioneering Innovative Urban Educator. He Is also an accomplished muralist, designer, composer, DJ, VJ, poet, and resident visualist for NYC Beat Collectives, In Plain Sight, & Beat Haus & one-half of super powered multi-media project Children ov Jupiter. Social media: @spazecraft

TYRANNY OF MIRRORS
BY ABSOLUTE NSYTE

Tied to the memory of darksides where u hurt me/

Can't stop the visions be apparitions of apartheid division b/ fields of
distant slavery conceived beneath the sea/ long before where the hustlers
be/ they taught heat one lash at a time pushed the creed in me/ trickery
from the start modeled after Joan of Arc/ no more sacrificial than an
awkward fart/ soulless nations that tear their first borns apart/ look at
how we model art/ teach no one then cause a spark/ greater than a
revolution pollution park with misty skies of acid mix with rancid parts/
Tell me we ain't Joan of Arc and Moses to we model well oh yes we do/
can't face ourselves yet we eat cake/ on top of the backs of millions from
their tables we take/ to afford our lux-jewelry it's so deluxe can't tell us
much we too hot to touch/ we fail in ways we will never see/ as we hail
ole hitler to a new dixie-cratic beat/ Take a seat and receive this talking
too/ I guess I got the right 'cause one half of my family is just like you/
too racist to see the races between both of us behind them sheets/

The Tyranny

of your mirrors

caused cuts on my face

and whips on my soul's back

Breonna My Taylor McDonald My Laquan

Come Eric My Garner Yes come see what I'm ON

Feeling like heaven is over

Where there's no MECCA for the DONS

We were raised with high stakes

over the hot coals and ONES

The crossroads where heart breaks with the CON

When it rains it pours better run or ring the ALARM

No happiness leaning over the CLOSED DOORS

YET my people are true warriors ready to EVEN SCORES/ Have 'em like legendaries ASKIN' FOR MORE/ I'm the gifted and most prolific all up in YOUR CORE/ MY ENERGY feel the frequency of my people B/ Sensei in my GURU mode hibernating TOURS G/ Next dimension meditation flying through the floor B/ there are no ceilings that are too great for me/ Wutang like imagery cross alignment symmetry/ Jean Baptiste and Mavis Staples cross biology/

The Tyranny

of your mirrors

caused cuts on my face

and whips on my soul's back

SO your house is on FIRE do you care if it burns?/ It's the most central question while sweat out your perms/ We fighting for FREEDOM while you fighting with GERMS/ We bringing the JUSTICE you will never LEARN/

The Tyranny

of your mirrors

caused cuts on my face

and whips on my soul's back

Absolute Nsyte

Absyte

Absolute Nsyte is a Brooklyn-based emcee, songwriter/producer, poet and Global Enterprise IT Program Manager with two Bachelors and a Masters in Enterprise Software Development. She has produced five independent albums and mixtapes while also working for some of the foremost leading innovators in IT & Web Development such as Dun & Bradstreet, Verizon, The City of New York and Mastercard among others. Her email is absyte22@me.com and you can follow her on Instagram, @absolutensyte

SKIN
BY ANDREA "KELLI" HIGGS

Do you hear the skin I'm in?
Is my voice too loud or low?
Does my melanin clog your ears?
Do my words come too slow?

When asked for input at a meeting, could you
        acknowledge my response as clear and concise?
Why do my words get lost in translation, they're deemed
        not worthy, and easily dismissed as trite?

Do you hear the skin I'm in?
It's exhausting repeating what was previously stated.
I guess the framed parchment and awards on the walls are
        less than adequate or simply overrated.

Would you prefer I turn down the sound of my skin,
change the tone, perhaps change the station?
I cannot and will not accommodate your request.
Ida and Sonia expect me to represent truth and justice
        for the next generation.

If you only hear the skin I'm in, your silence will
        reverberate.
There's no need to adjust the volume.
History's cacophony beats like an 808.

The revolution will not be televised.
Wake up, listen and pay attention.
From 3/5ths to whole persons,
People and their hues, they are a-changin'.

No justice, no peace.
No one accountable for the slain.
Emmett, Trayvon, Eric, George, Breonna and more.
We honor their lives by saying their names.

Please stop. Do not deny what is hiding in plain sight.
Skin has fueled the cost of discrimination
      fo[u]r centuries and generations.
Who's paying the persistently escalating price?

Do you hear the skin I'm in?
Does my melanin clog your ears?
Do my words reveal the audacity to hope for a time when
      the content of my character trumps the color of my
      SKIN?

Andrea "Kelli" Higgs is an attorney based in White Plains, NY, adjunct professor, grant writer, speech writer, and guest columnist for the Westchester County Press. Her email is kelli@kellihiggslaw.com and you can connect with her on LinkedIn, www.linkedin.com/in/kellihiggs.

THE GREAT DIVIDE
BY ANGELINA RIVERA

What an eerie state we lived the past 4 years,

with outrage, anger, hate, divisive-causing fears,

with enemies sought to kill nations fathered by sin,

Obama warned us we'd fall back in the space within.

The compromise was breached he didn't have his win,

that state of marring collapsed the leaders' power within,

the very fabric of the change he aimed to make,

but race dynamics took another higher stake.

and claimed some lives and brought up hate that ceased

　　　　to grow,

that killed the mama, sis' and father we all know,

that hate that brewed and manifested in our face,

was testament to the monster that took his place.

and Trump was born out of the lies his father told,

he was elected by hidden men underground and old,

with massa politicking mindsets within their hold,

the men who tightened borders killed a culture cold.

and he's the orange man who kept that nation's place,

awaiting boys and boys to rise up and fill space,

in a world eradicating their entire race,

wiping out their hateful sin that disgraced grace.

They wanted to erect the slaves we laid to rest,

by citing century old tactics and just to test,

test the minds and thoughts of peoples who laid wait,

to see the fostering of global rage, anger and hate.

pissed us off we fought to stand strong in nomadic state,

and we took back our sweet country on this date,

you were blindsided by our united comeback win,

we got a sistah on our side with our own skin.

that represents the thing you feared would now begin,

eradication of old sins fate lied buried within,

those foundations that we built with our own hands,

the ones that poked and prodded us to build what stands.

the bedrock of the lives we live out by YOUR plans,

circled back took back what's ours, which is this land,

and we look back at the time we have come from,

to see the beauty of our culture, rise up as one.

so now we waited all this time just to exhale,

to breathe a sighed relief after the grand telltale,

of a country gone astray went straight to hell,

now we're back ready to start a brand-new tale.

tale of harmony and peace, justice for all,

won't be easy those Reps have just been told,

that our peoples, now the force, will reckon all,

and ancestors' ready watchmen on the wall.

to write the history that awaits us as we hold,

hold on to grace that God has rendered us as bold,

if we stick together this time and stay strong,

we will conquer victory yes, all day long!

Angelina Rivera is a native of Newark, New Jersey, where she began writing poetry at a young age, where her poetry became the voice of her quiet inner self. She is employed as a report writer for the State of New Jersey, she is a certified master herbalist, and is a soon-to-be meditation instructor and her email address is linguisticrtist@gmail.com and you can follow her on Instagram @iamangelinarivera.

TAX EVASION
BY BENIN LEMUS

The newspaper printed the story.
Turns out, he's just like us, debt-wise anyway.
He's trying to figure out if he can get a
pay-day loan, but the interest is high and
the loan officers are more like loan sharks-
if you don't pay, they bite.

The president is broke.
He likes nice things and instead of going
to Goodwill, the 99 cent store, layaway,
like the rest of us-
            He charges it and calls it,
an investment.

The president is broke.
But unlike you, and unlike me,
he doesn't have student loans.
He probably spent his money on hookers
and Adderall and tacky McMansions
that no one would ever want to live in
and no one will ever buy,
and yet, someone lent him money.
How does he have 421 million dollars' worth
of debt?

The president is broke.
He is a liar.
He knows how much we need $600 and yet,
he wants us to work for our money,
save our money, in a damn pandemic.

This broke president,
with his $70,000 hair cuts, hiring his daughter,
to read shit to him, explain shit to him,
to be his consultant.

The president ought to be ashamed of himself
instead of shaming us.
The people he scams, the people he locks up,
the people he allows to die from COVID.

The newspaper laid it all out today,
The President of the United States is broke:
morally, spiritually, financially,
broke.

Broke like $2.23 in your checking account.
Broke like ramen until payday.
Broke like putting $3.00 in your gas tank.
Broke like no insurance and late on rent.
Broke like too much month at the end of the money.

And yet, he golfs on the weekends and
instead of eating beans and rice,
fishing quarters out of a coin jar to wash clothes,
being humbled and figuring out a way up and out
of a tough situation,
like the rest of us,
he bobs and weaves, ducks and dodges,
to avoid paying taxes.

The president is broke and like the rest of us have
been
            doing
            all our lives,
he's going to have to figure it out
            because we,
got nothin' for him.

Benin Lemus is a Los Angeles-based poet, teacher-librarian, and social justice activist. You can follow her political and social musings on Twitter @Bookishgirl_LA.

MARCH 30 YEAR OF THE PLAGUE
BY BOB HOLMAN

Who thinks of language rights at a time like this? In the US, the Wampanoag tribe certainly is – just as the pandemic hit the US, these Native Americans had their tribal status revoked by the Trump administration. The Wampanoags are the tribe who greeted the Pilgrims in 1620. The last speaker died over a hundred years ago. Now, the Wampanoags are a model for language revitalization, with a Tribal center that has dedicated language classrooms and an ever-increasing number of speakers. This is the moment that Trump makes his power grab, to take all this away. Be vigilant to government intrusion under the cover of the Pandemic.

In New York there's plenty of poetry online, including the Bowery Poetry Club. I am self-quarantined above the shop on the Bowery in downtown Manhattan. But of course, all the cultural centers are closed – the vitality of live performance cannot be replicated on Zoom. The homeless own the streets. Essential workers, mostly Brown and Black folks, are on the subways. Masks are required by law – not everybody obeys the law.

I've been in my apartment for two months. I have one poem to show for it. It's based on the words of John Donne, British metaphysical poet of the 1600s, who wrote,

Ask not for whom the bell tolls
It tolls for thee

My poem goes like this:

    DONE
Ask not for whom the siren wails
That's you in there

My friend, Carmen Bardeguez-Brown somehow got stuck in Thailand for the pandemic, but that didn't stop her from writing the quintessential Nuyorican (New York + Puerto Rican) Spanglish poem about the Pandemic. I love to read it for its polyglot sensibility.

New York is not a ghost town (Boom-bang)
Boom-bang despierta despierta
high peaks rascacielos
stores money money money clubs
Human misery miseria
You seduced me with your fast paced walk
Horny greedy motherfucker my love mi amor

Times Square dirty pretzels overpriced everything carajo
Gazillion restaurants fresh coconuts en las bodegas
Italy in the Bronx PuertoRicans con su guaguanco
Living in the streets while celebrities pretend to hide their
diamond glittering
United Nations in the house while the South Bronx was
burning down
What Now?

Horny greedy motherfucker mi amor my love
your dirty streets from Broadway to 125
The New York Times howling at El Diario la Prensa
Nueva Yol
You're bleeding now
Don't cry for me yo soy New York Tu eres Mi Nuyol los
5 Boroughs y en control.

Carmen Bardeguez-Brown, April, 2020

I can't wait to be with you all again. Take good care. As they say in
Occitan, Lo men tribalh qu'ei encuentà's deu nenet. My job is to take
care of the baby.

Previously published in *Ostana Endangered Language Alliance*

*Founder of the Bowery Poetry Club, Bob Holman is best known for his work with
the oral tradition, poetry slams, spoken word, digital poetry, poetry films and
endangered languages. bobholman.com, @bobholmanpoet*

LAST DAY I COULD SMELL: MARCH 16, 2020
BY BRIAN SHAW

Walking in

There was this

Weird smell, it

Came over

Me like a

Blast of air

A strong scent

For a Tuesday

A hospital

Whooshed into

The school I

Teach at, this

Industrial

Strength Febreze.

What's going on?

I thought.

Oh, a crew

Came and cleaned

Last night,

An aide said.

You could feel

Blowing through

Vents of this

Classroom like

Damn. I walked

In my class

It was quiet

There was this

Silence. A

Moment when

Nobody

Said much, they

Were gagging

From the fumes

I'm guessing.

I sat down

Six feet away

From someone,

There was this

Sense we would

Maybe to

Day, a week

We had no

Idea.

Next class to

Us had three

Total students,

Emptied out

The teacher

Called out sick,

So and so

Equaled 23;

This damp from

My jacket

It was strange

I soaked

Through it though

It was a

Cold room in

A basement;

A room so

Crazy you'd

Usually

Have to tell

Calm down man,

This is a

Classroom, stop

Yelling, Kobe!

Then I write

Up a plan

On a piece

Of paper.

Today, one

After the

Other walked

Up and said

I wasn't

Tryna play

No trash can

Basketball,

I'll see you

Tomorrow,

Fist bumping

Yeah, I said,

Choking up

Giving them

An elbow

Back, knowing

Brian Shaw is from Salt Lake City. He is a school behaviorist, a producer/ sportswriter who publishes Brian Vs. Utah, *a sports insider newsletter on Substack and author. Twitter @ExUtahSports*

HALF IS STILL WHOLE
BY CARLA VEGA

I am a caged silenced songbird

Dreaming of unforeseeable freedom

to soar familiar skies

to view the world from high above...

I am

LOVE

laying sedentary in my Heart

Waiting patiently

Making art to pass the time

until I find

my match

to light a steady flame...

I am rain come to cleanse

Jagged rock before diamond

First note of unsung Song

Bouts of crying, wailing, longing...

I am Wild without prey

No access to the jungle

No humid breath from trees

No cacophony of cries in camouflage...

Painfully isolated. cold. alone.

In hiding from an enemy unseen

I can't breathe… locked up. in a camp. with barbed wire.

watched.

I am limited funds,

rationed until I soon r u n o u t…

Then what? I cannot stay here forever.

This

Is

Not

Sustainable.

I am the temporary Artist in Residence

with unbounded imagination as my friend

with time to catch up to Self…

I am Wealth

Beyond the old ideals.

I am the cozy bear in its cave

safe to sleep in peace

stored up for Winter

no need to emerge anytime soon.

Wrapped still in cocoon

I breathe and know

I am being born anew…

I wonder…

about my kin. my clans. my ancestral relations.

My two sides spanning opposite ends of Earth

½ Filipino, ½ Puerto Rican

Which side will visit me this day?

Who will emerge to bring me closer to Me

connecting these fragments of my Soul?

What Magic was I made to forget,

but am now remembering?

I am remembering…

My intuitive ways

The magic of my hands

How Spirit speaks to me

Visually, aurally, with tingles and heat

and raised hair on arms on back of neck…

I am remembering the deep conviction

surging through me

when a message is coming through for You...

I am remembering the way plants speak to me

through scent and curiosities arising, like...

'Who are you?'

'What is your medicine?'

'How can you heal me?'

'What must I learn to harvest?'

You are giving me permission to know you...

And I see how you grow so freely

Relentless through the concrete

No matter how many times they cut you down.

You are hearty and meant to Be, so please...

Let me bring pieces of you home with me

to soothe my senses and help me remember...

I am remembering the spirit of my forefathers

Greeting me...

Calling me closer to the root through food...

Ah, I found Malunggay!

The farmer at the stand is Filipino

and he promised Saluyot

and Eggplant

and Bittermelon

and Okra

and Opo in a few months…

Oh, and I can make Adobo!

and add Soy Sauce

and Ginger

and Bay Leaf

and Vinegar

and steaming White Rice starched with Pride…

I am remembering words, the few I know…

Maganda / Beautiful

Salamat / Thank you

Pahinget ng mangga / Can I have a mango?

Isa, Dalawa, Tatlo / 1, 2, 3 …

I only know a handful… but I can remember!

And I know I am loved beyond forgotten language

Whole and Worthy of the Magic…

She told me I had Magic Hands...

"Ay, Jusko!"

Not just a cry from Grandma Luz's aching bones

I am 'Ablon'

A call for healing...

She, High Priestess Healer, tried to teach me

In repetition

In touch

In the prayer in Latin to keep the Devil away

In offerings to ancestors on the altar...

And I am remembering... I can still learn from her

She is willing to teach me from B e y o n d t h e V e i l

Bridging me gifts

In nature

In people

In feelings

In visions

In communion with Elders-

wrinkled hands and stretching skin,

slow shuffles and greying eyes...

I remember the perseverance of my people.

Our People.

All those who weathered the storms that came before

Survived to live to let us thrive.

We are more resilient than we think.

I am living on the brink...

Remembering more and more each day...

Hands. Energy. Land. Herbs. Ilocos Norte.

Dirt roads. Farmland. Family. Clans.

Holiday singing in the streets. Nine day Novenas.

Secrets of Sungka. The memories never end...

Lineage and Legacy live in me.

This mix of Browns in me

Not only ½...

It blends in Me

Whole.

Carla Vega is an internationally recognized Los Angeles-based, San Francisco-rooted multi-disciplinary performing artist and writer: SAG-AFTRA actor, voiceover artist, solo theatre creator, poet, singer, dancer and teaching artist. She believes that the performing arts and storytelling are powerful catalysts for healing, inspiration, compassion, and positive social change. All social media: @iamcarlavega www.CarlaVega.com

GUNS FOR HIRE
BY CELILLIANNE GREEN

In 2020, the police, policed
In Black America, there is no peace

The police kill unarmed Black people at will.

Running away, at home, asleep in bed
Choked in the street, Black people are dead

Slave patrols were used to control.

Police today behave in a similar way.

Cell phone videos have allowed the world to see
Police brutality is a Black reality

Unarmed Black people are killed by police violence
Black people are buried under the blue wall of silence

The police and White people interact differently
Police treat White people as if they are free

White people survive police encounters alive.
In contrast, Black people face systemic inhumanity
They are disproportionately a police casualty

Police are trained to kill with qualified immunity
Black people are routinely subjected to police scrutiny

Police act as tax-payer-funded, guns for hire
Black people pay taxes too. They are not inspired.

In fact, Black people are sick and tired.
Black people want brutal police convicted and fired.

There is nothing in this world like being Black

Black skin is under state-sanctioned attack

Is the killing of a Black person a police initiation?
Why is the trigger pulled without hesitation?

Adults, children, teenagers, females, and males
For taking Black life, police rarely go to jail

Instead, police receive paid administrative leave
Black people attend funerals, cry, and grieve

They grieve their loved-one and a natural fact
A fact to which White people negatively react:

BLACK LIVES MATTER

CeLillianne Green is a poet, awyer, speaker, and author whose books include That
Word *and* A Bridge. *Her work provides cultural observations about life, love,
spirituality, relationships, history, and politics, and she can be reached
at www.CeLillianneGreen.com.*

COVID POEM
BY CHARLIE R. BRAXTON

We are bearing witness
to murder en masse
The wholesale slaughter
Of the blameless
At the bloody hand
Of benign neglect
As the cup of greed
Runneth over
All of us are not guilty
Yet none of us are innocent

Charlie Braxton is a poet, playwright, and cultural critic. His current book is entitled Embers Among the Ashes: Poems in a Haiku Manner *from Jawara Press.*

2020 ELECTION
BY DARA KALIMA

Part 1: A Week Prior

Disaster and tears and
teeth gnashing and ripping
of clothes; all things
biblical sans
the burlap.
But mostly stressed
people operating in
stressed ways.
Heightened
everything
as we all watch and stare
looking for Santa
to deliver us the gift
of a new president.
People will be armed with
picket signs and guns...
anarchy and militia and
sheltering and drinking.
Alcohol poisoning
for one and all.
Hospitals filled with
competitively peak
blood poisonings and
COVID-19 cases because
folks voted with no masks.
Heartbreak and maybe
joy, elation.
Election babies
conceived and delivered
in this crazy need
for carnal escapism.
Each and every person
grabbing their vice

to help them cope
through a forever long
night and in the morning
no decisions garnered;
just more counting
and court cases...
so many court cases...
too many court cases...
it will be a calamitous
mess really.
But I will be home.
Safe behind my walls.
Sitting vigil in hopes
we make it through
to another tomorrow.

Part 2: The Day Of

The day where nerves
are on end
as oppositions lock horns
stating irrefutable "facts" and
sad lived experiences.
No one budges,
votes were already submitted.
Hard to focus in on work,
every meeting is
laced with anxiety that
suffocates the digital
gathering spaces.
Hairs gray a bit faster and
tea is not nearly strong enough
though hard drinks are
too much of a depressant
on a depressing night.
"Did you vote?"
"Go vote!"
"I voted early!"

"In line for hours now, but I'm here.
Ain't going nowhere"
"See my sticker!!"
That's the crux of conversations
while internally you debate to
sit, eat, sleep, creep,
cry, phone bank,
exercise or stress clean.
Stress is clinging
to every action.
But of all the options
the best is to stay inside
because businesses are boarded
in anticipation of the unrest
destined to come
caused by either side
if their candidate is denied
their aspirations.
Heart experiences palpitations
as I try circular,
then five-second breathing
intermittently between prayers.
This will be
the longest
night of my life.

Part 3: Victory?

Despite the wished for
victory,
bodies are still filled with
unease.
We freeze
with the fear,
burdened by care,
this victory
is not sweet.
Who can enjoy it

when knowing others weep,
some slip into eternal sleep,
while others plan
the ways in which
they will creep?
Guns are loaded,
lungs are coated,
America's belly is bloated
from the vile digested.
And the dread,
though less,
is still there.
Days are still
filled with fear,
especially when
rallying cries
are yelling lies.
There were no lies
other than
the ones coddled to
and sought.
The battle,
though slanted,
was well fought,
and despite the hurdles,
we hurdled to victory.
I think
we won...
They said we did...
And,
for an hour or two,
smiles took over,
bodies happily swayed,
tears joyfully fell,
voices delightedly cheered
but...
    but......
        but.........

the
dread
is
still there.
There's still
71 days more,
with no clue
as to what is in store.
No certainty as to when
internal peace will be restored.
And well,
there's
so much more
work to be done.
Someone will still
get their neck
crushed
tomorrow,
but they say we won…
They say we won…
At what price?
And how great
is the prize?

Dara Kalima, aka The Community Poet, is a Bronx resident who explores the concepts of love, equality, and healing all through lived experiences and personal observations. Kalima has authored four books, including Two X Chromosomes with an Extra Shot of Melanin *and* Still Laughin'. *www.darakalima.com IG: kaliskamera*

SEARCHING FOR ANSWERS
BY DARRYL KING

There is no escape from the swollen tears
Born from the promise of lives...
That beat no more.

Every report captured by
Cell phones
That
Document the evils,
Festering from among the bowels of Americana...

They
Administer...
Throbbing pains
Penetrating...
Amongst our wounded hearts

And bring our world...
Every idea,
Every thought,
Every step...
Into slow motion
Unable to focus upon
The desires of the day.
The ills of a wretched society
Percolating among us like a cancerous virus,
Contained... maybe not

Dismayed forever by
Mothers without words
Fathers without peace
Children without answers
A time without a conscious

For we are now witnesses to
A sorrow that can't fathom...
Surreal circumstances
That now flow like rivers of blood.
The decadence of a burning society
Revealing...

Silent killers
Unmasked
Exposing ugly
Showering us with a quiet suffering
The dispensation of hatred,
From heart to hand

A place where anger displaces reason
Stupidity surpasses wisdom
Animalism... rising above humanity

And as
Escalation
Becomes the order of the day

It destroys
A menu of many choices,
Filled with diverse fabrics,
And
Unique characters...
Who no longer have their say.

So listen...

Will the chickens come home to roost
Like Prince Malcolm once proclaimed?

Will turn the other cheek thinking
Become tattooed by villainous footprints?

Will those with the power for change

Ever stand for anything more than the status quo?

For this call vibrates throughout
Whenever a rudderless ship... has no captains
Seeking comfort from among the individuals
Ejecting bland leaders...
Becomes our quest
Who are
More concerned with self
Who then
Retreat to their shelters,
Filled with empty fodder.

Brothers and sisters...

We must protect our families
Teach our young
Hold one another strong

Because darkness and light
Don't share the same address
Wickedness
It's true nature,
Eventually
Rises like fermented dough
And unveils its hidden agenda.

For we can not fall for the...
Three card monte,
The banana in the tailpipe,
The pie in the sky,
The by and by,
The American Dream...
That never sought to include...
Everyone

'Cause what truly matters most
Is found within...

The divine nature of our yesterdays,
The shadows of our today,
And the visions of our tomorrow.

Band together... we must
Like displaced straw,
Seeking solace

Gather together... yes
Carving out...
Bushels of possibilities

So as we search for answers
To capture the now

Pause...
Meditate...
Pray...

And maybe, just maybe
We will hear...

One another
And perhaps...

What's next?

Darryl Eric King -- film director, screenwriter, producer, poet from Philadelphia. Dedicated to making a difference in the lives of people. Author of the book Voyage To Lyrad. *His email is Kingdk65@comcast.net. You can check out his work on Euphoria Media on YouTube.*

A NATION OF WEAVERS
BY DE'ANGELO DIA

inspired by A Nation of Weavers by Opinion Columnist David Brooks,
The New York Times, Feb. 18, 2019

start with the pain
social isolation
fragmentation
eyes flood with tears captivated by silence

7:55 a.m. - I gently squeeze her shoulder
trying to be present
the crying never stops
empty spaces
the rush of adrenaline
left with fragility

Dec. 7, 1941 countless Americans
official death toll 2,403
Navy personnel, Marines, Army service members, civilians
a nation in peril
recruiting stations
a pivotal moment of solidarity
and yet when 47,000 Americans kill themselves yearly
as a result of depression
and 72,000 more die from addiction
isn't that a silent Pearl Harbor

when basic norms of decency, civility, and truthfulness are
under constant threat
isn't that a silent Pearl Harbor
when Black and Brown youth are
five times as likely to be incarcerated as White youth
isn't that a silent Pearl Harbor

this is not about comparing pain

this is an epidemic
a dedicated nurse navigates 12-hour shifts at a VA Medical
    Center
providing care to COVID-19 patients
at the sacrifice of self-care

a furloughed hotel culinary worker processes the days to
    come
questioning God and where his next meal will come from
witnessing the self-indulging nature of others

a concerned neighbor in Greenville
indignant because once again
Black youth continue to face intentional injustice
just as gross as 1955

a college student in the Midwest
convinced that she is the only one haunted by compulsive
    thoughts
about her own worthlessness
equated by mathematical theories and agents of poverty
    alleviation

the Trump-supporting small-business man in Louisiana
silently clenches his fist in rage
as presumptuous dinner guests disparage his way of life
    and theology
trickle-down theory

this pain is a common threat
lack of healthy connection, an inability to see the full
    dignity in others
the resulting culture…fear, distrust, tribalism, shaming,
    strife
an obsolete system operating on the basis of
    one-dimensional perspectives
conceived by the Holy Spirit

start with the pain
social isolation
fragmentation
processing insecurity yet confronted with collective reality
attempting to understand
why there was ever a need for weeping to endure for a
    night.

de'Angelo Dia is a poet, theologian, and comic books scholar who investigates public opinion and contemporary beliefs on cultural, social-political, and theological issues. He is a member of the Goodyear Arts Collective and a Cave Canem Fellow. His work can be found at dia1518.com

SCARLET TRIANGLE
BY DEE ALLEN.

Desperate bid
For re-election
Social media master plan:
Twist public perception

Of who the real
Public enemy is
The real dangerous mob
The real security risk

"And you shall know them
By this distinctive sign":
Scarlet triangle
Inverted design

Bright red as anger
Hardly concealed
Bright red as blood wrath
On these streets so real

Resurrected old
Nazi death camp symbol
Mark for political foes—
Divisive, un-civil

Yet Antifa, the so-called threat
Fights for community
Fights for all races
Fights for unity

Smear campaign by advert
From a national security angle—
Only Fascists would dare
Use a scarlet triangle.

*Dee Allen. is an African-Italian performance poet based in Oakland, California. He is the author of five books [*Boneyard, Unwritten Law, Stormwater *and* Skeletal Black, *all from POOR Press and his newest from Conviction 2 Change Publishing,* Elohi Unitsi]*and has 32 anthology appearances under his figurative belt so far.*

KNEELING
BY DOROTHY RANDALL GRAY

a prayer
a plea
a please
a cop kneels on a neck
and the world inhales

seven bullets
pull Jacob to his knees
seven children
watch their father
kneel
did Breonna
pray beside her bed
'if I should die
before I wake'
kneeling

Poet, award-winning artist, global activist, and bestselling author of Soul Between The Lines, *Dorothy Randall Gray has shared the dais with the Dalai Lama, and the dance floor with James Baldwin. A Hedgebrook Fellow and LA Poet-in-Residence, her acclaimed writing workshops with incarcerated youth, post graduate students, and professional authors reflect her dedication to social change and transformational empowerment. www.DorothyRandallGray.com*

THE PINK SLIP
BY D.P. MARTIN

SHOTS FIRED!
Mistrust must end, I have reached my limit.
Three years and counting each day and each minute.
Sixteen to twenty declined our democracy,
Ego and ethics of divisive hypocrisy.

Recall new year hyped, focused, and driven,
Pandemic robbed hopes, dream, and clear vision.
Hit wall amassed from work ridden woes,
Felt safely remote, then position got closed.

SHOTS FIRED!
Black voices turmoil, unheard and abandoned.
Needed amusement though selective and random.
Unrisen power, our human worth maligned.
Red devil, white fear, blue lives unkind.

Black body toll rises due to targeted alliance.
Exposed knee-kill through lockdown's reliance.
No justice! No jury! Delivered death as a fate.
No plan! No aid! They "stand by" to hurl hate.

SHOTS FIRED!
I dare you not... for those straddling fences.
With memory of prior failed-to-elect winces.
Unblinded we see; deceptive freeform proclaim.
Unequaled in bad, not the "good trouble" vein.

Echoes of smoke... Shifting sleight of hand.
Flourish in darkness, avoid transparent stand.
Clouded minds replace masked tortured souls,
Though shaken and stirred, we now know our roles.

SHOTS FIRED!
Poll clusters sought early votes, unmask distress.

Feelings flow encouraged; favor hopes of redress.
Now is the time to show up in all places.
No comfort in hiding behind manicured faces.

World rises in anguish, steps out comfort zone.
Fake claims of fraud; outrageous pleas thrown.
Victory! Too close to call... concession speech we await.
Bets are off! For greater good, shut it down...
CHECKMATE!!!

D.P. Martin is a NYC-based writer, social justice advocate, facilitator, model/actor, and spirit-led Renaissance man. Formerly, he was the director of communications and public affairs at In The Life Media and managing editor of PULSE magazine. Kevin Powell's Writing Workshop was inspiring and re-energized my passion for the art of writing. Follow me on Instagram: @dpm57.

SILENCE
BY ELLE CEE

After yet another long winter of discontent, I yearn for spring.
The promised newness of it all seems a beacon of light in
    the dark reality I have created for myself.
I know I cannot sustain this perpetual meager existence
    much longer.
Here and now, I vow a vernal emergence from my cocoon.
I will spread my wings and rediscover myself.
Instead of surviving vicariously on orts of others'
    escapades and dining on daydreams,
I will thrive finding sustenance in soaring toward my own
    lofty pursuits, leaving nightmares where they lie.

This is what I said, what I believed.
However, this covert COVID operative led me to a place I
    had seemingly long avoided.
As this insidious cloud overshadowed summer's bounty,
I was thrust toward autumn.
Yet, in many ways, it appeared as if time had stood still.
My cocoon ripped from me; I was exposed.
My eyes opened and shut and opened and shut
and, with each blink, I found in my perpetual solitude the
    stillness I feared but needed.
I had grown accustomed to what I perceived and professed
    as being alone.
This silence however forced me to acknowledge the others
    here with me.

Blink.
I saw the joyful face of a scrawny scrappy girl
perched on her great grandmother's counter tearing collards
    and wasting leaves much to her elder's disdain.

Blink.
There too was the trepidatious adolescent
drowning in ill-fitting garments and judgment repeatedly

failing to fit in where she would never be let in and
later trying desperately to blend into the wallpaper.

Blink. Blink.
I recognized the thick-thighed, light-skinned, long-haired
    teenager
who fell prey to the gazes and grabs of greedy grown men.

Blink.
Then, there was the fatherless young mother
who gave her untethered self to (and excuses for) the
    unenthusiastic young father of her own child
and shouldered the shame and the blame for them both.

Blink.
Off to the side was the silently long-suffering, socially
    inept and broken 20-something ingenue,
dispossessed of her power and woefully unaware of her
    body as she gave it for nothing in return but,
    instead, at the expense of her light.

Blink. Blink.
The seven of us and countless others, each with her own
    ticket crumpled in hand, readied for escape.
This motley crew,
this stew,
this gumbo of emotions and reflections,
experiences and perspectives,
wants and desires,
fears and dreams,
hems and haws,
yeses and nos
(so many nos)
have all been sitting here together for months now
(OK, years)
just waiting to see who will step forward and speak first.

Ahem…

2020: The Year That Changed America

Blink.
More silence.

Elle Cee is a DMV-based cook, artist, poet and serial dabbler (when not working her good government job). "Ellementality" is how you will find her on most platforms (e.g. Twitter, IG, Gmail etc.).

2020 WHAT A YEAR IT HAS BEEN?
BY ERIC "E-ELEVATES" NELSON

2020
2020 what a year it has been?
Therein loss wins
Therein obscurity and solidarity
2020 humans grinning.
Grins unseen and seen

2020 what a year it has been?
Therein protests togetherness,
Therein war of words.
2020 seeker of transfusions.

2020
Grace deprived, grace revived.
Race emphasized
The skin of 2020 peeled.
Humans of kin.
We are all human within.
2020 what a year it has been.

Eric Nelson is a community activist, journalist, teacher, and poet. His email is darnellnelson16@gmail.com and you can follow him on Twitter, @MrNelsonBMT

DUMP TRUMP ¿Y AHORA QUÉ?
BY GLADIRA VELÁZQUEZ

I. 11/3/2020

Wrestling with the angst,
of not knowing what fate will be chosen.
By a vote.
By the vote,
of the American people.
How many lifted their pens to raise their voices
And be heard?
How many sealed their envelopes to stamp
their right to be counted?
How many stood in line with 6 feet of distance,
but clutched together in hopes of
Not "Making America Great Again"?
No!
Making America our dream, and not again;
finally!
Breaking free of the Satanist chains, of the venomous
    stings; hissed out hatred and conspiring hymns.
Demand that we, Brown, Black, Creole, Mulatto, Blasian;
scratch Caucasian!
A term created upon the hills of hypocrisy and racist
    superiority.
That we, Black, Brown, Immigrant, Native, Descendent of
    Indigenous, Descendent of the Brave;
a creed that all women, men, LGBTQ, working, middle,
    upper class;
be honored through a nation that respects who we are and
    who we Be.
We all deserve a nation with a government that rings
    democracy and disputes Trumpocity.

2. 11/11/2020

¿Y ahora qué?
Sacamos a ese diablo,
pero de todo mal no nos
hemos librado.
¿Y ahora qué,
les pregunto?
Abrazamos a nuestros hermanos
en la Florida,
que por tanto que le rogamos
siguieran y votaron por ese
racista malvado.
Por la ignorancia, sí los culpo.
Se dejaron llevar por los malos recuerdos de regímenes de
Videla, Chavez, Castro, Pinochet y Maduro.
¿Y ahora qué?
¡En esta lucha seguiremos!
Porque es cierto, que
Trump era un veneno.
Pero ojo!
Los ingredientes siguen
en el gabinete
de los senadores, jueces, y chapuceros.
No nos rendimos, pa'lante seguiremos
con la valentía de Alexandria Ocasio-Cortez,
con la certitud, siguiendo los pasos de nuestra ángel de
justicia,
Ruth Bader Ginsburg,
hasta que por fin
llenemos los asientos con representación justa
para nuestra igualdad de derechos
y la equidad de recursos y reconocimientos.
Para que nuestros hijos no sean el próximo sufrimiento de
este género.
¿Y ahora qué,
les pregunto?

Gladira Velázquez Cruz is a Diversity, Recruitment, Retention Coordinator and Human Resources professional for the Ithaca City School District in Ithaca, NY. She can be reached at gladira.velazquez@gmail.com.

MY STORY ENDING
BY GLADYS DAE WEEKS

WHAT WILL I BE
When this story ends
When you return to your worlds
of peace and tranquility

WHAT WILL I BE
When this
MOVEMENT
becomes
A MOMENT

WHAT WILL I BE
When ABC's
become AP courses
You don't see
the need
for me to challenge

WHAT WILL I BE
When our children frolic
FRIEND OR FOE

WHAT WILL I BE
When I seek employment
Passed over for someone
with no qualifications
My FOUR DEGREES
collecting dust

WHAT WILL I BE
When I want a picket fence
not silver elevators
you deem enough
AND
still move far away

when I move too close

WHAT WILL I BE
at the end of your stethoscope
A declaration of pills
or thoughtful healing

WHAT WILL I BE
When I enter your stores
followed like a criminal
When your weekly salary
is my hourly rate

WHAT WILL I BE
When I scan pages
Magazines of beauty filled
with everyone except me

**WHAT WILL I BE
WHEN MY LIFE
DEPENDS/
ON/
YOUR/
ACTIONS**

WHAT WILL I BE

WHAT WILL I BE
When this story ends
When you return to your worlds
of peace and tranquility

WHAT WILL I BE
When this
MOVEMENT
becomes
A MOMENT

WHAT WILL I BE
Some of that
depends
on
YOU

MY/STORY/ENDING/DEPENDS/ON/YOU
DEPENDS/ON/YOUR/ACTIONS

During this tumultuous moment, which **BIPOC** have experienced for centuries, I implore you to look at the end result. When this movement transcends into a moment, how will you have changed? Will you do your part to stand up for what is right?

Will you help to ensure that my life too is one of peace and tranquility?

Gladys Dae Weeks, a Brooklyn native, is a retired educator, child advocate and poet. You can follow her on Instagram, @gladysdaeweeks, where you can also access the link to her book, Poetic Imagery: A Journey of Love, *or email her at gladysdaeweeks@gmail.com.*

LOVE AND HATE
BY GLENN HODGE

He was saddened by what he saw.

The television and news were filled with sadness.

Not that this was unusual for American news.

Indeed, it was the norm.

And as he began watching, as is generally the case like most over time, he was ill-affected.

But as he watched, this story touched him.

He recalled as a child, his mother telling him, as he cried over having received a reprimand he deserved, "There is a direct relationship between love and hate."

At the time this comment didn't stop the tears or make him feel better.

Indeed, he wondered if his mother was telling him that while she loved him (she always began the morning by giving him a hug, looking him in the eyes and saying, "You know I love you, right?"), she also hated him? The statement was confusing at the time.

The television showed pictures of people, white people, demonstrating with signs stating "White Power"...."There was NEVER a genocide of the Jews"...marching with their fists held above their heads. Among them were children, parents, pregnant women, and people of all age groups. Directly across from them were a group of other demonstrates. Shouting at them. Telling them to go home! Calling their actions shameful... un-American... Racist...

Then the television showed a car suddenly appear and began running through the crowd as people ran, screamed, crying, shouting expletives... Now he understood his mother's statement.

Glenn R. Hodge is a West Indian-born American, tax and business attorney, and writer who lives in New York City. His first book, entitled A Proud Monkey In Iceland, *remains in search of a publisher. He is currently working on his second book,* Victims Rights *and continues to write poetry.*

COCK OF THE CROW
BY GRACE BENIQUEZ

Will we ever see a redwood?
Will we ever stand under its canopy and peer
up at its majestic branches?
Families fleeing a fiery Katrina
Thousands of charred dreams
Lives to embers

Will the children, separated at the border, be found?
Will they recognize their parents and slumber in their
    arms?

Someday,
they will move among us
waiting to slit our throats — an act of mercy

Will the reservoir of our tear ducts
be replenished, so that we
may once again shed
tears of boundless joy?
Darkness recedes only
to gather its strength.
Let us not be fooled again.

So many of us
were caught in the headlights of denial,
our fight or flight response
hampered because we were holding
onto a fleeting illusion

So I ask,
Who will you be?
Who will I be?
Who will we be when in the light of day
they drag our neighbors from their homes;

their bare feet scraping
the pavement seen nevermore
Who will you be?
Who will I be?
Who will we be when they extract
a coworker, and threaten
us with brutality if we dare to intervene?
How many times
will the cock
crow before we
are given away?

Grace Beniquez is a poet, artist and educator who was born and raised in the South Bronx. She is the author of Lazarus Bread *and* phthalo blue.

SOCIAL WORKING
BY DR. HELENA D. LEWIS

My place of employment has labeled me essential.
I feel more sacrificial than respected
This essentialness has not been reflected in my paycheck
I was broke before the pandemic
And I'm still broke
If I was to die today
My family could not cover the cost of my funeral
I am the only breadwinner
The soul caretaker to a parent who is 91
Most days I don't feel like getting out of bed
Brushing my teeth or taking a shower
I want to lie with the lights off and cry
But I force myself to put on a brave face
And cover it up with a mask
I go to work
I sit in my car
I am overcome with anxiety
I pray to God to give me the strength to get out
See, I'm the person in charge
My job...
Take care of everyone, but me
I'm not a doctor
I'm not a nurse
I am a SOCIAL WORKER
Social working in the pandemic
If I do not make it
Please tell my story

Dr. Helena D. Lewis, DSW, LCSW, LCADC, is a New Jersey-based theatrical scholar-practitioner and former Nuyorican National Slam Team member. Her website is www.hdlpoet.com and you can follow her on Instagram @hdlewispoet.

THE BEGINNING, OR THE END?
BY JACOB EDWARDS

Two Zero Two Zero... Oh the things you have shown us
    this year,

Unpredictability...Confusion and Fear,
It is as if Mother Nature approached you with eyes full of
    anger and tears,
And asked you if this time 'round you would give us proper
    ears so that we may properly hear,
Her cries,
Which turned to sighs,
Then quickly into a feeling of deep despise,
For our cruelty and indifference with a promise to darken
    our skies,
And with an assist from 2020 a plan was devised,
To either permanently open or forever close our eyes,

We must know that we are all defenseless to her might,
We either work with or against her knowing against her is a
    futile fight,
And if we fight...we all die and learn the hard way that she
    was right,
But if we humble ourselves then we just might,

Remove ourselves from under this dark cloud and back into
    the light,
Our collective decision will decide if she appeals to Two
    Zero Two One to continue our plight,
We can begin on December 31.....the first day after that
    night,

The Floods...The Droughts...The Famine...The Rains,
The excess of tornadoes and hurricanes,
The Wind...The Heat......The Flames,
The Virus...The Murder Hornets and Quakes,
The only question is if it was enough for us all to wake.

Jacob Edwards is a musician, environmentalist and poet from Chicago, IL. He has published one book of poetry titled Resurrecting The Art. *His email is bleedingpoet@yahoo.com.*

PROTECT YOUR FAMILY
BY JENINE CORNEAL

Whispers of…
"arm yourselves –
protect your family"
…linger in the air

End of January…
on a work trip,
I shot a gun
for the 1st time…
guided by an experienced colleague
at a range with co-workers

Never wanted to before…
They were amazed –
…apparently… I was pretty good
But could I do it alone?

Whispers got louder…
"arm yourselves –
protect your family"

Mid-march
all over IG,
facebook,
group chats…
My black power friends,
Muslim friends,
my be self-sufficient,
grow your own food,
don't depend on "them" friends…

Whispers got even louder
"arm yourselves –
protect your family"

As violence increased
protests increased –
became more violent in response

"arm yourselves –
protect your family"
My heart cried – HOW?

Family & friends - some court officers,
some police, some COs…
males - closer to home,
they can shoot…
some have legal firearms,
some maybe…
they just have 'em
…and won't tell me…
as they know I'll be against it…

Family and friends all over the East coast and beyond…
from NY/CT to Florida and NC/SC
to TX and CA to the UK and sweet T&T…
There's no organized group of "us"
that I know of …is there?

Yet ALL these people keep saying
"arm yourselves –
protect your family"

Are we organized?
Is there a code I'm unaware of…
some silent Handmaid's Tale-inspired language?

Guns and ammunition selling out in LI…
Why am I recalling
movies about our history, our past…

My… child… is in MD
I just want her safe,

I want her friends safe,
I want her professors safe,
I want my family and the U.S. safe…

"Arm yourselves —
protect your family"
But WHO is the REAL enemy?
Trump supporters come in every size, shape & color…
Do they hate all of us?
Blindly lumping our multi-faceted spirits into one persona —
"the enemy"?

Where do we begin?
Is it already too late?

I'm determined to be hopeful
Biden won — right?
Kamala Harris is VP elect — right?
Or is our right to choose who leads us...
the latest casualty in this domestic war…
we never signed up for

Arm yourselves…
protect…
your family!

Jenine Corneal was born and raised in Brooklyn of Trinidadian heritage. She performed poetry at Cornelia Street Café in Greenwich Village and was published in a local magazine, Mahogany Blues. *Her IG is jinjin213.*

UNDER THE CLOCK
BY JERRY W. WARD, JR.

exquisite orchids
are pandemic eyes

an end arrives

apocalypse is
an elegant dance

an end survives

mover and motion
coordinate and conduct

an end archives

undoing of bodies
demise of minds

an end contrives

these lies, boldly saying
entering eternity is easy

Jerry W. Ward, Jr., a Richard Wright scholar, is author of THE KATRINA PAPERS, *Fractal Song: Poems, The China Lectures, and* Blogs and Other Writing *and co-editor of* The Cambridge History of African American Literature, Black Southern Voices, *and the* Richard Wright Encyclopedia. *Professor of English Emeritus (Tougaloo College), he lives in New Orleans, Louisiana.*

RAMADAN 20 VS COVID-19
THE CALL TO PRAYER IS LOUDER THAN
THE DEATH TOLL
BY JESSICA CARE MOORE

On the first day of Ramadan
April 23, 2020. There are millions
Of reasons to fast.

Three of my girlfriends are expecting.

The Jesus children
wearing rosaries 'round their necks
Praying death will leave Salt City

News repeats itself, therefore, is
No longer news.

We are not people of color
In Detroit, we are black

Upsouth people. We are
Not for Sale or consumption.

We, right across the street from Lebanon.
We tout the biggest masjid in the country.

We have always removed shoes
Before entering our sacred homes.
Wujud our bodies clean beyond 20 seconds.

Detroit hijab wrapped covered beauties
Watching them all rocking burkas, now.

The projects remain the cleanest kitchens.
Smells of Clorox Bleach and metal ironing boards
Creased into our daily routines

Cleanliness is next to Godliness
Sunday best. Friday is Ju'mah.
We all praying to any ancestor
Still listening.

The food that fed us, will kill us
In the new world.

They are trying to kill the vegetarians
Dick Gregory whispered in King's ear.
When he was 8.

Tell your mother...

Smiles taste like tears
Songbirds begin at 4am

My friend has lost her mother
Grandmother
& Aunt. My best friend, her sister.
Maria.

I am brushing off the dust of my red prayer mat
Listening to Jon McReynolds and Kirk Franklin
I need everyone.

Even black Jesus
to help get us all through this.

Yes, race still matters.

Ma Sha Allah
Ma Sha Allah

The call to prayer is louder
Than the death toll

The call to prayer never silenced

We never die anyway.
Abiodun Oyewole reminded us.
We return, we move on, we become.

Psalms 23 won't finish the day
The clocks are flying across the room

Which day is it? Whatever day you feel
Is necessary for right now. Pick one.

Which day do you feel the most beautiful

When he sends me music, I fall in love
With writing. When I write I hear music.

What else to do with this time
'Cept tell somebody it happened.

We were alive when the world stood still.

Music never pauses.
Mahogany, Ryan and Randi
Are all pregnant during a pandemic.

These resilient babies won't stop
For outbreaks. Wait for it to end.

Life continues

Even when we decide it is over.
When humanity is finally white flagged
& all the oxygen from the Amazon
Is bottled and taxed like new shoes.

The magnolia tree will still blossom
The same time every year in the backyard

All those thick colossal roots laughing
At our fragile bones

How we climb, how we dream
To be so bold as you.

How our arms shadow your branches
How we wish to be song birds worthy
Of your protection.

The playing field is not playing.
Nature is calling. Science is searching.

Spirit has this all figured out.
And it's not in any of those books
Made from dead trees.

Faith is not a word.

It's knowing.

Belief that there is something absolutely
Beyond this place.

Something that will heal the wounds
Inflicted on a continent.

Sami Allahu liman hamidah

Praying 5 times a day
May not be enough

To purge the sins against the
womb of the earth
against the hungry bellies of
The chosen people

The unshackled reality of hope

Will not eat away the truth

Balancing itself
between dusk and dawn

Fasting may be the only way
To clear out the noise

The sirens the gunshots the lies

No distance
Between faiths anymore
Pick a book, any holy book.

We all die in the same position
Legs spread open, mothers pushing out
the next tomorrow

It doesn't matter
how we die

Or at what speed.

Fasting

or Slowly

It only matters
what we are willing to die for.

Let it be for the first cries
Let it be so the world is made

anew

jessica Care moore is a world-renowned poet, institution builder, advocate for artists and the founder of Black Women Rock! Her 5th book, We Want Our Bodies Back *was published in 2020 by Harper Collins/Amistad.*

THE NOT SO HIDDEN AGENDA
BY J. HAMMAD

Misrepresentation and character assassinations are increasing in frequency in order to spread misinformation across the nation because it is clear the underlying goal is miseducation.

J. Hammad is a writer, researcher, and consultant currently based in Maryland with New Jersey roots. J. Hammad's email is jshammad8@gmail.com.

A SIGN IS JUST A START
BY JOSEPH POWELL

I see your sign—
Yes,
I see you
marching on tired feet
filling the streets
raising your voices
singing
shouting;
yes,
I see you;
we all
see you.
But,
at the end of the day,
when the sun has gone down
and the singing stops
and the tired feet
have marched
all the way home;
and the signs are put away
in garages
and closets
filled to overflowing—
what then?

I ask,
what is
your takeaway?
what is
my takeaway?
Mothers
are still losing sons;
sons
are still losing fathers;
women

are still going missing;
men
are still going to prison.
Laws
are being broken
by those
who make them
and swore
to uphold them;
the rich
still do not care
about the poor;
the poor
still see no relief.

Yes,
a sign is just a start,
but
I know teachers
who are having to take
second and third jobs
just to make ends meet;
I see roads and bridges
crumbling all around us
and we're talking about
paying for a wall
that may or may not
protect us.

A sign is just a start,
but I have friends
who are getting sicker
because we still
are arguing about healthcare.

And who are we
to think
that we are better

than someone
who doesn't look like us
or believe what we believe
or love...
who made us
the arbiters of love?!

One man
or woman,
no matter how powerful
in stature
or wealth,
is going to make
a lick of difference
if we, the people,
choose not
to come out
from under our signs
and from behind our masks
and see each other,
not as
the "other",
but as
the other side of
who we are.
We the people,
all the people,
have to decide
to become better
than what we are
what we've been.

A sign is just a start,
along with your marches,
your singing and
your shouting;
but,
at the end of the day,

I want
to see you,
all of you,
all of US,
getting to work.
A sign
is just a start.
A sign
is just a start.
A sign
is
just
a
start.
So,
let's get started!

Joseph Powell is a Nashville-based poet and spoken-word artist and author of four collections of poetry including The Spirit Of Baldwin Compels Me. *His email is jobypoet@yahoo.com and he can be followed on Instagram, @thespiritofbalcompelsme and Twitter-@jobypoet*

BLACK AND BLUE
BY JOSEPHINE BASCH

United, we fall.

The bile-spangled banner flew high and proud. Raised my
glass...
knowing exactly what was to come.

The message.
The conscience.
That which passes us by, and can never be brought back...

Emotionless.

Metal cages to blueprints to cell blocks... Can I borrow an
original thought?

Plotted out ways to leave a mark... Spray can replaced by
the pen. And
around here, neither are as mighty as the sword. Most were
busy
throwing darts. I searched for my bow and arrow. Tried to
inject some
love into this ocean of hatred. Inhaling the memories,
because they
were so much sweeter than reality. Waited to exhale.
Asphyxiated.
Prayers for the merciless... Dripping. Entangled.
Empty gestures and fabricated testimonies. Catchwords for
clones...
Taking advantage of tragedy.

Drowning in the shallow end of their lies. Sailing on like
Amerigo Vespucci.

Raised my glass...
Egomaniacal and docile populace... thank you for the many

woes... mental menstruation and such...

The home of this brave new world. Land of the illusionists.
     Purveyor of the many holograms.

Vacated once and for all.
Grand opening.
Grand closing.

Josephine Basch is a writer and editor that has lived in Berlin, Toronto, Paris and New York City. In addition to poetry, her works include Hip-Hop profiles, graphic novels and material focusing on climate change. You won't find her on social media, but you can reach her at: jo.basch@icloud.com.

CONSTITUTIONAL HARDBALL
BY JOSEPHINE WILLIAMS

"Constitutional hardball"
tastes like
blood
orange
COVID
skies
at a distance
behind a window
masked fear
rot
stomach pits
gnawing
hungry kids
in rich countries
let them eat cake
— fake cake —
gathers
in our feed
we straddle
the thin blue line
between safety
and
Kyle Rittenhouse
we, the untouchables
— without bailout
they,
too big to fail
we, the embraceless,
— too small to win
we crowdfund
dignity
in contactless coin
group-scrounge
bail funds
Minnesota Freedom

too far off
Then it hits you
we no longer
share
oxygen
our viral soundtrack:
the treasonous chanting
of unmasked militias
and sanitised
excess death
chilling
Amazon delivered
body bags
and gritted teeth
Freedom?
freedom to die
— precarious —
— yet essential —
and drive-by funerals
Choice?
either I win or I win
he said
like a forced pregnancy
an unwanted hysterectomy
survival of the
fastest cars plowing crowds
leaving quarantined
untouched widows
to watch dusty orange
sunsets behind windows

Josephine Williams is a London-based student of international law. She maintains a blog on technology, race and human rights at medium.com/josewil2. You can follow her on Twitter @yoyomorena.

NOT GOING GENTLY
BY KEINA FIELDS-SMALL

I ain't sorry!
I say, YOU CHEATED
Because, I didn't lose.
We are white America,
The BETTER AMERICA
You stole it from us!
You! The Blacks.
You, cattle from Africa.
YOU stole it from right <u>under us.</u>

<u>You worked the earth.</u>
You built a community,
<u>You built The White House!</u>
<u>Make America like it was before.</u>
<u>I own the house and you can get the door.</u>

DIGGING Up the truth,
KNOCKING down the statues!
It's mine! It's mine! Dirty America.
Violent and bloody!
You better not take away our guns.
You Black Aliens!

We're still taking all your ideas.
You Sittin' still yet Moving forward! (I don't know how
    you do it.)
Shuffling. Singing.
I called you lazy!
I said it! I wrote-ed it in A HIS-STORY book!
Everybody likes you! I hate you - Go clean the toilet.
Scaffolding on Inequity!
Making something from nothing. It's impossible! You
    cheated.
Somehow you swarm the earth.
The Earth, The land.

I'm Earth, your land.
What did you say, My land!
   Sad. Disheartened.
Disheartened.
So many of YOU voted.
Elated! Victory!
We are Victims.
We voted!
You cheated!
   You voted!
   We voted.

Not going quietly. Please Leave.

Keina Fields Small is a Speech-Language Pathologist in New Britain, Connecticut. She specializes in teaching tweens and teens social language competency skills and taking the perspectives of others. She spends her free time sending handwritten love letters to friends, family, and strangers.

REMEMBER
BY KEISHA-GAYE ANDERSON

The poets see things
others want to
disappear
or forget
like bodies stacked on trucks
moving quietly
after midnight
or forged documents
to make a child a wife

We remember for us all
the head-on collisions
of who we perform
and what we really be
We can see
the bottom of the glacier
in new moon sea
and the cracked cog in the
big machine
We feel the electric charge
in the air that spins itself
over great distances
into thunder, lightning
revolutions
We sense the confusion
that creates runaway egos
turned leaders turned despots
We urge you to

STOP

Listen to the
strumming of the threads
of life that

weave us into a wave
a being
that is no less separate
than water
We want you to
remember who you are

We are
a star

Keisha-Gaye Anderson (keishagaye.ink) is a Jamaican-born poet and visual artist based in Brooklyn whose books include A Spell for Living, Everything Is Necessary, *and* Gathering the Waters. *She is a past participant of the VONA Voices and Callaloo writing workshops, and holds an MFA in fiction from The City College, CUNY.*

THIS MUVFUCKA
BY KENNETH CARROLL
for Amiri Baraka, Gaston Neal & my father

I wish my father were an analyst for CNN
He'd show up on the set…late
With a Tupperware tumbler of ice water
His shirt open, exposing a clean white tee
His name in red cursive above his pocket
A joint behind his ear for later
A Miles tune in his head

Thanks for joining us Mr. Carroll
Wolf would say, give us your thoughts
On president Trump's …

My father would sip his DC tap water
Adjust the toothpick in his mouth
Look dead at the camera and offer;
"This Muvfucka."
Silence.
Wolf, 'cause he don't know about
The ways of old black men
Would not get it, would ask for
My father to elaborate

But "This Muvfucka"
Is both intro and exposition
Both preface and full thesis

My fathers and my mothers know
"This Muvfucka" as pillager
and kidnapper, enslaver and treasonous
rebel, as nullifier and cowardly mob
as terrorists and hypocrite
as discriminator and exploiter
and denier of restorative justice

there are volumes in the economy of words
there are collections in the canon of terse cursing
there is revolution in the deep voiced delivery
"This Muvfucka" my father knows
is the same muvfucka of poplar
hangings and magnolia rapes

The president is the same "This Muvfucka" of redlines
And segregated housing, nigger schools, church bombings
blues man say, "don't get me to talkin,
I just might tell the whole thing."

I saw my father arrested one day
For sitting on the porch, with other black
Men, the white lady across the alley objecting
To their presence and laughter

Black men rounded up by white police
Tossed into the paddy wagons for existing
A price for their freedom

When he returned home, my mother asked
Who called the police, my father said,
"This Muvfucka"

and so it does not surprise him, him who sat
on his porch, digging the smell of honeysuckles
blown by a breeze from oxon run and Jimmy McGriff,

that the country had elected "This Muvfucka" a diseased
        genetic
remnant from a long line of muvfuckas who think
their ugliness can reverse time, who imagine black
people won't take the toothpick out their mouths, remove
their clean work shirts and give him these hands

If my father were an analyst for CNN

He'd walk off the set in mid-argument
As the legion of talking heads
Tied their tongues to their asses
In feigned corporate debate

He'd dap up the union workers
On the way out, spark up his joint
Knowing there was never a time
When we didn't resist.

He'd sip from his
Ice water, as the cabs passed
Him like restless clouds over the city
He'd shake his head with a wry laugh
And say
"dese muvfuckas"

Kenneth Carroll is a poet, playwright and fiction writer. He is past president of the African American Writers Guild and former director of DC WritersCorps and the proud father of three talented children.

COVID-19TH STREET
BY KIM YAGED

New
York
feels
dead
because it is
the place
of the dead
and dying
Demystifying
race
and Race
Segregationist hate
doesn't skip
any place
I can't breathe
You can't erase
Forget you're home
to money street
Capitalist rampage
Less exceptional
than Exceptionalism
You too
have to look yourself
in the face
Progressivist shame
trying to escape
your share of the blame

Kim Yaged is an award-winning script, short story, and children's book writer whose work has been published by Random House, Applause, and Ballantine Books, among others. Visit www.kimyaged.com to learn more about her work.

REVELATION 23
BY KS HERNANDEZ

1. And every form of oppression vomited out of his veins onto streets slick with blood, sweat, fear, disease, and hate.

2. The very essence of humanity screamed for relief. As man dominated man and children begged in grief.

3. His final breath becoming a roar releasing the rage of a thousand seas into the hearts of woman and man.

4. Those hearts are torn asunder weeping tears and fire.

Is this really it? Will it happen for us this time? Many times in history when the vile and deplorable became too much for the human psyche to bear, the world would scream out in either agony, or joy.

Watching George Floyd be murdered over and over on the news, on social media, via text message in bright vibrant color was too much, again. Emmett Till's face beaten beyond recognition where every cell in his mother's body seemed to be saturated with crippling grief.

The world screamed.

Time and technology mercifully only allowing, my generation, a black and white photo of this child so mistreated.

Like the dreams of every Black man, woman, and child pulverized and choked with barbed wire, driven to insanity, to the end of what no one else would ever dream is acceptable. Are we willing? Do we have the courage? The madness of being repeatedly denied and unheard, and unknown, and mischaracterized. Can we look?

The concept of freedom is not strange. It's quite common, in fact. Birds are free to fly. Cats are free to purr, dogs are free to wag their tails, and a roach is free to creep and multiply. Black folks are free to consider themselves free until the birth of our individual consciousness offers us an option to either be burdened or to live burdenless. Reject it all, and take on a fight where there will be no victors?

We have an option to be preface-free as bonded to a past where no one and everyone is to blame.

Is this really it? Will this really be our turning point? I hear the word revolution thrown around with the desire to tear away the power addled and to tear down a world solidly built on the backs of the dead. Booker T Washington said, "You can't hold a man down without staying down with him." Where would we be? Like New Zealand or Canada? Nations such as these also have a past deeply driven by class and caste where if the bottom crumbles, then the guilt of the past burns the top to dust? I've given myself permission to be angry, to be disgusted, and not hide it.

To allow it to lay bare

the rotting stench of hatred

lingering in your nose.

A discarded pie, dropped top down on a dirty floor.

Look at it.

It was beautiful, my peace.
Then you choked him.

You shot her sleeping.

You killed her in your jailhouse.

You hung him from a tree, in the year of our Lord 2020.

Is this really it? Is this the revolution that we've been waiting for? No. I don't think so. A revolution requires the destruction of economies, and crumbling of currencies with foundations beaten to an unrecognizable pulp—like his face...

Beneath all that we think we want lies beauty so terrible, and blinding
that, I believe, it will be the threshold to our end.
For it is brilliant and blindingly painful. Can we look?

We see distractions attempting to appease an angry mass teetering on the
edge of revolt. Senseless murders continue. Murderers continue to live
freely. Monuments of bondage torn, and tossed
into the sea. Why?

Blatant racism in the US, like that of the1950s and 1960s. Leadership
utterly despises our existence as inconveniences because we demand.

To live, to shop, to work, to grow and be—without the proverbial knee
on the necks of our desires with our efforts gasping for life.

What drives us? Why have we not yet been extinguished?
In the words of Howard Thurman, "We stand at a moment in
human history with our backs against the wall... we have to
get the courage to look at what we want... and the clue to what
you want is you begin to understand what you are for...
before you begin relating it to these great issues."

What will that be?

*KS Hernandez residing in the state of Virginia, Is a Wellness Advocate, Freelance
Writer and Blogger having published multiple ongoing blogs about the writing process
and self-care through writing. She is currently penning her first novel, her email is
kshernandezinc@protonmail.com and you can follow her on Instagram,
@KSWriteshere*

OCTOBER SURPRISE
BY LAUREN SUMMERS

This Great American Experiment has a crack in its frame.
The family photo is tilted,
        slipping out of the side;
there's a shard of glass piercing the face
of the melting clock.
How long will it be before our…

Time has stopped on the hour of our
reckoning with a family that was never anything but
        dysfunctional,
yet dreamed of being free
to love itself,
like long lost sisters,
daughters of bastard fathers who never knew whose mother
        they'd fucked.
None of us was born into this family out of love.

The photo in its broken frame,
with its broken glass,
hangs crooked on the wall
above the Sunday dinner table,
set with a bounty of rotten food.

There is no straight road home.
It was only ever an experiment.
Sometimes they fail.

Lauren summers has been writing poetry since childhood but was moved by the upheaval of 2020 to publish it for the first time. And this just might be the start of something. Reach her at laurensummers@alumni.harvard.edu.

CONVERSATIONS WITH BLACK CONSERVATIVES
BY LAWRENCE CHAN

According to your Republican thesis
Trump was chosen to lead by Jesus
You say he the best thing for blacks since Lincoln
And I say what the fuck are you thinking?
Conservatives got you thinking they care about your kind
But throughout history they been robbing you blind
Instead of 40 acres and a mule settlement
You're forced into a Jim Crow tenement
Living in some neighborhood looking like it been bombed
Like it's 1960s Vietnam
Fighting against KKK elements
Caught in the loophole of the 13th Amendment
You could have a degree from Harvard and Yale
But they still want you locked up in jail
Price your freedom so high that you can't make bail
The government got you blackmailed
Before you're born, they got your life set
To enter the prison-industry complex
Straight from the inner-city projects
These prisons need slave labor to feed the cash cow
That's how they got blacks still enslaved now
Like up to 15 years for one gram of crack
'Cause people who smoke they are black
But the Whites who snort cocaine they let them be
Sentenced to probation and then let them out free
And if you got three strikes in your life story
You locked up for life as mandatory
And if you avoid jail
Welcome to the trickle-down economy
A way to keep people stuck in poverty
Conservatives have set up this scheme
For over 400 years to get their cream
And they don't care if you're a witness

To them it's just business
They don't care about the optic
As long they make a profit
Now COVID-19 got bodies filling up the morgue lobby
Bags filled with brown and black bodies
On the border they got kids underage
Without their mama trapped in a cage
And you're just sitting here, where is your outrage?
Like Eric Garner, Trayvon Martin, George Floyd and
many more Killings have been going on for years in
this undeclared war
How many deaths did you ignore?
You tell us we need to wait for them to investigate
While we wait for some unknown future date
Tell that to the moms of the sons that were slain
And when the cops get off how do you explain
How to live with the pain that remains
The last memory of her son buried in a coffin
This shit happens way too often
You ask me when will all these riots cease
It's when unarmed blacks stop getting killed by the police
I see you scared with the country's current affair
You feeling the coming revolution in the air
Black Lives Matter protest everywhere
But you're still defending all of Trump's lies
When he's gone next year, be too late to apologize
You still want to be a part of this redneck agenda
Promoting these lies and Fox News's propaganda
Why don't you do what Donald Trump preached
And go drink some Clorox bleach
I can't believe the conservatives you embrace
Why don't you just get the fuck out of my face

Lawrence Chan is a lifelong resident of Brooklyn, New York, who is just trying to figure out life in this crazy world. His email is lawrence.chan.poetry@gmail.com

ELECTION 2020
BY LENARD D. MOORE
for Kamala Harris

We
walk out our houses: honking
to blow blues back
where they birthed.
Clap our stories
into now (toward evening).
At the crossroads
we howl
jubilee as if carrying
big brown buckets of joy.
We accent our footsteps
with whistles tuning tales
we course like rivers
in our veins.
We
want work now
so troubles can set
like the sun
never to rise
again.
We, wearers of masks,
Keep going
Keep going
Keep going

*Lenard D. Moore is a poet, essayist, book reviewer, educator, public speaker,
photographer, author, and editor. He is author of* The Geography Of Jazz,
among other books, and editor of All The Songs We Sing, *among other books.*

WHAT YOU TOLD ME
BY LOIS ELAINE GRIFFITH
for Miguel Algarín

Seems like you told me in the beginning

this ending would come.

But nothing ends beginning.

Seems like it was this way

before I knew

there is before — in front of me.

Seems like I always knew

what I didn't know

that I knew what you were telling me.

And now, asking why

can't change why it is

what it is.

Words are spirits you tell me.

Words are tools to write the wrong answer right—

explaining what doesn't change the question:

why have you touched me—

why do I feel your touch

when you're not touching me

to make me know

you're touching me?

And we drive park-side Fort Greene—

feeling the scent of night — spring

you tell me like loving—

your love is disinterested.

And I need disinterest at home to think

why double entendre spirits mischief to make me ask:

why is it all over at once—

this ending to begin?

Then, again, I didn't know

that I knew I'd work love hard with you

to word the questions

that don't dare answer

why we love to care to love.

Lois Elaine Griffith, one of the founders of the Nuyorican Poets Cafe, is an artist/ writer/ teacher living in Brooklyn.

STRANGE FRUIT
BY MAKISSA LEWIS

The smell never goes away
You just learn to live and live it away
The smell that inspired Strange Fruit that Billie sings
You know the smell because it is one of those black things

Like, being programmed to hate your black skin
Fighting others that look like you, so they don't win
The smell is just another fact we know all too well
Our ancestors do not need to tell

Of what was done and what was not done
Because we either experience it or know of someone
And, no white washing can take that smell away
For there is always going to be another body the next day

It is a black thing that makes us aware
Makes us overly cautious and living in constant fear
But, we also know we must not overreact and we must
remain calm
We do not have the luxury of raising the alarm

Or, the consequence is that the strange fruit we smell
Will be used in the story of our short-lived life they tell

Makissa Lewis is a combat disabled veteran and founder of the nonprofit My Seester that serves female veterans of South Florida. When she is not engaged in female advocacy with her nonprofit, she is working on an anthology that documents her experiences during and after her military career. She can be reached via email at founder@myseester.com or on Instagram @my_seester.

SHIFT
BY MANUEL GONZALEZ

I.

We need to shift consciousness
Artistically shift awareness
Create a new pedagogy
We define the world
Each of us has a unique perspective

Shift the narrative

With powerful vulnerability
We speak truth to power
Armed with our hearts
We create change
By creating connections
With our stories
Our voices
Our ancestors
The vibration of the Uni-Verse

OM

The revolution has begun
The revolution has never stopped spinning
Revolving
Evolving
Encompassing
Including
.............Because
Ain't nobody free until we're all free
..........One voice
..........One heart
..........One mind
Mitakuye Oyasin

WE ARE ALL ARTISTS!
And as artists we create culture
WE ARE ALL ARTISTS!
Critiquing social structures
WE ARE ALL ARTISTS!
We are the organizers
...........The leaders
...........The storytellers
...........The watchers (observers)
...........The narrator

Shift the narrative

II.

What they don't know
What they'll never understand is
Arte es mistico
It must be felt
Can't be explained
Heartbeat rhythms
In syncopation
With universal truths
One band
One sound
Until all that is left
Is the resonance

We stay grounded in history
Standing on the shoulders
Of untold stories
Voices
Silenced by the passage of time
We are simultaneously
Forward looking
And
Historically relevant
Dancing the rain down from the sky

Us
Collectively
Multimedia poetry
Power and prayer
Shift the narrative by
Weaving our unique perspectives
Into public spaces
This is what we mean by community
Cultural sustainability
Intersectional connections
Protection of sacred land
We understand
Systematic environmental racism
The violence of industry
Colonization
Assimilation
But remember...
THIS IS TIWA LAND!

III.

The sacred circle has been drawn
The eagle and the condor fly together
All signs and symbols are signaling change
The ceremonies and rituals
Have called upon our spirit allies
Ashe
Power
The Orishas come to witness
And some ride us like the wind
So we can create art
With intention
THE MOUNTAIN HOLDS POWER
PRAY IN THAT DIRECTION!

Spiritual mercenaries
We nonviolently
Obliterate the patriarchy

Living every day of our lives as ceremony
And our very existence
Is an act of resistance
We shift the narrative
By bringing the medicine that we carry
In our arte
Healing ourselves in the process
Finding forgiveness
Redemption
Breath
Acknowledgement
And release
So we can
Shift the narrative

Manuel Gonzalez is a Albuquerque Poet Laureate, teacher, and spoken word artist.

THE COUNT IS STILL OUT
BY MARTINA GREEN MCGOWAN, MD

Rising,
Still feeling a bit tender.
The election is over
But the count is still out.

The world has shifted
Slightly.
Maybe I will only need to install a dash cam front and rear
Or be strapped with a body cam
Every time I exit my vehicle,
Or simply an open carry
Each time I want to leave my home
But perhaps not all three
As I had thought.

After the declaration of the winner,
We will sadly still have children in cages
Snatched from their parents.
We will continue to destroy the earth.
We will still hate those
Who don't look like us
Or act like us
Or agree with our every thought and whim
Or still be hated because of how we look

But perhaps
We can begin to heal.

Character and behavior move slowly.
We are, after all,
Only human

Inching our way along the paths
Of evolution and enlightenment.

The final count is still out
On whether we can ever change
Or simply continue as we have until humankind is
annihilated.
It is a choice.

Martina McGowan, MD is a poet, public speaker, an activist against social, racial, human, and sexual injustices, and the author of i am the rage, *a poetic exploration of living inside injustice being released February 2021 by SourceBooks. Her email is martinamcgowanmd@gmail.com, blog- MartinaMcGowan.com, and you can follow her on social media: Facebook, Instagram, LinkedIn, and Twitter @martinamcgowan.*

ELECTION ANXIETY
BY MAYA GOSS

Election Anxiety
Is a real thang.
Not a catchy phrase CNN coined
To describe the stress of waking up to
a Pandemic-cloaked world.
Just as the spring air was taking a
Breath.
Thought us Boomers had seen it All
Vietnam, riots, recession, AIDS.
Drugs, sex and rock n roll.
Retirement blossoming on a
Pear Tree...
fragrant and sweet
Singing and swinging
My way to days of rest.
Contemplation, the last mile.
Until the curtain dropped.
Now I Know how Europe felt.
How our parents in the 20s felt.
Days are endless
unrecognizable now.
Marked by
Isolation, fear, rationing, masks, 6ft apart
Breadlines via your car, stimulus checks, unemployment,
mass graves, working from home, compromised immune, positivity
rates, Dying alone, virtual school, uncaring president, nightly
body count.
The unspoken question
When will it go Away?
No tp to be found Anywhere.
Will the mask become part of our facial décor?
Is this the End
Or the beginning?
Election Anxiety

Replaced by Uncertainty
Perhaps 2021 will reveal…

Maya Goss is a Virginia born Author, Blogger, Educator, Griot and Foodie. She is the author of 5 books for young readers from the award-winning Exploring Ancient Africa *series and the upcoming memoir,* All the Lies are True. *Her email is mpubl@hotmail.com, and you can follow her on Instagram @mayapubl.*

WITHIN WALLS
BY MICHAEL SINDLER

Microscopic menace meandering on the wind
Hanging in droplets of life's sweet breath
Invisible sentinels posted by the door
Ready to pounce and possess

Even the most benevolent visitors –
Mail, meal, or grocery deliverers
Are now suspect
All attempts to touch are forsaken –
Seen as tantamount to suicidal
We wait out elevators until solo passage is possible

And yet, once safely ensconced
One cannot escape the lingering passenger – Despair
Knowing many will not escape:
Scathed survivors – scattered ash

One cannot escape the flame of fury
The jowl-burning bile of disgust
Anger towards those who propagate and propel death
Through willful-ignorance-born
and bigotry-led disobedience

None are immune and few are innocent
But care and compassion and the desire to hold on
To help and hold together
Are what we have left
Hold these jewels dear

We are within walls
But love for all must radiate globally
We are in instead of out
But are all in it together

Be well
Hold on

There is more than menace dancing on the wind
There is also Hope
And Hope can find a home wherever it is blown
And wherever it lands

Let Hope land on your tongue and dissolve
Rushing towards you heart
Let yourself breathe Hope into your lungs
Let it cover you head to toe
Let it be your food, your garb, your elixir

Let Hope be your strength
Listen to it when it tells you to stay safe
When it tells you to keep others safe

Then – Spread Hope
(The opposite of disease)
In whatever way you can

Use your gifts-
Your art, your will and enthusiasm
Spread Hope
Give Hope
Be Hope

Abide in the shelter of Hope with all humanity
Until the doors reopen

Michael Sindler, a native of South Carolina, has called Denver home for well over a decade. His work crosses genres and includes fiction, non-fiction, memoir, poetry, theatre, and songwriting. He has been published in various Denver-based print and web venues and he has collaborated with and participated in a number of media bridging projects and productions with museums and arts organizations throughout the region.

ME, IMMIGRANT, ME
BY MICHELE RANNIE

it was the sun
that baked it in
to the seams of my skin
and the dents of my pores

my honor
swagger
and song
timed to the rhythm of the Caribbean Sea
beating into shores that I love

And now
ride with me on the train
and into high-rise buildings
scaling escalators and chasing dreams

and planting good seed
with my seed
just as the father and mother before you did
so that
there is nothing that separates my claim from yours
except perhaps
a generation ranking in era and time

Michele Rannie is a poet, civil litigation attorney, and immigration/civil rights activist based in New York, and born on the Caribbean island of St. Kitts. She considers her highest calling to be that of mother to her thirteen (13) year old daughter. Her email address is michele.rannie@gmail.com and her Twitter handle Is @MicheleRannie.

PLAGUED AMERICA
BY NANCY MERCADO

It takes a plague to crystallize
the malignancy occupying the White House
that churns out death
a gross carnage of humanity
stockpiled inside U-Haul trucks

It takes a plague to breach the lies
we live in this America
bearing its mercenary truths
its decomposing laws
scavenged by elected vultures

A plague is what it takes
to realize red baseball-capped buffoons
can freely amass assault rifles
the privileged scant illiterate and starved
lined up for miles to reach food banks
gleefully waving soiled confederate flags in tatters

A plague must be what it takes
to discover our illusory lives
the hamster wheel we've been sold
traveling on it all along
toward manufactured dreams
toward nowhere in reality

It takes a plague to recognize
we are orphans in this America
sparing no expense we're marked for ruin
by the slothful elites who bask
in swimming pools of our blood

A plague is what it takes
to wake up from this American dream
to see our children encaged

our mothers our fathers
butchered in broad daylight
our homes mired in soot water
our lands laced of oil pipelines
discharging at whim
scourging valleys filled of life
decimating our future
under a foul dark layer of evil

A plague must be what it takes
for our redress in the streets
of this America
our decisive rebellion
our final renaissance.

Nancy Mercado was named one of 200 living individuals who best embody the work and spirit of Frederick Douglass, on the occasion of his bicentennial, by the Frederick Douglass Family Initiatives and the Antiracist Research and Policy Center at American University. She is the recipient of the 2017 American Book Award for Lifetime Achievement presented by the Before Columbus Foundation.

2020 VISION MEANS NOTHING IN THE DARK
BY NATHANIEL SWANSON

Most days I don't want to turn my camera on,
my eyes have made railroads of my face and
the lights are dim, it's getting dark.
Class is at the back of my mind behind the growing dread
        that I might die.

Someone made a threat on my life back in 07-09 and
I still think a knife is on its way to my spine.

And I'm Black,
        smack dab on a campus bordered by KKK members
            and Trump flags.

]And these cases keep rising higher,
and white people got cars. Nice cars.
And pockets that burn deep enough that they can't sit still.
I'm talking money for plane tickets and
hospital bills.

If I catch COVID because they caught flights imma lose it
even though I can't afford to. I'm here for a reason.

My room has become a coffin.
My reflection knows my shadow,
and my shadow knows my day down to the minute.
He hasn't seen light in a while.
My reflection knows my shadow so well they start to
        look alike.

The mirror shows the darkness.
The camera shows the darkness.
I can't remember the last time the world wasn't dark.
I can't remember the last time the world wasn't dark.

Nathaniel Swanson is a poet, scholar, and youth activist who serves as the 2020 & 2019 Youth Poet Laureate Ambassador. He was a member of the 2018 Urban Word NYC National Slam Team and has been published in Joy and Hope and All That: A Tribute to Lucille Clifton. *Nathaniel is now a Posse Scholar at DePauw University. Follow him on Instagram @n_ate_the_great*

THANK GOD FOR THE INTERNET
BY NICOLE JOCLEEN

I know you're probably wondering how we got here.
Well it all started when y'all doubted Hillary
Over some emails.
Nah be for real
It was 'cause she was female.

You exposed your chauvinism that year
And for me that's when things began to become clear.
Trump won and black people thought they'd died.
But why, 'cause you never supported Hillary in the first
    place.
Now where's the lie?

It was starting to look like the Trump legacy would end
    with a successful run in the white house,
then 2020 came and I began to have my doubts.

Remember those Pastors that said Trump's victory was
    ordained by God?
Well I'm starting to see what the purpose was all along.
A police officer routinely placed his knee on an unarmed
    black man's neck.
Thank God for the internet.

Young black people called their white friends on the carpet.
Said, "we ain't really friends if my marches ain't your
    marches."
White, yellow, brown; united for one cause.
I told you I'm starting to see what the purpose was all
    along.

This time it wasn't peaceful. This time the flames weren't
    headed our way.
This time we got their attention. This time we changed the
    game.

Thank God for our ancestors who gave us the play.
Am I the only one that thought about Tupac on that day?
Wished he was here to see it?
Hoped he was hiding out in New Mexico,
Afar, but still viewing it?

Then like a dark horse the Coronavirus became a name.
Shook the core of our very existence;
Nothing was the same.
Politicians said this is the new normal
Like it was some sort of checkmate.
Like they knew something we didn't know;
That's politics though.

Trump thought they were exaggerating,
Said it was just another flu.
We went with it and the party continued.

I mean we believed him on the low.
He is the Commander and Chief of this country,
If anyone, he would know.

We looked up one day and we were masked up,
Policing each other;
Making matters worse.

Then we shut down.
What a time to be alive.
We fought over toilet paper
and asked God why.
The numbers are going up.
People around me afraid of COVID
But they don't want to hear that sea moss talk
'Cause the doctor didn't prescribe it.
They don't want to hear that dairy mucus talk
So unfortunately people are dying
And anyone making sense is suddenly a target.

What does our president have to say?
Oh he's somewhere meeting with Kanye
'Cause elections are near
So it's time to kick things into gear.

Anybody else wondering what Bush had to say
Watching the man who accused him of not caring about
    black people
Relating to Trump in this way
It's funny how things change.
We laughed 'til we saw his name on the ballot.

I ain't mad he did what he set out to do
Something no rapper before him had the guts to do.
His kids will be able to say my dad was a part of the 2020
    election too.
And 60,000 votes from a person with no political history is
    an accomplishment too.
But somewhere in my heart I felt like black people were
    screwed.

They said they voted for Ye cause he's a real nigga.
Come on he's splitting the vote let's be real, my nigga.

My people talked bad about Trump for 4 years but
    suddenly
The closer we got to elections black Trumpers began to
    appear.
This made it clear that Biden had to make his next move his
    best move.
Insert Kamala Harris. Hey Queen. You know what to do.

And this is when we really saw people's true colors.
Because in 2020 we were finally teaching black men how
    to have our back.
Cue internet Kamala Harris attacks.

They attacked her political history.

They didn't know I was just happy she had political
     history.
They said her spouse is not black.
Neither is Ye's, okay.
But we're not discussing that today.

When it was all said and kinda done
America had enough.
I mean the election was intense
But Americans came through and voted like they had some
     sense.

Trump is doing everything but bowing out gracefully.
Biden's preparing for our shut down.
I'm preparing my mind to say "only in 2020...what now?"
Some people are still waiting for things to go back to
     normal
Waiting to attend big family reunions
Waiting to return to the Essence Festival
Waiting to take off the mask
Waiting to go to a sold-out concert and stand neck to neck.
Me, I'm just waiting on my second stimulus check.

Nicole Jocleen is an Oklahoma City-based poet, screenwriter, and author of 5 books, including Don't Be Afraid of Men and Their Faces. *Her email is nicolejocleen@hotmail.com and you can follow her on Instagram @nicolejocleen*

2020
BY NIKKI GIOVANNI

I don't understand why the virus took
Over two hundred thousand people
But not trump and that third foreign woman
and that half-wit boy who either can't talk
or doesn't speak English
or spies for Russia

I do understand that republicans
Are cowards and so are those nazis
Cheering
And those kkk we now call police killing
Not to mention father and sons chasing unarmed Black men
and running their cars into crowds
Pretending they are brave or something

They are not only cowards
And nazis but evil fools
who go to bed white
Wake up American
And hate themselves for having
To share this earth

They will not overcome
And we will not love them

I don't understand why
Biden doesn't know every time
From Pilate and Lincoln and all the rest try
To forgive they are murdered
And I hope this is not the case

But what does 2020 mean to me

A chance to learn how to open oysters
Talk to friends

Catch up on my reading
Tell myself I am going to dust the house
Lie about it

Enjoy the cold weather coming in
Improve my hamburger making
(add a smidgen of nutmeg/fry slowly in butter)
Enjoy my own company not to mention football

And remember there will be tomorrow

Because there will be

And evil will go and good will come

I am Black
We have seen much worse

Nikki Giovanni is probably the only poet who does not email. She is happy.

AMERICA, YOU'RE BEAUTIFUL.
BY NINA BREWTON

America, you're beautiful.

Your beauty the manifestation of the very best of
everything that is within you

Your shores shimmering as gold refined
A glimmer of hope across waters
A glimpse of home in the distance
To those who have fought your battles
Stood their ground on your behalf
On soil that does not bear your name

America

These heroes proved

We prove our love in the ranks of your stripes
Our love made evident from our core

I affirm my love for you in my core values
Integrity first
Service before self

Excellence in all I've done for you

America, you're beautiful.

You make it easy to love with your empty promises
Hearts set on the imagination of all that you are
All that we can be

My heart has swelled for you, America
Self-love nearly abandoned
Set aside in the name of unity and inclusion

Your comfort, my duty
Your freedom; not my freedom
It is not our freedom
My reality not yours
Yet you refuse to see

America, you're beautiful.

Your allure pouring over praying hands with every sunrise
We give thanks for your daily bread
Grains golden, rich with life
Nurturing generations of

America

The waves that carry dreams to your shores
Are waters of meditation
Flowing like the tears of dreamers

Each drop gathers as clouds in your spacious skies
Raining down on your majesties
Peaks purple like bruises in the hearts and on the backs of
your countrymen

By Grace, you pour over us with your beauty
As your children pore over you
Your symbols of superiority
Lifted high upon your mountaintops
Honoring, always
America FIRST
Your eyes fixed on
Your banner of war
In all her glory

Dignity, perverted
Saved for ghosts of those representing the worst of who
you are
Romanticizing the sins of

Your four fathers and their brothers
These American idols

Casting their shadows down on the least of these
Their images carved into stone in the minds of your people
America, you're beautiful.

However
You are
The uncle no one speaks of
The abusive, violent, drunk uncle
More than a mere black sheep
They say he's the worst of our lineage
Tearing his own family apart
Battles with principalities fought at dinner tables

His hatred masquerading as pride and patriotism
Thanks given every time he leaves
Carrying his anger, regrets and greatest insecurities
with him

Fear, hypocrisy and hatred
He holds close like the family Bible
Yielding to its every word
Holding it tightly, twine of discord
Sewing into the hearts of his own children
The tradition of abuse the family has long denied
Perverting their love calling it, pride

He's taught them to see "others" as the enemy
A threat to their way of life
He fought on the frontline for freedom
Yet demonizes those who fight for their own

America, you're proud of the seeds of your bloodline
Your children becoming
Teachers who teach half truths
Congressmen passing laws exploiting the oppressed

The great grandchildren of slave hands
Becoming those who swore to protect and serve

America, you're beautiful.

But you can no longer afford to fall into the shadows
Of a past rooted in
Darkness
Hatred
Evil

You have violence sewn into
The very fabric of your being

This fabric the rope used to hang the sweetest of fruit from
trees
It burns the hands of those refusing to release
Tugging, holding on to their allegiance
To the myth of Liberty and Justice for all

So, we fight
We stand in
Liberating strife
Infernos burning city to city
From the splendorous mountains and lush valleys of the
land of gold
Eastward to the streets of the capital of the Confederacy
Northbound throughout the rotten apple illuminated by
the light of Lady Liberty herself

We fight
We march
We pray

We lament for his...for your deliverance
So much beauty and potential
Worthy of love
The grace we're all worthy of

Even I, stand enveloped in grace
Somewhere between the love of Christ
The words of Baldwin and
Paul's letters to the Thessalonians

High atop Mercy's billboard
We be the Light
Creating space for grace to abide
Yet exposing lies
The shadows in the corners of our minds

Light begets light
Illuminated by Love
Reflecting off of mirrors
Forcing our brothers and sisters to see themselves
As they are

We be the light
A light on the path forward
To the America of our best and brightest imaginations
Teaching your children to cease fleeing from reality
Showing them how to change it for the benefit of all
    lives…

Even if the reality is not yours

America

Nina Brewton is a host, performance artist and social mentor, based in Chesapeake, Virginia. She is the author of two books, Dramas of a Bald Head Queen - a memoir *and* Heart of a Queen - Poetry and Prose from the Soul. *You can follow Nina on Instagram and Twitter at @baldheadqueen and always learn more at www.webethelight.com.*

THIS NEW AMERICA
BY NOEL A. FIGUEROA

Is this the America you want me to accept? One where it's okay for me to be downgraded, degraded and disrespected because of the color of my skin by people who are bent on believing that this country only belongs to them? Yet this country was never theirs in the first place. Isn't that ironic? Is this the new America you want me to accept, where racists, sexists and instigators of strife and division get to be president and encourage more bold and brazen racist behavior and rhetoric with no accountability or responsibility on the part of the offenders?

Is this the new America you want me to love when it's been engraved in its DNA to hate and despise me perpetually through the generations? Is this the new America you want me to celebrate when my people are still oppressed, stressed through systems designed to hold us back and diminish our intelligence and contributions to society? Is this the new America I must stand for when it chooses to continually stand against me? Why must I live in a country that my ancestors bled and died for to help build and be treated like a second-class citizen? So quick to be told "go back to Africa" but my ancestors didn't ask to be brought here against their will, treated like animals and machines for profits they never got to enjoy.

Why should I go back when your ownership of this country is based on lies, scandal, stealing and crooked politics? Is this the new America you want me to support when it's done everything in its power to systematically dismantle the black family, emasculate black men, degrade black women and convince black children they are no greater than the systems put in place to hold them back? Is this the new America you want me to oversee where my people constantly have to justify their worth and scream at the top of their lungs to be heard because of the stereo of double standards turned up full blast?
This new America does not, and has NEVER provided liberty, freedom and justice for ALL.

Noel A. Figueroa is a Poet, Author, Blogger, Event Host and Facilitator of the "Poets With Purpose" Poetry Workshop. You can reach him at PoetsWithPurpose@gmail.com & follow him on Instagram @TheAnointedPen

THE WORLD IS CLOSED
BY PETER D. HEHIR

They said the world was closed today,
so I went to have a look.
I found it with the shutters down
and the phone was off the hook.

So I stood there for a little while
but no one was around.
Then silence came and startled me,
with the most alarming sound.

I asked him where the others were
and why the streets were bare.
He whispered, 'Life had ran away
while death was playing there.'

'Oh no,' I said. 'It can't be true,
for life is not afraid.'
'But no one ever goes,' he said
'where death has ever played.'

I understood and walked away
as Hope was standing there,
with Courage in her afterglow
and the sunlight in her hair.

She said, 'Go home to those you love,
this is no place to be.
For if we walk these streets today
then no one shall be free.'

She threw her light to lead the way
and showed me where to go.
The very road that life had gone,
where the future flowers grow.

Then death showed me another way
but I didn't want to look,
so I stumbled home in time for tea
and I read another book.

It was called, The World is Closed Today
And the streets we shouldn't roam.
The first line said, 'Just please be safe'
And the ending — 'Stay at Home'

Peter D Hehir is a Poet and Author from Birmingham, England. He has three collections out now and available to buy, you can find him on Twitter @thebrummypoet and on Instagram Thebrummypoet. He has a new website - petespoetry.co.uk and his email address is thebrummypoet@gmail.com

SOLDIER OF SOLITUDE
BY PETER M. SCHEPPER AKA PMS

All alone,
I'm isolated,
All my loved ones, miles away.
Stuck at home,
And suffocated,
Afraid to go outside and play.

Out of shape and overeating,
I only want to watch TV.
Mouth agape,
I watch our leader,
On his stage,
He lies to me.

Resentments surge,
I crave escape,
I'd like to take that magic pill.
I'm on the verge,
It's taking shape,
I hatch a plan with all my skill.

Alarms go off,
I see red flags,
I know the way this story ends.
I stand aloft,
Temptation nags,
I need support of absent friends.

I can't succumb,
And jeopardize,
I've got to fight to carry on.
An answer comes,
I raise my eyes,
I need the help of number one.

Can I be brave,
And shirk this fear?
The future is an aimless trod.
The answer came
To me so clear!
I march along the path of God.

Peter M. Schepper, aka PMS, is a New York City-based artist, actor, writer, and framer. He is best known for his handmade marionettes.

CONTINUITY
BY RANDI MCCREARY

grab

grab. grab. grab. grab. grab.
grabbing, and then he still grabs
stop grabbing; pussy.

apricot

apricot tantrums
leaving children in cages
twisted war wages.

boundaries

it's much too often
that the huffmans and loughlins
sentences soften.

while...

mothers of dark child
considered to have gone wild
out of the district.

youdontknownan

smirk. shine. smize and clap
nancy had him in her lap take note.
that's a wrap.

sheshed

the last time i checked
blood shed from my ovaries

belonged all to me.

shock

mouths falling open
from the audacity of pride
how dare we love us.

no

no means no means no
from the turtle-necked martyr
to the let it all flow.

lost

our moral compass
has become fogged and cracked thin
leading us nowhere.

mac

aorta colder
than a football sized platter
of preserved big macs.

safe

we don't say, "i'm home."
we say, "baby i made it",
language barriers.

Randi McCreary is a Kansas City-based poet, writer, speaker, educator and the author of two chapter books including A Beautiful Mess *and* Sweet.Water.Horizon. *Her email is randiwriter@gmail.com and you can follow her on Instagram @randiwriter.*

IMPOTENT GODS ARE THEIR OWN DEVILS
BY RASHELL R. SMITH-SPEARS

Victor Frankenstein never made a monster,
just a man
who became his own thing,
and Victor didn't like it.
Because he wanted to be the god.
He took what didn't belong to him
parts of lives
that once shaped whole men
and puzzled them into his picture
of a man that he could know.
But his knowledge was short
and this frightened him,
gave him nightmares.
So, trained on the man, Victor's eyes
reflected the monster in his head.

Victor's American brothers never made a monster either.
They plucked men from African soil—
Ibo
Bantu
Ashanti—
and planted them in American dung.
Parts of men they tried to fashion into
a slave
because they wanted to be God.
And when they couldn't control them
they cried monster and ran
at the men waving guns like torches
to show they were afraid.
But the real monster? Their arrogance
coming back like zombies
to decimate justice.

RaShell R. Smith-Spears is a poet and fiction writer who has published in numerous journals and anthologies, including Sycorax's Daughters, Gumbo Magazine, *and* Dying Dahlia Review. *She teaches English at Jackson State University in Jackson, Mississippi, and can be reached at rsmithspears@yahoo.com.*

#45
BY REGINA HEAD

4 years of pure madness!
Was it simply a dream
or a nightmare?
Just unbelief...

He displayed no respect for others!
He showed no compassion!
There was no empathy on his part!

Only cared about himself —
not me, not my children nor my
grandchildren,
not the elderly,
not the homeless,
not the poor.

Constantly spewed out —
division,
divisiveness,
hate, and
rudeness!
 #45
that's how I referred
to him.
I couldn't say President Trump.
I couldn't say Mr. President.

Please God, let his era
be over!
Guide him right on out
of that White House!
He has already indicated
that there may be some
resistance, resistance,
resistance.

Regina Head is a retired Detroit Public School teacher. She has a love of children's books for ages birth to 7 years old, and is in the process of writing her first children's book. Her e-mail is rhead3@yahoo.com and you can follow her on Instagram @head.regina

THE URBAN WALL
BY ROBERT VAZQUEZ

Skellzies, Off The Curb, Stick Ball from Sewer to Sewer, Kick The Can...

Quarter Waters, Bazooka Joe, Chips & Fun Dip... "We are short on money, can we repay you later, Mr. Bodega Man?"

Public School, Pledge of Allegiance, Passing notes to the cutie up front, I hope she turns around.

We walked the halls, shared some classes, and traded lunchroom tickets with kids from all different backgrounds.

Pinstripe Lees. Le Tigre shirts, Puma kicks, V-Bomber jackets were all the Craze...

Black or White, Different Skin, Allah, God, Jehovah that's who you praised...

It didn't matter; we were all family, that's how we were raised.

Fast-forward to now; I walk the streets where I grew old.

No street games, no children playing, just streaming videos where only half the story is told.

The streets are empty; the kids are hiding, buried in their phones...

Virtual friends, apps and games, NO house parties, No late-night dances with unwanted chaperones.

Who can blame them; our world is crazy; they say our neighbors are "Illegals".

We tell them they may be "Bad Hombres," Drug Dealers, and Rapists who should get hauled off to jail and shouldn't enjoy the beauty of our country. No Statue of Liberty, No Ellis Island, No American Flag, No Bald Eagle.

What are we doing? What are we teaching? What happened to
Give me your tired, your poor, your huddled masses, yearning to breathe free?

Are we destroying our paradise, tainting our children, is this the equivalent of eating the forbidden fruit from the poisonous tree?

I'm often asked, "What do you think of the next generation, where are they headed?" My response is "I don't know…but always remember we reap what we sow."

They tell me our children have vision, they can move forward through it all.

I pause, process and slowly respond…

"How could they do that, when their minds and hearts are stopped by a border wall?"

Robert Vazquez is a Bronx-raised writer, marketer, product developer, advocate for the youth, and the author of two published children's books. You can follow Robert's journey on Instagram @RobertVazquezAuthor.

WHITE WRONG RIGHT
BY SEAN HILL

I keep looking
I keep looking

I almost squint to black

to see the reason
excuse
justification
mistake
slip up

the moment
where a cop
doesn't mean

to execute someone

the knee
he thought wasn't too much
since the suspect could still say I can't breathe
apparently someone can breathe
to speak that sentence like Mr. Garner
Mr. Ambler, Mr. Ellis, and Mr. McClain spoke
before their breaths were stolen
choked into hashtag

maybe he threatened the cops life
and the cop had to retaliate
with two other cops
restraining his body
forcing him down
one with knee to throat
hand on thigh
comfortable

but
threatened

yeah…
I get it

but something is off with this story
that's right

I'm looking for answers
of why I am abused
from abuser

I am asking rapist
to explain why they raped me

I am Iraq, Somalia, Vietnam
asking the U.S. to heal me
after you lie, invade and bomb me

I am a torso
asking a knife
to not stab me
after being sliced
for centuries
I can look for reasons
all day and night
all week and month
all year and 400 more

I know
the answers
have been there
the reasons are clear:

our current police
evolved from slave patrols
preventing uprisings and revolts

then when slavery ended
they were still used to keep tabs on Black America
even helped enable the white fable of protection
from the "scary black man"
since the birth of this nation
helped the setting of fires
and dropping of bombs
on black cities like Philadelphia,1985
back to Black Wall Street, 1921
Tulsa, 30 plus city blocks
burned
300 dead
800 injured
black children, men, women
integrated
with white
building rubble
buried in mass graves
no funeral

the white murderous mob
had no arrests
no peaceful protest
yet, they got their "justice"

we keep getting attacked
or hung
with ropes
and ropeless lynches
bullets to chest or knees to neck
until life flinches slowly
out of our bodies

he called for his mother
who is already what he will soon be

. . .

a knee
so many
Caucasian patriots
didn't enjoy
when a football player took one
for his fellow citizens fallen
an idea suggested to him by a green beret
to show respect in his protest even more
twice, two black men
raised fist at olympics
the time still wasn't right
or appropriate enough apparently

when a King fell assassinated
during his unpopular
peaceful protest 1968
when another King fell in 91 from cops
beating him in a circle with batons
brain damage from 11 skull fractures
he learned to forgive
but should we

I don't enjoy
I don't want
to keep being right
about the idea
that so many of

you

don't care

about black

life

you keep adding "more" or "only"
to "black lives matter"

you keep stuffing words in us
      like lies in police reports
      like drugs into black cities
        like bullets into children
please
      prove me wrong
        I'm trying to be wrong

I
want
to be wrong so much

show me
show me

that I'm
wrong

I need
to be wrong

if you are white

I love you

don't confuse pain for hate
see all hate as pain
relate
please
kindly prove me wrong
with your actions
not just your words
with your compassion
not just your logic
with your humanity
not your politician
with your love
not your sympathy

with your honesty
not your shame
with your empathy minus the blame

since somehow
we keep dying
because you say everything
is in my mind
that America is fine
a few bad apples
even though
those good cops who whistleblow
are cast out as rotten
you say everything is alright
just some reform
just more body cams
that they keep turning off
that they keep not wearing
that they keep recording us being murdered
I know not all cops are racist
I know we had a black president
I know he was white, too
I know about black crime in Chicago
I know that's not the topic, let's talk about you
I know white & all people get brutalized
I know that's true
but your heartfelt truths
your well meaning lies
your constant race debates
that always deflect

they are just
another arm
another rope
another knee
on my

International actor, US touring poet, school building humanitarian & TEDx speaker Sean Hill supports & manifests world peace through inner peace with poetry in a realistic & fun way. All social media is @LetsBendReality and his email list for community events, writing workshops, and passionate positivity is at www.LetsBendReality.com

JOURNAL ENTRY: TUESDAY APRIL 2ND, 2020
BY SHANELLE GABRIEL

Something about death
Clears the sky
The blues bring blue
The sun shines on sadness
Amidst the madness
I remember,
9/11 was a clear day
The perfect condition for ashes
To float and greet us in Bay Ridge
The same way
80 degrees hit palm trees
And the wind wheezed warm
The last time
I kissed my mom's cheek
The sun shines on sadness
The same way
Flowers resounded
With the hum of visiting bees
The grass a sea
Gleaming the greenest
Shade of emerald
I'd ever seen
On the day my nephew's
Left his 5 year old body
Tragedy
Seems to cause nature to display
Her full glory
And now,
45,000
Are missing the lavender
Christening this sunrise
That I watch from
Inside the house I'm confined
Locked in a gorgeous world

Beyond belief
A scene at the end of a sci-fi movie
Where heavens part
Clouds leave
The sky in contrast
To the array of black
Rays through church windows
As if to return the color
The face in the casket lacks
As if nature is the path
Calling them back to the Creator
Every time I've witnessed death
I've seen it push precipitation back
Nimbus clouds refusing to compete
With tears that flow
Reminding us
No matter the storm inside
Over this world
We have no control
Cherishing the robins and sparrow
Serenading amidst the crows
The dazzling daylight
Playing mediator between
Our goodbyes
And God's hellos

Shanelle Gabriel is a poet, singer, educator, and lupus patient advocate from Brooklyn, NY. She has toured internationally, and released 2 albums fusing poetry, hip-hop, and R&B. Visit www.shanellegabriel.com and follow her on Instagram @shanellegabriel.

VOTE
BY SUZEN BARAKA
Commissioned By Poetic People Power

My mother relies on me, to help her save her Korean BBQ
    restaurant in NJ,
She does not understand that this country doesn't care
    about either one of us, or our survival,
All she knows is that Shake Shack got $10M and how
    come she hasn't gotten anything yet
I tell her what the SBA representative told me,
That we filled out the application too early, just before
    quarantine when Asian businesses were already
    struggling because of the virus,
They streamlined it since then, and threw out our
    application without telling us, there's nothing left
    for businesses like ours,

I can tell this does not reconcile with the version of
    America she dreamt of in a country where freedom
    must of felt foreign to her the way freedom feels
    foreign to me,

The way simply breathing feels revolutionary in a country
    that targets Black bodies,
The way, at 36 years old, this Black body is afraid to make
    more Black bodies,

Like Black bodies ain't the people I love, like Trayvon
    don't remind me of my nephews, like Sandra don't
    remind me of my sister, like George don't remind
    me of my daddy, like Elijah don't remind me of me,
    an introvert and different and unbelievably fucking
    strong, LIKE being Korean and Black during
    coronavirus in Trump's America don't make me want
    to burn it all down.

I've applied for the NJEDA, the PPP, the EIDL of the SBA,
And I'm looking for the words to say…
I don't know how to help you Mom, I don't know how to
    help you Dad,
I don't know how to help Trayvon, I don't know how to
    help Oscar Grant,
I don't know how to help Breonna, Dominique or Tony,
But here I am talking to y'all about voting because I
    know…

Moses is a Black woman
Shirley is a boss
Sojourner Truth is a verb
And they been telling us what happens to a vote unused,
It becomes an American dreamer deferred…

Just ask Stacey Abrams
Voting is the bare minimum

You can lead a horse to Maxine Waters, but you can't make
    him think,
Alicia Garza in the Black Futures Lab tryna bring y'all
Black to the Ballot, and back from the brink,
So here I am trying to get people to vote because I know…
That between 2012 and 2018, over 1.4 million voter
    registrations were cancelled, with 700,000 cancelled
    on a single night in July, and that's just Georgia

Here I am trying to get people to vote because I know…
That in 2017, 99 bills to limit access to the ballot have been
    introduced in 31 of these here United States

And I'm looking for the words to say,
If our vote wasn't important, why are they working so hard
    to take it away?

Vote because
Flint Michigan. Still. doesn't. have. clean. water.
Because over 5,460 children have been separated from their
    parents at the border.
Because…children are being tear gassed…
Because…children are being tear gassed during the
    pandemic of a respiratory disease…
Because children are being tear gassed during the pandemic
    of a respiratory disease for protesting the murder of
    a Black man by a white police officer via asphyxiation.

Vote

Because the war on drugs led to Black fathers being ripped
  from Black babies, slavery,

Because the war on drugs led to Black bodies being
  stopped, being frisked, like it don't matter if Blacks
  live?

Because the war on drugs led to ONE in 13 Black Americans,
  losing their right to vote due to a felony conviction,
  THAT was 2016, the same year as Trump's election,

I said ONE in 13 Black Americans without a vote,

The same year as Trump's election,

Vote because you want to make facts, facts again

Vote because the first step to co-opting a system is
  engaging in it,

Just ask the FBI, the CIA, Justice Roberts and Brian Kemp,

Vote because when you're standing in the voting booth
  trying to decide between tweedle duh and tweedle
  dee, you'll ask yourself why isn't there a better
  choice,

Vote because when they try to dismantle our bodies from
  our breath, we gotta use our voice.

Suzen Baraka is a lawyer, poet, writer, actor and activist who has been performing and touring nationally for over 17 years. She can be reached via Instagram @Suzen_Baraka.

In power & gratitude,
T Bailey 2021

NORMALLY
BY TERRI L. BAILEY

Today I woke up with a cough
And my throat was a little scratchy
Normally
This wouldn't have bothered me
Because yesterday
I hung with the sun for a day of play
And working spiritually
For some emotional relief
And I have these allergies
That would normally
Make me sneeze anyway
But I have to say
It ain't normal times
And that cough planted a red flag on my mind
And made me sweat
Which I do randomly
'Cuz I'm over 50
And this hotness that would normally
Just annoy me
Now sets off an alarm in me
Because the threat of fever stalks me
And the hint of temperature rise
Implies
Viral impurity
And I don't want to take my temp again...
But maybe I should

Normally

When I'm just sitting around, and my comfy couch makes
me sleepy
I'd just lay down and take a damn nap you see
But now a nap may actually be perceived
As fatigue

And a regular old additional sleep need
Could signal the death of me

DAMN! DAMN! DAMN!

Normally
In the good old days of last month
I could give a hug or a fist bump
I could kiss my momma and share a meal
But now giving her some sugar is a big deal
Because age decreases her likelihood to heal
So we use the telephone and window as a protective field

Normally
I'm an extroverted introvert who is fickled certainly
I love to be at home but crave interacting socially
So I be in the community
Organizing or reading poetry
Or participating revolutionarily
But now I'm desperately
Trying to meet on Zoom
Using Facebook Live in my living room
To participate in society
Distantly and safely
Visiting via a computer screen

Normally
My woke people be crying LOOK! LOOK!
Them dirty ass crooks
Trying to keep us shook
Using the corona news
As an economic distraction
Increasing the divisions of the already fractured factions
So we be fighting just to breathe
While the powers that be
Are coming for us stealthily and yet blatantly
Fuckin with the have nots
Who are defending themselves against the think they gots
While those in charge are meticulously planning

To take what's left of the poor who survive
And have no idea that they'll have to keep fighting just to
stay alive

Oh yeah, while we speaking financially
Let me give somma y'all a read
'Cuz since I don't work in a normal taxable way
You don't think I've earned a stimulus payday
Yet if y'all ass lose that last taxed check
You'll be broker than me and twice as vexed
So you better spend wisely and keep in mind
We are living and working in a new time
And you gon' wish you was the entrepreneurial kind
'Cuz job security ain't what it used to be
And you existing in a state of false reality

Normally

My differently abled child would be out in them streets
Fishing or hanging out eating sweet treats
But the quickly increasing infection rate
Cancelled them dates
So I sit here with my daughter
Being all smiley and shit
While imagining a lamb in slaughter
and bracing myself for a hit
Are my rapid breaths and heartbeat
An indicator that death is near
Or is it just a visceral reaction
From widespread corona fear

Normally

I would say chile have several seats
Go and sit your crazy ass down
Stop predicting imminent defeat
Apocalypto ain't coming to town

Tap it out, breathe and meditate
That's what you should be doing right now
But it's hard to stay calm and focused
While anticipating a final bow
And then I read an article
'Bout disabled lives not worth being saved
So I'm honestly concerned
That y'all will send my daughter to an early grave
Cuz normally you can't see
All her fabulous abilities
And a ventilator wasted on her
May deny an ableist's need

Normally

I pray and make Ebo so things don't get any worse
But y'all challenge my faith in Orisha
And post another damn Bible verse
This paranoia trying to oppress me
But my ancestors come in dreams
Telling me my blood has survived
Far worse than we've ever seen

So suck it up!
And let the healing begin
Love up on my family
And pick up the goddamn pen
Write stories of our victories
Dictating how this shit will end
And choose to create how my life will be
As I triumphantly ascend
And realize on the other side of this mess
I'm still highly favored I'm still truly blessed
And with my pandemic survival
I'm certainly guaranteed
Success and greatness unrivaled
And the knowledge that I'll be
Stronger than I would have been

Had I just lived normally

Terri L Bailey, MA is a Florida native, a Yaya, Poet, writer of Black horror and Afrofuturism, a community educator and activist and the first runner up for Alachua County's first poet laureate. You can contact her at terribaileywrites@gmail.com and follow her on IG & Facebook @terribaileywrites

A HAIKU FOR SOME WRITERS
BY THANDISIZWE CHIMURENGA

I

A haiku has rules
But as a sista told me
'Free' and 'rules' don't mix

We ain't gon' get free
By following some ol' rules
Especially "his"

You know who "His" is
To be free men and women
We do our own thang

II

The work of haiku
Says a lot with a little
Sonia Sanchez asks:

What work does this do?
She asks poets and writers
Does your work free us?

Does your work heal us?
If not what does it do, yo?
It must do something

It WILL do something
It will not exist simply
To exist it will

Heal us or hurt us
Fight for us or not for us

It will flee from us
Or it will stay put
It will muddy the water
Or bring clarity

It WILL do something
Tell us, what it gon' do, Sesh?
What'chu writing for?

III

Toni Cade Bambara
She also spoke to writers
Said we had a job

The job of writers
Is to make revolution
Irresistible

That sounds hard, don't it?
How do we do that, you ask?
How else do you think?

Write, Revise, Write, Rest
Write, Revise, Resist, Rewrite
Write, Rest, Write Some More

Write Revise Some More
Procrastinate like a mugg
Write Resist Revise

IV

Langston Hughes spoke too
One of the first of Our Greats
I ever studied

He loved Black people
I said he LOVED Black people
He wished we all did

How he wished We loved
Ourselves How he wished that We
Would look within Us

Our inspiration
And our Beauty and purpose
Can be found within

The Negro Artist
and The Racial Mountain is
An essay he wrote

What did his words say?
In Nineteen and Twenty-Six
What was the message?

He told us to stop
Wanting to be white because
That's what we're doing

Subconsciously true
'Universal' does not mean
What you think it means

We must look within
For all that we need is there
We need a new way

The planet needs one
The planet needs a new way
More than the US
needs a new president and

THE UNITED STATES

DOES NEED A NEW PRESIDENT
QUICK FAST HURRY UP

Earth needs a new way
We will not find a new way
Following old men

Old white men who are
Committed to death we need
Common sense and Life

Life and common sense
These people have proved themselves
Unfit for Adults

Unfit for Humanity
Unfit to Govern
Unfit for Living Beings

Move on over now
Get out the way your time's up
The planet needs peace

We had it before
In the beginning, we did
We'll have it again

We must look within
We must look within Ourselves
We must look within

The job of writers
Is to make revolution
Irresistible

What are you writing
For,
Sesh?

*Sesh is the Kemetic word for "writer"

Thandisizwe Chimurenga is a Los Angeles-based writer. She is the author of No Doubt: The Murder(s) of Oscar Grant, Reparations... Not Yet: A Case for Reparations And Why We Must Wait, *and has contributed to several anthologies.*

CHAINS
BY VALENTI PHILLIPS

The world as we know it has changed
The world as we know it has chains
Chaining us to a new reality
Chaining us to a lucid mystery
For we know not what tomorrow brings
Complete annihilation or a curing vaccine
Curing that which has no definite symptoms
Curing that which kills yet remains invisible
We mask up to avoid infection
The assimilation renders us indistinguishable detection
Now we all really do look alike
We've been inducted into an army with no tangible enemy
    in sight
And yet we fight
With all our might
Not to succumb to an unpredictable pain
To that which already has us in chains

*Valenti Phillips is an Atlanta based poet. Her email
is valentiphillips@gmail.com and you can follow her as well on Instagram
@i_am_valenti_p*

PART III: FICTION

A GLORIOUS WIN
BY GWENDOLYN CAHILL

Copyright 2020 Fourth Edition

Based on an excerpt from *Whispering Arising*

After another successful radio broadcast, Donetta Iglesias walks into the break room. Several radio jocks are engaged in a hot political conversation about the 2016 Presidential race.

DJ Delicious shouts, "This is a mess, there's no written qualifications for the position. I mean, it looks like anyone can run for the Supreme chair. You would think that the President of the United States should have experience in governing at the State or Federal level. Seems like this race and other races are contingent upon the candidate's war chest. I'm going to throw my hat into the ring."

Donetta ignites the room with laughter, "Your war chest isn't big enough to fight a billionaire. Hold on to your dollar. Trump is going to buy the supreme chair."

A small crowd slowly gathers in the break room.

DJ Delicious replies, "When the absurd becomes a way of life, it is time for a radical revolution. Radical change is often brought about in the election booth."

Donetta shouts, "You're right. Clinton has the power. There are too many debates, personal attacks and negative political tactics prevail in this campaign. I know one thing; all of you need to vote for the person who has your best interests at heart. They promise you the world and fail to deliver. Oprah hasn't spoken."

Donetta laughs and then she places her right hand close to her right ear, "Wait a minute. I hear Oprah."

"There really is no choice. She's not coming to your house. You don't have to like her," Oprah says.

Susan laughs, "Wait a minute Oprah. She came to my house. She came to the YWCA in Yonkers, NY. I swear to God. I lived there for a moment. I stood in the same room with Hilary Clinton."

That was the 2016 election. Trump won that election because of the electoral college votes, but he did not win the popular vote.

No one in the room can stand up straight. Everyone is bowled over with laughter. Donetta picks up the phone and fakes a call to Oprah Winfrey.

That was how it began. This year Biden took control. Donetta waves her hand in the air, "Trump ain't for us."

Fear of Trump campaign antics has begun in the 2020 elections. Steve Harvey's Morning Show minced no words. Every morning there was a commentary about the urgent need to change the guard. "Our vote matters," became the chant. "We will not be afraid to vote, we're voting."

Politics became a frequent topic in the break room.

The crowd grows too big in here, shouts the station manager. "Go do some work." He quickly disperses the crowd, but that did not deter them. Someone mutters, "That killjoy."

The sound of heels, squeaky sneakers and flip flops walking down the hallway leads a raucous chorus of laughter. After a while, they slowly depart from their desk and congregate in the lunchroom. Donetta stands on a chair and shouts, "Listen up everyone, this a no brainer. Cast your vote for Biden-Harris."

CNN was the first network to report their win. Trump's Election Apprentice Show will finally end in January. When I reflect upon the Trump Era, I see a man who was unable to "Make America Great Again." For us, America was never great. There is no such thing as a great country. Every country has issues. It could be worse. Lest our country is built on Democracy.

Donetta replies, "That's what they say, but there has always been a racial, class divide here. It seems like the racial divide has widened. Clearly, the needs of the bulk of Americans were overlooked. Relationships formed were broken. Our First Lady was mute. He did not fulfill his promises. In my opinion, COVID-19 sealed it. During the pandemic, Trump withdrew his support for the World Health Organization. All of us are forced to wear a mask, but even after testing positive, he still refused to wear a mask. He did not get us a second stimulus check."

The quest for the supreme chair was interesting. I did not think the Biden/Harris ticket was a good match when I heard his announcement, but I am not a political pundit. That June 27, 2019 debate was turbulent. Perhaps Kamala's ability to stand toe to toe with him intrigued him. Senator Kamala Harris does not seem to be intimidated by anyone. She pointed out Biden's record on school busing in the seventies and his work with segregationist senators James Eastland and Herman Talmadge.

The video of Kamala Harris phoning Joe Biden saying, "We did it, we did it, Joe. You're going to be the next president of the United States," was full of warmth. They were able to overcome their differences. This history-making ticket has led to the election of the first female Vice-President of the United States. Kamala Harris is Jamaica/Asian-American. She is married to a Jewish entertainment lawyer. Mrs. Kamala Harris is one of the most powerful females in the world!

In my opinion, Joe Biden's decision to pick a fifty-six-year-old running mate was wise. Momala is remarkably interesting! It is going to be interesting to see how they will address COVID-19, engage the nation, the world, and how they will reunite a divided country. Issues of inequality in the criminal justice system continue to plague us.

We pray that the transition will be peaceful. We needed a person who could walk into the Oval Office and take command of the controls, repair foreign relationships and fulfill promises. November 7th is a date that will remain in the hearts and minds of many. President Trump's refusal to publicly concede is disheartening. The people have spoken. President Donald Trump, you lost. Lawsuits filed by Trump to challenge the outcome have largely been dropped or dismissed.

Gwendolyn Cahill, resides in Richmond, Virginia. She has authored poetry, a political thriller, collection of short stories, children's pictures books that include her artwork and They Shall Swoop, *a mystery that received an unsolicited movie proposal from Pierson Media. Her email is OmariIrene@yahoo.com.*

WHEN THE BUBBLE BURSTS
BY JOLON MCNEIL

I knew I should look at him directly in the face and I didn't want to. I knew that if I did that I'd start crying. And he didn't deserve to feel like a better man for trying to console me after shattering me. So, I took a big gulp of the margarita in front of me and stared at him. Not in his eyes though. I could barely handle looking at just the space between his eyes. occasionally my gaze would drift to his long enviable eyelashes. But never directly in his eyes because I knew that it would trigger my undoing. Nothing could have prepared me for this moment in our timeline. How could he be getting married…and not to me?

The words that I could hear told a story of heartbreak long ago and a surprise reconnection. Part of what hurt in the moment was that I had never heard this love story. And this one thought spiraled inside my head, what else don't I know about this man after 15 years in a friendship?

It pained me to be present in the moment; I could literally feel something breaking inside of me. Every word that fell from his lips pierced the bubble of the life I created inside my head about us until it burst. But there was no way ever in that moment that I would let myself fall apart for him to see. At that moment we were still friends so the joy in his voice was supposed to be a happy moment, right? Still nothing could break through or push away the growing creeping sadness transforming my mood. He asked me if I was listening. I nodded and took another big sip, took a tortilla chip from the basket the waiter put in front of me. I wanted to vomit. I was overwhelmed by errant thoughts crowding my mind and by the mental work to make sure that I did not tear up. I don't remember how the story ended or if it ended at all. Somewhere inside of the story of found-again-love, I ordered another round. I had decided that I would not get through this night remaining sober. I do remember thinking 'I'm so ready to go."

I recited multiplication facts in my head to ground myself against any impairment. I could repeat the 12 times tables, but I had no memory of how I walked to the parking lot or got in the SUV. My insides swirling, I put my head against the window and closed my eyes. I wonder now how I didn't just jump out of the moving car.

"Say bruh, you ok?"

I lifted my face off the window and grabbed onto his arm that was resting on the middle console. "I don't...I don't feel well." My face sank back onto the window.

"Watch out." He put the window down. The air was not welcomed neither was his attempt to make me feel better.

I lost track of my heartbeat though having one didn't seem useful at the moment. I started singing songs inside my head to distract me from the utter destruction happening to my heart. I wanted to scream. I wanted to punch him. I wished that I could undo the last 15 years. I wished that there was some way to empty him of the life and love I poured into him. I didn't have anything left, except the wind in my face.

Back in the apartment, I took a shower, without a shower cap, which I never did when I visited him. Fuck it. I'm taking these braids out soon anyway. I was glad to be going home the next day. Leaving him to go back to my solo reality was always tough but not like this. In my heart I knew it was our last goodbye. More than just my heart knew it. And still I needed to protect him from my loss, my grief. I needed him to know that I was happy for him, whether it was true or not. It was not true and I longed to be home in my own space to deal with the annihilation.

I got out of the shower and went to the 2nd bedroom where I kept my suitcase and computer. I've always slept in the bed with him...15 years of sleepovers, the second bedroom was just somewhere to store my stuff. I checked to see if there was an earlier flight, knowing that he'd made plans for us to go to brunch before my flight. Yet I didn't care. I wanted out. I preferred to cry in peace, in a place where doing so wouldn't bring questions, couldn't bring solace. I didn't choose an earlier flight because I'd have to explain why.

His knock on the door surprised me and it only occurred to me then that I had shut the door. I'd never shut the door before, not even to get dressed.

"Bruh, you need anything?"

What I needed he couldn't give, wouldn't give. What I needed wasn't that easy— I ached for him to love me the way that I loved him. And that ache existed on all my personal fault lines and now eschewing every desire to keep it together, this quake was ripping me apart.

"Naw, I'm good."

"When you coming to bed? I feel like I'm on punishment," he said mournfully.

I didn't answer. I got up off the floor and walked to open the door. I allowed myself to look in his eyes. Doing so shook me and I walked into his chest. He moved his arms to put them around me, clasping his hands together in the small of my back. The silence enveloped us. Next to him my breath slowed and we breathed in synchrony. He exhaled and I felt his breath cool the exposed areas of my scalp. We both knew it was our last night together in this way. And that hug was the confirmation.

We separated from our embrace. Standing on his left side, I hugged his arm and put my forehead against his collarbone.

"Come on, it's time for bed," he told me plainly. And I did what I knew to do, what I always did— follow him to his bed.

The music from the stereo alarm woke me up. Slowly it dawned on me that I was on the sofa and not in the bed. I sat up and stretched, looking around his apartment. There's a memory in every corner of this place. I was sitting on the sofa I helped pick out, across from the reclining leather chair that I sent him the link to. My feet now on the rug that I had heard about for weeks before he bought it. I walked to the balcony doors and opened the curtains. The last time I opened the curtains, I was in a towel and I met him there to smoke cigars after a night out. The cigar wasn't the only thing in my mouth that night. Dawn was approaching, the pinks and oranges danced together in the Tampa morning sky. I thought to myself, "This is dope. And I'll never see it again from here." I felt my breath catch in my chest. My bottom lip trembled. I can't cry. I won't cry. This place will not be watered with my tears. I'm a bit dramatic. I inhaled deeply, counting 4 seconds as the air filled my lungs. Exhale for 7 seconds to center myself and not cry. I didn't cry.

I closed the curtains and went to the fridge to get a cup of black cherry Greek yogurt. It was the last of the ones we bought when I arrived 3 days ago. I sat on the counter stool I always sat in, the one I considered mine. Over the years, I had claimed my own things in his apartment, my stool, my towel, my coffee mug, my water cup, and the mason jar for drinking…my side of the bed. though I would never leave things there that I brought with me. There would never be a woman that he could invite to his apartment that would have any inkling of our relationship because I left something by accident. The women in his life would have to learn about me on purpose.

While I ate the yogurt, thoughts of the previous night rushed in. I followed him into the bedroom and took off all the decorative pillows and stacked them on the floor. A makeshift table, I put my phone on a pillow stack to charge so that it was easier to reach when I leaned over the bed. I got in the bed with my back to him. He squirmed around, trying to get comfortable. He grabbed one of the other pillows and hugged it, settling his body down into the comfort of his personal cocoon. He was shirtless and I could feel the heat from his skin. Normally that heat would be like a magnet for me and I'd push myself over to him to lean on his back with mine. In that position, I would find sleep easily. Not that night.

I put my fingers through my braids and pushed my chin into my chest to stretch my neck. I reached my right arm over to my left shoulder and somehow knocked over the spoon from the yogurt cup on to the floor. God. I hope he didn't hear that. I went to the sink to wet a paper towel. Before I turned around, I heard him. Big yawn followed by "shit." I turned around and there he stood. Rubbing his eyes, pulling his gym shorts out from between his legs. Damn. "Good morning," I said, walking over to the spilled yogurt. "Yeah, good morning." He walked over and picked up the blanket off the couch. "Why did you come out here?" He walked over to open the curtains, the sun was really shining. I finished cleaning up the yogurt and threw the paper towel into the touchless stainless steel garbage can that I convinced him would be worth the money since he was a germaphobe. He went to the counter to turn on the coffee pot. "Huh, bruh?" I decided to sit on my stool again, knowing my possession of anything related to him would soon be gone.

"So…" I paused to exhale. "Before I answer, I need to ask you a question. How did you think last night was supposed to go after telling me you were getting married? Like really, what was going to happen?" I looked at the waistband of his worn basketball shorts that I've known for years and bit my nails. In my mind, I flashed back to one of the many times I'd laid next to him naked and to last night when I remained fully clothed. He reached in the cabinet to get a mug. I don't think it was an accident that the one he pulled down was the only one in the cabinet that I had bought for him. I bought it in Bermuda while on vacation.

"Let me finish making this coffee." Of course, we would only have a conversation on his terms. I should've been used to that. There's never been a time in this relationship where my need for answers was more a priority than his timing. His discomfort or apprehension always ruled the day. Everything happened in his timing, shoot this trip especially was according to his timing; he asked me to come this specific weekend and I jumped to buy the plane ticket immediately, because everything he wanted, if I could make it happen, I did. Happily. Mostly. Almost never did he get a "no" from me. While I waited, I tried to smooth out the ridges of my bitten finger nails with other fingers and tried not to cry.

Finally, he sat in the stool at the end of the counter, leaving a stool between us. I found it symbolic of the space that would have to define our relationship going forward. I chuckled quietly as he sat, another thing that I didn't want to explain.

"Look, I don't know. I don't know what was supposed to happen, except that this is what we do. We sleep in the same bed. I hog the blankets. I fall over on you. You push me off and over. I wake up and you're there. And that didn't happen."

"So us together in the bed, you laying on me naked, is the thing to do on the night you told me you were getting married? I mean, when you asked me to come to bed, I just did, because I didn't know how not to. It's just automatic. But it's been a decade or more since I felt uncomfortable in the bed with you. So on a trip to the bathroom, I decided to stay out here."

"Hmmm." "Hmmm…I don't want to make it weird."

"I'm not sure weird is the word, but…it is what it is. We still going to brunch? I need a mimosa." "Yeah, bruh, we still going," he said while standing up. He walked over to me. stood in front of me and put his arms around my neck and pressed his chin on top of my head. In a different time, I would have thought that was sweet and I would have relished it. In a different time, I'm sure it wouldn't have happened.

Brunch was awkward. We ate mostly in silence. Thankfully we were seated by a window of the restaurant which overlooked the bay. It was quite the beautiful distraction. He noticed that I was looking outside the window and attempted to engage me. I tried, but I had neither the will or the skill to participate in anything other than drinking as many mimosas as I thought appropriate before getting impaired- I still had a 2.5 hour flight to manage. He asked about my students and about my strained relationship with my principal. I answered what I could feebly and looked away from the window when the waiter came with more champagne. He paid the bill, I left the tip and we left. And two things occurred to me, he had never let me pay the tip ever and that it was probably the last time I would have a meal with him. Only one of those things bothered me.

More strange behavior followed. He left his chair and waited beside my chair until I got up. He walked beside me, not in front of me as usual. He opened the door for me to leave the restaurant. He opened the car door and closed it when I got in. Asking questions about this behavior might reveal yet more sentiments that I had no capacity to accept or reject. Luckily it was a beautiful day and I could focus on the clouds passing by.

The competing thoughts of wanting to wish him well and wanting to hate him filled the space inside my head. He wasn't speaking and part of me was happy for that and I wanted him to turn the radio on to interrupt the silence. The other part was numb in disbelief.

We've had a normal routine at the airport at my departure for years now. He pulls over and parks. He gets out of the truck and walks to the passenger side to get my suitcase. When he closes his door, I unbuckle the seatbelt. I reach into the center console and get a piece of gum or whatever candy he has in there. I get out of the car only when he opens the back passenger door. He takes the suitcase to the curb. We hug and he reminds me to text him when I land. He gets into the truck and I go inside the airport. Today was not normal and maybe he needed to mark these final moments together. We hugged much longer than normal; he hummed something as I pressed into his chest. He hugged me tighter. Into my braids, he told me, "Don't worry, we'll get through this. You know how much you mean to me. I hope you do. You are indisposable. Nothing has to change about us." I felt him inhale and exhale forcefully. Normally, he was the first one to break the hug; he never wanted anyone to tell him to move the truck. This wasn't a normal regular goodbye. He knew it. When I withdrew from the hug, I mustered the courage to look him directly in the eyes. His kiss on my lips startled me but not as much as his next words to me. "I love you. I always will. Not nothing or nobody could ever change that." Though I had never heard him say he loved me, I knew in my heart that he meant those words. I wanted to reject the words, the kiss, I wanted to reject my whole pitiful attitude. I questioned why he would say it at this particular point, but I knew he knew it was the last goodbye for us. He knew, like I knew, that there would be no more "us." The tears welling in my eyes constituted my response. Conscious that I still had to get through the airport and to my flight, I wiped the tears away and pulled myself away from that emotional space. I told him goodbye and walked into the airport. I couldn't even look back to confirm that he had gotten into the truck and pulled off.

For years, I wanted to hear those words from him. Finally hearing them in that particular context unglued me. I couldn't figure out what to do with his words. So, the words decided for me; they just swirled around freely, integrating with all the questions I had, and the negative ideas about myself that were a constant. I got to the TSA agent and handed her my ticket and passport. She looked up from the passport picture and paused. "Are you o.k," she asked. "You look like you've been crying. Whatever it is, I'm sure it will be ok."

Jolon McNeil is a Philly girl and a career educator. You can find her at www.jaemacwrites.weebly.com

THE LEGEND OF SWEETIE MAE BROWN
BY KATHY HENRY

In spite of her name, Sweetie Mae Brown was the meanest woman in Sugar Shack, Mississippi. She was linebacker big. She once picked up Scooter Davis, who was six feet tall and two hundred pounds, up by the back of his neck like a mother cat would do to one of her kittens, and tossed him off her porch. She had beaten up on her last three husbands and was currently scouting for number four. The men in town lived in fear that she would put her roving eye upon them. The women in town gave her a wide berth because she had accused them of wanting her husbands' when she had them. Yeah, Sweetie Mae was a mean ass bitch. Mothers used her name as a threat to keep wayward children in line. The religious would do the cross when she walked past them. She lived in a raggedy shack on Dead End Lane. No matter how hard the sun shone in town, no light reached Dead End Lane. Spooky looking trees seemed to reach out and grab at you if you had the misfortune to walk past her house. No one wanted to tangle with old Sweetie Mae. Every night, she would leave her shack and go to one of the local juke joints and get her drink on. Her favorite drink was Jack Daniel's, no chaser. After slugging down a few rounds, drunk and ignorant, she would proceed to harass anyone who took her fancy. One night it was poor Charlie Jones, whose only crime was to politely decline her request for a dance. Before Charlie knew what hit him, she had him trussed up like a hog for the slaughter. Tossing him over her back, she threw him into the garbage can in the back of the joint. Everyone stared and then started drinking. Nobody in his or her right mind tangled with a drunken Sweetie Mae. They had come to think of Sweetie Mae as the nightly entertainment. Yes, this is how Sweetie Mae rolled. She terrorized the citizens of Sugar Shack on a regular basis until the night she met her match. It was a typical night at Papa Charlie's Bar & Grill, her favorite joint, and Sweetie had just downed a pint of Jack Daniel's when a stranger walked in and sat down. She was a pretty, petite thing with big brown eyes and a confident attitude, so she immediately took everyone's attention. Especially Sweetie Mae's. She hated women like her, with her womanly ways and little body. How dare that bitch come into her spot and take the spotlight! With Sweetie's eye on her, the young lady sat down. A gentleman asked her if she wanted to dance. Since he was a cutie, she said yes, and to the small cramped dance floor they went. Sweetie Mae's eyes got big. That bitch was dancing with Cletus Taylor, her future husband! Of course, Cletus had no clue about this, but that didn't matter. She had marked him as her own and for that, that bitch was 'bout to get beat down! They were getting their juke on something serious when Sweetie Mae came up behind the girl, grabbing her by the arm. "Look ho, this is my man, and no one fucks with Sweetie Mae Brown's man," she snarled down at the girl. There was complete silence in the bar. Cletus didn't say a word. He didn't want to be trussed up like poor Charlie. To everyone's amazement, petite drew herself up and snapped back, "He told me he didn't have no woman, and I know a man-looking bitch like you is not his woman." The crowd watched in silent, thrilled amazement. Petite had game! Sweetie Mae's mouth fell open. She couldn't believe this little sawed-off broad was talking crazy to her, Sweetie Mae Brown, the meanest bitch in town. With a quick move of her hand, she slapped the girl, knocking her against the bar. With only survival on her mind, the girl grabbed the nearest bar stool and started to beat the shit out of Sweetie like she stole her last pair of panties. Old Sweetie was laid out on the floor, with drool running out her mouth. Making her way to the entrance, the girl ran out and jumped in her car, sped off into the night, never understanding the magnitude of what happened. The patrons of the bar cheered like crazy. Sweetie Mae had finally gotten her ass kicked. Sweetie Mae slowly got up from the floor, tears of humiliation running down her face. Oh, the shame of it all! Her ass kicked by a girl who was five feet tall and a hundred pounds soaking wet! She would never live it down! She slinked from the bar, with her head hanging down, never to be seen by the citizens of Sugar Shack again.

Kathy Henry is a graduate of Roosevelt with a Bachelor's Degree in Sociology.

MAKE PLANS
BY KEVIN SCOTT

If you want to make God laugh, make plans.

I had been single for most of my adult life. The 42 candles on my most recent yellow cake with chocolate icing baked by my flour-thumbed brother was evidence. I blamed my fickle and shallow self for my relationship status.

I didn't know who or what the perfect person was but long-term never worked out. My last real relationship was three years ago to an earthy, artsy, sleep butt-naked, walk bare-footed, eclectic, finger-painting Alabama belle named Sarina. She sold art in a rented corner of a larger space on South Street, Philadelphia which featured African carvings, rain sticks and furniture. She loved her Kush and her finger paintings. She even painted, photographed, and displayed pictures of her nudity at a Temple University exhibit. I loved her free spirit but my brother advised me our family would never accept Sarina.

My traveling sportswriter occupation could account for my singlehood as I was never in one place long enough for a meaningful connection. I was a hustler to the craft and the job. Relationships took a back of the bus perspective.

February 29th

I flew to California to cover the Sixers' West Coast stint against the Clippers, Lakers, Kings and Warriors. This was my first trip since Kobe's death and this was going to be a weird trip not seeing Kobe and Gianna courtside. The wound was still fresh, but the weather was a great deterrent.

I had a few friends in LA and a specific ballerina named Tracy who enjoyed my occupational visits because it routinely led to sexual trysts, twists and turns which would leave me in a euphoric state of elation. I would ask myself, "is she the one?" Her love for California and a contract with the Los Angeles Ballet would keep her stationary. I was not a fan of the LA scene to become a permanent resident and our conversations were superficial.

March 1st

Philly played the Clippers and Shake Milton wowed everyone with 39 points. Though the Sixers lost the game, I received additional writing assignments to cover Shake's performance. I had a day to myself before Philly would face Lebron and the Lakers, so I contacted Tracy. My schedule was open and I hoped she was available for lunch or something, centering on the something. Her excitement to see me left me thinking, "is she the one?" We visited the California African American Museum in Exhibition Park. Sula Bermudez-Silverman was the featured artist and the exhibit featured molds of Sula's childhood dollhouse, created in casts of sugar which was historically traded and used as a commodity and trade of her ancestors.

It was difficult to digest lunch at the Greenleaf Chop shop by USC village. Tracy voiced her passion for her Afro-Puerto Rican heritage, about colorism, and our placement within the African diaspora. She amazed me. She was not trivial. I consumed my roasted spaghetti squash and turkey meatballs. Tracy had a salad with a unique combination of green and black olives and artichokes. We laughed about our obsession over hummus and I surmised we hadn't spent enough time together. I thought, "is she the one?" I could get used to the LA weather and bogus behaviors while getting to know the Puerto Rican ballet dancer.

My cell phone settings alerted me of sports and major news just in case I had to stop, drop and write. The recent alerts centered around the coronavirus' impact around the world. Tracy was concerned her trip to France would be postponed. The entire world grappled with the unknown.

March 3rd

Though Anthony Davis dropped 37 points and the Lakers beat Philly 120-107, the sports world wanted Lebron's take on COVID-19. He said he'd follow the NBA's protocol and decision but hoped the best for everyone impacted. I took the liberty of interviewing Rajon Rondo and asked him about COVID but he waved it off.

Tracy and I met before I headed to Sacramento. We had dinner at Shaquille's at LA Live. Tracy ordered Roasted Beets and Deviled Eggs. We joked about her ballerina's diet and she noted it was seasonal. I confessed my feelings and she asked what took me so long. She had mutual sentiments. We spent a pleasurable night in my hotel room and ordered room service for breakfast in the morning. As I boarded the plane, I asked myself, "Is she unquestionably the one?"

March 5th

Philly handled the Kings 125-108 behind Tobias Harris' 28 points and Shake Milton was at it again with 20.

March 6th

I landed in Oakland to cover Philly's last game of their West Coast trip. I was looking forward to flying back to LA and spending more time with Tracy. It was reported twenty-one people tested positive for COVID-19 on a Carnival cruise liner and the ship was being held at sea instead of docking in San Francisco.

I drove from Oakland to the other side of the bay and checked in at the Hyatt Regency Embarcadero. Lobby patrons watched CNN's report as the virus made its way to America.

March 7th

I was too preoccupied with the world events to focus on a decent story, although the game was exciting to the final buzzer.

The world was closing in on 500 thousand reported cases. My editor told me to head home. I shared my plans of heading to LA but he said, "No can do. This is serious."

I changed my flight and informed Tracy. She understood and said we'd chat soon about future arrangements.

The World Health Organizations declared COVID-19 a Pandemic and the 45th President declared a national emergency. Travel bans had been issued and toilet paper and paper towels vanished.

Tracy said we were living in the last days, read Revelations 6 and write about it. I told her my editor would have an issue with me mixing religion and sports. She urged me to find a way.

Tracy died from COVID April 6th, 2020.

She was the one.

Kevin M. Scott is a Phoenix-based writer and creative who has worked in several areas of media. He is currently working on releasing a collection of short stories and a novel. His email is kevin@thekevinmscott.com and you can follow him on Instagram, @thekevinmscott.

BAD DREAM
BY LONDON LOME'

As she begins to wake, her eyes slowly open and her body shifts so she is now laying on her back. Her eyes adjust to the light. Now fully open, she looks towards the window in her bedroom. The trees gently sway in the wind and blue sparkles between the branches. She tries to sit up, but is groggy. She slowly raises, then scoots back to sit against the pillows on her headboard.

"What a dream," she thinks to herself. "Fire, death, destruction, lies, murder. Killing in broad daylight, gas masks looking like a zombie apocalypse. Like a bad reality tv show or maybe a video game come to life. Yeah, definitely like a Grand Theft Auto come to life."

Grabbing the bottle of water on her nightstand, she slowly gulps it down. She is amazed, as she typically doesn't remember much of her dreams. "It was so vivid. Probably because I am just getting up. Let me move around and get my day started."

After getting out of bed, she walks into the kitchen to get the coffee started for the day. As the coffee is brewing, she uses the bathroom. "Why am I still trippin'? That dream felt real as hell."

Finishing up in the restroom, she sings the ABC song as she washes her hands. She stops and looks at herself in the mirror.
"I am in my 40's, what triggered me to sing the ABC song?"

Turning the faucet off, she then wipes her hands on the hand towel. Walking slowly back into the kitchen, she hopes the grogginess will subside when her daily coffee fix gets into her system. Coffee made to perfection, with just the right amount of cream, she heads over to the living room window. There is a lot of noise outside. Living downtown has its perks, but it isn't usually so noisy. There are so many people in the street. Upon closer look, they are dancing.

"What is going on?" she thinks to herself as she opens the window. People are chanting, yelling, dancing and with all kinds of signs. She looks through the window, trying to make out what they say.

Glancing over the signs, they are hard to make out, until she comes across one that reads, "The 4 Year Nightmare is Over!", another reads "Move Out, You're Fired!"

Her coffee kicks in. The dream was vivid because it wasn't a dream. It was the last four years of her life. Not a video game. Real life. The fire from a police station being burned to the ground. In her lifetime. The destruction, from people being tired of witnessing killing in broad daylight. The lies from a leader, someone who is supposed to be in charge of leading the greatest country in the world. The police committing murder. Who polices the police? Nine months into a global pandemic, constantly washing her hands and staying indoors.

Her coffee is flowing smoothly through her veins. The initial grogginess was from watching the 24-hour news cycle for the last five days.

Though a portion of the nightmare won't fully be over until January, the weight that has been on her shoulders the last four years, has lessened. She smiles, as hope, enters back into her system. She wants to join the jubilation in the streets. She wants to chant with them. But she is aware that the pandemic has not ended. She is cautiously optimistic for future change, but until then, she will keep her Black ass in the house.

London Lome' is following in the footsteps of her author mother AJ Questenberg. Be on the lookout for London's debut novel coming soon.

A KHARIZMA VALENTINE
BY LUJIRA COOPER

Sunlight passed through the Amethyst Mountain and blanketed the entwined and entangled lovers in purple. The aroma of Kharizma Gold coffee wafted upstairs and tickled Moore's nose. "Ahh, a new day."

She had experienced a harrowing time after Lauren's agreement to accompany Hawkins back to Earth. Although the rescue went better than expected, her frightened wife experienced six months of confusion about where she was and fearing Hawkins would have her raped. She'd never forgive him for scaring Lauren. It had been a long road back to the idyllic.

Moore left her sleeping butterscotch-skinned beauty to prepare a champagne breakfast. Buttery soft scrambled eggs, crisp bacon, and hot croissants. They sat at a small table in the bedroom that faced the mountain. The lovers toasted and fed each other plump strawberries and cream.

"Ri, stop nibbling on my fingers," Lauren said laughing.

"Hmm, I can think of other parts of your sexy body to nibble on."

"Ri, you're insatiable."

Continuing her finger snacking, "And you're not. I remember you thinking I was a breadless ham sandwich."

"No. You're my big milk chocolate baby. What's on your agenda today, other than devouring me?"

"Nothing much. Need to pick up some things."

"When will you be back?"

"About three hours," Moore replied, swapping fingers for croissants.

They drifted into the companionable silence of lovers, lost in thought.

Moore finished, took a shower, and dressed in her signature black and teal. She kissed Lauren goodbye and got into her skycar.

***

Flying to Crystal City, she saw a world of safety, love, and beauty. A place she'd brought three thousand folks from the clutches of Hawkins. She thought of the extra years and children given them by Kharizma. Her teal and black skycar landed, sending up a plume of red dust. She hurried to Kai's Jewels. The window showcased unique handmade jewelry of platinum, gold, and silver. Exquisite was an understatement. Entering, a bell tinkled.

"Well, my favorite customer returns. Thought you'd abandoned me," said Kai, dressed in a crimson, ocean blue and forest green kimono. "How are you?"

"Better. Is it ready?"

"But of course," giving Moore a hug. "Lauren better?"

From a velvet pouch, she poured out a platinum and emerald necklace with accompanying earrings.

"Yes. Wow, each piece gets better. Love it. And the other piece?"

"Oh, my impatient friend." Kai produced a six-inch cuff with scalloped images of Moore, Lauren, and their children.

"Now that's an exquisite piece. Lauren will love it. Gives her an excuse to go bare-armed. Next thing order, flowers, then get home."

Kai laughed at Moore's surprise and delight. She wrapped it all in red velvet boxes. Moore gathered up her presents and kissed Kai's cheek and left whistling.

***

Lauren laid out a blood-red V-backed dress with a thigh high split. Cued up Celine Dion's *Because You Loved Me*, Aretha's *Bridge Over Troubled Water*, and *Drown in My Own Tears*, and added some others. Scooting around the bedroom, she hummed and danced to Tina Turner's *Addicted to Love*.

Karen, Moore's majordomo, answered the door to find a baby-faced man holding a long box.

He said, "Are you Ms. Moore?"

She reached for the box. "No, but I can take it."

"No, my orders were to give it to her."

Karen smiled, invited him in and buzzed Lauren. "Messenger demands you. He'll be sorry."

"Be down in a minute."

"Must be a busy day," Karen said. "Would you like some lemonade?"

He nodded.

Lauren's rich honey-soaked voice asked, "What's in the box?"

The young man turned, and his mouth dropped. He shook his head. *Was it a vision that floated down the stairs? Damn, she's gorgeous. No wonder the flowers.*

He heard the silky voice say, "Not polite to stare," as she reached for the package.

"Here…"

She opened it and squealed, "Kharizma Blues, wow."

He stood there. Karen shook him, tipped him, but he didn't move.

As she ushered him to the door, Lauren said, "Thanks," and kissed his cheek.

"He'll embellish that kiss to all his buddies."

"I know. Wow, these are gorgeous," she said, putting them in a blue crystal vase.

"Twenty-four. Your husband knows how to treat you."

"And I plan to show my appreciation. You can take off now and tomorrow."

"Yippee. Gives me time with my girlfriend. Sure, you don't need help."

"No."

Karen had time, so she watched the prep. Little wrapped and stuffed seasoned hens appeared with pink asparagus, smashed turnips with white and yellow potatoes, and small biscuits. Lauren placed all in the warmer, then whipped cream for her personal feast. She set the table with blue crystal plates and glasses. Sandalwood scented candles sat in sconces. She got on a step ladder and retrieved a small, long velvet box out from behind some bottles on the top shelf and placed it at one end of the table.

Karen's furrowed brow questioned.

"Ri's sneaky. I put it somewhere she'd never look."

Lauren heard Moore's skycar and rushed to the door. "I guess I must wait to jump in your arms."

Moore put the packages down and scooped up her wife. "You look and smell delicious. Maybe we'll skip dinner, which also smells good."

"Ha, not a chance. I've got plans for you. The flowers are gorgeous."

"Not as gorgeous as you, my wench."

"You two are about to get mushy. I'm out of here," Karen said with a big grin. "Have fun."

They chorused, "Oh, we will."

Lauren cued up the music, then climbed onto Moore's lap. The kissing and nibbling began.

Lujira Cooper is the author of Theft of Trust *and runs a writing playshop for SAGE, a center for LGBTQ elders. Email: defiancemoore@gmail.com. Website: shadowfeather.com*

FLOODLIGHT
BY LULU ALICEA

You are a liar I know it and you know it and you know I know it!

Eliza thinks of the best emoji to signal the trash, garbage, beautiful liar, Tocca is and then three fading gray dots slide on the screen.

U r crazy. I'm no liar. OMW! B there in 5.

Eliza rolls her eyes and puts the phone on the glass counter. She swipes her finger across the tablet to finish the chapter on parasitic organisms and notices the time on the corner of the screen. It's just past eleven. She can lock the store's front doors.

"I already counted out the drawer and set up the shelves for tomorrow morning. It's a stupid night to be open." The election is two days away and yet her boss still thinks people want greeting cards and googly eyed stuffed unicorns. The place is the last shop in a half dead strip mall, on the edge of town. Her boss lets her study and when her best friend leaves on time to pick her up, she's home in five minutes. She met Tocca working here. Besides being the only two brown girls in the entire town, they also were both taking community college classes.

"Which I need to get ready for. Even if it's a Zoom class, it's still a class."

Eliza hops down from the stool and twirls her navy-blue mask on her finger. The Biden/Harris stenciling flashes around and around. She opens the top drawer, grabs the key for the front door and looks at the closed-circuit monitor, the camera facing the empty parking lot, and locks the door. Black asphalt shimmers underneath the one working light. Nothing across the highway stares back at her dark night, a void, senseless thing, silent as most things in the town. They never yell out their hate, instead just a snide comment or a flag and a sign on their lawn. To her face a smile, with teeth, and a nod.

Eliza jumps at the buzzing behind her and chases the sound around the store. She puffs out a laugh. Her phone.

N traffic. B there soon!

"She is ridiculous." Eliza shakes her head and pushes out the cramping in her shoulders.

You are probably still in bed. I will walk home.
See you tomorrow morning on Zoom!

A car door slams in the distance and Eliza's eyes jump to the monitor. She squints at the figure approaching the door. She tastes a dark, metallic splash of acid in the back of her throat, her hand tightens on the phone. An arm appears on the other side of the glass and Eliza hears the clog, clog, clog of the locked door.

"Uh, hello?" The man's flat voice muffles through the air. Eliza turns and peaks out.

"Hey", a White man waves his hand. He's wearing a collar shirt, red loosened tie, and dark pants. Eliza steps closer to the door and sees the familiar white block letters on the red fabric of his hat.
She stands in front of the door.

"Yeah, we're closed." A cold shutter traces down her spine.

He looks at his watch. His hand pulls on the door again, knuckles pale with effort.

"Just open the door. It will only take a second." His voice drops at the end and sways up and down right before he smiles. Holding up a finger, he gestures the number one.

The pressure inside Eliza's head pushes in. A cramp travels across her forehead. She watches her foot take a step forward and can't recall telling it to do it. Another one after. Her fingers touch the key's surface.

"That's it, girl, let me in." The stranger's tongue slides out and licks the edge of his lips.

Eliza watches his mouth unable to shake the tunnel around her now, the store, lights, air all blurring and swelling out and then down. She looks at the man, for the first time, in the eyes. They are brown, deep dark brown, and then a thump inside of her head and she blinks. His eyes are black, raw around the socket, cracked, red veins webbing over his cheekbone and down to his chin.

Vibration in her hand breaks the gaze.

Almost there, don't WALK!

She moves her head, snapping back and away.

The man presses his body to the door and Eliza only sees the black pooling in his eyes, blotting out any white and the blood red of the hat. His mouth opens, hollow, gaping, greenish and rotting.

"Open the DOOR! Let me in! LET. ME. IN." With each word he jams forward pulling on the handle and jamming his body against it. Eliza thinks she hears a crack at the bottom of the door and her body snaps awake. Her brain drives through all the ways to get out. No to the front, there is a basement with no outlet, and a back entrance.

Sweat drips down her back. She turns and looks at the camera monitor, sees the man as he looks into the lens. Eliza stumbles back and drops to the floor behind the counter. Her torso knots and icy pain builds from her spine. If she runs out through the back, she can cut across the parking lot. She starts to crawl towards the back door.

"I can see you, girl. There is another way in." Gravel and low the voice winds in from outside clawing into Eliza and pulls her back to sitting. She closes her eyes and counts her breathing.

A horn blares one long note and then three more and the store floods with light. After a second a hard knock against the glass. Eliza looks up to the screen, Tocca is knocking on the door. She pushes herself up and runs over, opens the door and latches onto Tocca with both arms.

"OK. OK." Tocca pushes Eliza back. "Who the fuck was that White man?" Eliza smiles and tears run down her face. She pulls in for another hug.

"No matter." Tocca laughs. "He ran scared when he saw my black ass. Let's go home."

Lulu Alicea is a playwright, author, storyteller and advocate born in Arecibo, Puerto Rico and raised in the suburbs of New York City. A featured speaker at TedX, her Ted Talk on creating a space for storytelling can be seen on YouTube as well as her directorial debut for the dance film America Rise. She lives in a quiet suburb of Manhattan and makes time to tell a story every day. Instagram @hudielu_stages Twitter @Hudielu

A COVID BIRTH: INTERRUPTED LIFE LESSONS
BY MARCY BEST

My mother died when she was thirty-nine years old. Her mother died when she was fifty-five years old. Once upon a time, I didn't think I would make it to forty. When I did, I fell apart a little.

COVID-19 has impacted the world; killing millions. It has done the opposite to me. COVID resurrected something buried within me. Single, childless and quarantined in an apartment; COVID dug up the roots of my angst.

I was an anchor-baby born in Brooklyn, New York in the 1970's to immigrant parents who left the Caribbean island of Trinidad for America.

I was two years old when my mother filed for divorce. My father was flabbergasted at her audacity. Imagine a woman thinking they had the right to object to their husband's infidelity. If they were back in Trinidad, she would know her place and accept his indiscretions without "running her mudderrcunt mouth to everyone." These are the words he told his buddy; who happened to be my mother's brother, because the term and mindset of "bro's before hoes" apparently extends to brothers-in-law, even if that makes their own sister the hoe in question.

My mother was a teacher in Trinidad but, when she immigrated to America, they didn't recognize her degree. I was too young to understand, or to ask her how she felt about being told her academic accomplishments meant nothing in her new country. Mommy, landed a teachers-aide job, went to college at night, and raised me as a single-mother. She maintained this schedule for four years. Six months before her graduation, she died from cancer.

Since the age of ten and into adulthood, I have imaginary conversations with my mother. 2020 quarantine took that to a whole other level and DNice supplied the soundtrack.

What were you thinking as you lay in that hospital with me perched at the foot of your bed, regaling you with the story of how I want to marry Prince not Michael Jackson? No, I didn't see the movie Purple Rain, I'm only ten. How would I get in without you? I just love Prince more because as I sat in that dark theater and he began to sing Purple Rain, my tummy felt funny in a good way. Okay, I guess I did disobey you. I'm sorry I lied, but we paid Lori's older sister a dollar each to take us. You should punish me for lying to you. My punishment should be living with you for the rest of my life, just the two of us.

I think I'm mature enough now to learn how to cook. When you get out of the hospital and come home, you have to teach me how to make macaroni pie and callaloo and crab. Teach me how to get the crab in the pot before it pinches me. Then teach me how not to be a crab in the barrel. Teach me how to make your cake from scratch. It tastes way better than Betty Crocker's. I don't care If my friends don't like it, I love it.

Teach me how to press my hair with the hot comb without burning my ear. You have to teach me to love my hair in its natural state and to know when to put the hot comb away. Teach me to be proud of my skin color.

You have to teach me grace, not the one before meals. The grace that stops me from cutting people out of my life at the first hint of betrayal. You have to teach me what therapy couldn't; how not to kill a fly with a cannonball. You have to teach me how to live, in spite of your death. You have to teach me,...me.

The first Black Ms. America, the first Black President, Prince and Michael both died early, not as early as you, but early. Michael died looking more like the picture on those Betty Crocker boxes than the Michael you would remember. My first kiss, first period, prom, college graduation. First job. First heartbreak. No wedding day yet, maybe because after your betrayal, how can I trust anyone else not to leave me? You left me a long time ago. So much has happened since then. Cell-phones, the internet, Y2K, September 11th, much death, some life. So many things I can't begin to explain to you. Do you have anything to explain to me?

What were you thinking as you lay on what you knew was your deathbed and looked in my eyes? Did you think of my father, who divorced me when you divorced him? Did you realize that your death and my father's desertion made me an orphan? Did you wonder how a pandemic would affect a motherless-child? Yes, I'm in my 40's now, but I will always be your child. At the moment when you passed from this world into the next, were you able to see into my future and witness the neglect, pain, and abuse I suffered at the hands of people you trusted? Or did you close your eyes and surrender to the relief of no more earthly pain? Can you teach me how to do that, how to surrender, without dying?

You have to teach me how to trust God like you did, because sometimes I'm scared He doesn't hear me. Do you hear me? I don't hear you anymore. I can't remember your voice, but I do remember your cake and I promise to make it like you did, without frosting. Who needs all that artificial, sweetness. It just leaves a bad taste in your heart. You have to teach me how to make a cake that tastes like where I came from, not one that tastes like everyone else's. You have to teach me to make a cake so good that when it's finished, I can still remember the taste. Then teach me how not to cry when I eat it.

Marcy Best is a dyed-in-the-wool New Yawker who has lived in Toronto, Los Angeles and currently resides in ATL; where she tries not to be that obnoxious New York chick. She is currently working on her first novel and her email is marciaannbest@gmail.com

SUNNY
BY PAULINE BERTHOLON

The girl's blood was on the rise. One could see it, but only in her eyes. Otherwise, she was bubbly and bright. She had a pep in her step and her perfume gave her a glowing light. But rage ran through her veins and there was growing sadness in her brain. The girl stood five foot one and wore big shoes that had a thin sole and made her no taller. She was scrawny so her clothes hung off her as they would off a pole. Her short hair split down the middle covering angry brown eyes unvaryingly soft from crying.

Though terribly brisk that Sunday evening, the girl wore only a neutral grey button down with a hole in the side. She had pleated olive-green pants with fringed ends and wide shoes, one of them with the laces untied. She stood lonely, outside smoking a cigarette against the brick wall of the restaurant. She was interrupted suddenly by Debora, her co-worker's voice, importunate, constructive, addressing her from the bottom of the stone steps.

"Sunny, tell me you're not standing out here with five cigarettes going like I think you are-"

"Jesus Christ Almighty," The girl responded, taking an angry little drag, and shaking her head.

"Are you?"

"You know, there are times I see myself dead in the rain."

Debora stared up at the girl and the goosebumps on her arm, as droplets from the entrance sign, one by one, dropped onto her yellow hair. She had on a black puffer coat and a wool neck gaiter that covered the better part of her head. South of her eyes she wore a mask over her mouth and nose. In fact, the only way anyone could have been able to recognize the bundled figure was by her eyes. Debora's were very distinctive, without even having shed a tear, dark circles surrounded them. People always described them as stark grey, but when someone got close enough, they could actually be seen as a dull green.

"All that can't be helping your headache," Debora said with a lean forward, "what you need is water."

The girl rubbed her forehead with three fingers of her cigarette hand. Her heart beat out of her chest, she tried to slow her breath. Debora closed the door firmly behind her, letting the kitchen staff, along with numerous garbage bags, out first. Fumbling, she wiggled the key and was finally able to lock the door and make her way up the steps. With a to-go cup full of Cabernet Franc in one hand and a painted umbrella in the other, she looked anticipatingly at the cigarette in the girls lengthy trembling fingers.

Feeling the sober stare of her co-worker's eyes, the girl held the stick in between the ends of two fingers in her right hand and handed it over.

"Have it." She said.

"No. I only need one puff." With her pinky finger, Debora pulled down her mask, took a deep pull, and stared abstractly for a minute or two at the night sky, as the wind made the rough cold stronger and sparse droplets stop falling, then glanced back at the cigarette, took a couple of test drags on it and found that it had gone out. She passed it back to the girl who lit it. Before she could be tempted to take another, Debora announced that it was time for her to begin her trek home in the rain.

"Drink some water, it'll help you get rid of that migraine!" She yelled towards the girl, facing her route home.

"Well, you're gone now so I feel much better!" The girl said. She heard Debora's laugh. The road lamps on Fourth Street came on. They were faint and far apart. With no plan for being left alone in the cold, she stumbled down the street, her head buzzing and light from smoke. She searched her pocket for one more cigarette to calm the reverberate droning in her temple and stopped to see if she could spot one in the mess of extra matches and dollar bills.

.With her right hand, she lit another cigarette, curled her arm over to wipe the warm blood that started to drip from her nose, and lifted her eyes up to the stars. She loved to look at them even though they made her feel insignificant. She walked on the road in the mud by the cars instead of on the sidewalk, with no wherewithal to pass by strangers at this time of night.

.When she made it to her apartment, she temperamentally, as though she'd smoked, by god, for the last time in her life, flung it out onto the wet pavement with strife. She wiped her nose, in a different spot this time, hiking up her shoulder to reach her shirt.

Inside, she dropped the keys on the dining room table and the sound of metal hitting varnished wood echoed in her head as she walked with sopped shoes across the wooden floors. She stopped short of the bedroom. She could see her roommate was fast asleep, sat on the couch, soaked into the pillows, and gazed directly in front of her at the mirrored closet doors. She glimpsed at the yellow fog and fingerprints that rubbed its back along the edges where the doors slid open; while the yellow dust settled into the cabinet drawers. She looked directly into her own eyes, as if it were neutral territory, and saw a young woman whose talent was running away. Who, day in and day out, thought that this was her time. Whose eyes were soft from crying. Whose face had seen the eternal footman in his long overcoat, standing under the loft bed spying. Whose shirt had a hole. Whose cocktail of pills rolled.

This temper, tension, and grief built in her, she'd kept hidden. But now the cork burst out from the bottle, and the wine came flooding out from inside. Spontaneously, her head grew wide and erupted. The walls were painted red behind her.

Pauline Bertholon was born and raised in Jersey City NJ. She writes to create awareness for mental illnesses and promote mindful living.

GOODBYE 2020, MY OLD FRIEND
BY RISHAUNDA POOLE ROBINSON

I was there when you walked in. Without saying a word, you surveyed the room and proceeded to come forth. I saw intrigue in your eyes and the upward curve of your lips. I peeped the rubbing of your hands... slow and circular, as you contemplated the possibilities.

The long coat of shimmer and shine that you wore, unbuttoned and unapologetic, swayed briskly as you walked by, rustling a breeze that made me shiver at the thought. We locked eyes when you noticed me staring at its dark satiny lining and I must admit, a bitch got caught up.

Exposed, I relinquished myself, nestling my head in the bosom of your hype. Your forehead kiss was icy and instantly I knew you did not come to play; you came to slay. You had the time, and you had the range. You exhaled a deep breath of *"shookedness"*, so I named you *Mysterium*. Then I waited.

Without hesitation you started kicking hits and taking names. Straight to the grave, you took names. Too many to count, not enough to forget. There was weeping, wailing, and gnashing of teeth echoing in your wake; and yet you chose to trudge forward. Never looking back.

I scratched my head and thought, "DAAAAAAMN!!! Where dey do dat at?" and "Who raised you?" Because clearly, you were lacking manners. But as I tried to reach you to ask, you clouded my way with red bottoms and blue diamonds. Oh, how I laughed at the irony when it was crude oil that prevailed.

It introduced me to this black woman named Victory. Under the melatonin sky she danced naked like David, giving God the praise and my neighbors a fright. As I watched her dance, I forgot about you. For a little while, I forgot about you.

Then history showed up and reminded me that it would not be kind. So, I snapped out of it and dressed in my armor. With bated breath I contemplated your next move. My mental was on ten cause that False

Evidence Appearing Real be fucking with your girl sometimes.

One night I had a dream. You were on your way out and dressed in your concession cloak. It was beautifully adorned with tinsel and lights. I yelled behind you, "Hey! Can I now have some joy? Unspeakable?" You turned towards me and slowed down. You didn't stop. But you did slow down.

For a short time, our eyes met again. This time we each stared deeper and our gaze lasted longer. You were not as assured as before—I think I even saw a tear. Was it possible that you were afraid, too? Unlike me, the only place you had left to go was away.

Rightfully, I was angry. So, in my moment of strength from what I thought was your weakness, with boldness I shouted, "Did you do it? Did you do all that you set out to do? Did you conquer all that you set out to conquer?"

And there it was again…that intrigue in your eyes and that upward curve of your lips. My heart hastily dropped to the pit of my stomach as I watched you rub your hands slowly "…in that circular motion". You chuckled then answered, "Hell yep! Did you?"

Rishaunda Poole Robinson, a valiant survivor of the year 2020, is an author-in-waiting that resides in Richmond, Virginia. She is a wife, mother and grandmother. Her email address is rishaundarobinson@gmail.com and she can be followed on Twitter and Instagram, @theshaunpoole

PART IV: JOURNAL ENTRIES

A TALE OF TWO PANDEMICS
BY ANDREA WARD
June 15, 2020

Feeling poetic and heartbroken...this journal entry is for the crying artist inside of me.

Yesterday, I had big love. I woke up with a rose quartz heart and vowed to nourish my soul well. Ate some fruit and drank some tea. I had the desire to be a blessing. Checked on some of my friends and let them know that today was the day to keep going. I held familiar hands. Bent my brown sugar body towards the sun and let the wind fill my lungs; yoga at the pagoda was therapy for me. I found comfort in family. Built warm shelter from hugs.

Today however, yesterday's hope has been flipped on its head. It's been shattered against the pavement as despair flows slowly. I am not okay. Robert Fuller, a man with my father's rich skin, hangs in staged suicide from a Southern California tree. I knew only one, but somehow I miss them both. Oluwatoyin Salau, a 20 year old woman with a name wide enough to swim in, has become a casualty to a war she was barely old enough to fight. A warrior for Black lives, she was murdered by the light of the Florida moon. Killed senselessly by fragile, toxic, masculinity.

The weight of protest and pandemic has taken my scream. I feel distant from love. I'm worried/anxious/aware that I'm not good enough. Today, all I have is a whisper. It barely floats the 6 feet that COVID has carved between us. Exhaustion covers my face like a surgical mask. It holds my words hostage on my lips. More than tired and silenced, I am furious. Rage wraps around my core and plants itself 6 feet deep. I pray my anger will one day guide the steps of marching feet. May the buried-too-soon use my wrath as food for healing flowers.

Andrea Ward is a poet, birth doula, and maternal and child health advocate based in Norfolk, Virginia. Her email address is andrea.nicole2410@gmail.com and you can follow her on Instagram, @_andreawins.

I AM NOT A TRAINING FACILITY
BY APRIL CARTER

I am not a training facility to dump your shit on or to use as an experimental rebound. I am not a doormat or a play toy to distribute your abuse to in every facet you can possibly imagine, simply by gaining my trust. The other participant's mind is set to seek and destroy to cover their own inadequacies, meanwhile labeling me the stereotypical bitter Black woman who all of a sudden "doesn't want to see you win". The observations and critical thoughts alone growing into womanhood have not changed to date. Black love twisted with toxic intentions won't make you vibrate any higher than where you are. Broken people hide their cunning behavior very well in the world. As a result of all who are injured that begged for help by acting out, it always seemed that the chaos creator was relinquished of any accountability. Society (and family) has groomed those that can't see past themselves into believing that the anguish that was bestowed upon me was due to no fault but thy own. This is definitely not gender bias, but right now I'm speaking for those like myself and other warriors. Imagine an abused child with no counsel or support grows up in the world becoming a target of more abuse, fighting to get free, and getting blamed by the masses as if one deserved such treatment? Who's really out here covering us?

Providing all the reassurance couldn't fix that, but it's a start. Validation coming from the PUBLIC eye is acceptable; covering traumas of generations past is a sign of vulnerability that people can't afford to expose. My old broken ways aren't yours to use against me, and I did my work to heal. I refuse your personal insecurities, and that will NOT be my burden to bear! Yet, why seek change if the fallacies got you this far? There will always be someone like-minded to entertain and change the narrative to soften the blow to others to make you look like a scorned hero. Upbringing and lack of finances won't be the savior for moving negatively. The actions proved you chose self-sabotage including anyone in your path over help. The attention for a more interesting storyline of a fake power trip to cover up your shortcomings. For instance, most claim to never have endured or witnessed an abusive relationship. Some will go so far as to say it's the victim who knew better and allowed it.

Well, I bet a lot of the Nation that voted 45 in four years ago had no idea that a lot of them would be unemployed, losing their businesses, finances depleted, healthcare threatened, and people made to work for free, not to mention the utter disrespect for the elderly. He lies to your face, punishes you for challenging him. He does what he can in any destructive form, and if it doesn't go his way, taking a life or something of major importance will be your reminder of who controls you. The supportive team only backs him, because of what they benefit to gain. To gaslight you, he provides a stimulus gift to make you appreciate the little he's willing to give to counteract everything he just did! He threatened the public while people made excuses for him for years UNTIL he then failed the public. As if YOU were ever exempt?!

Welcome to your nationwide abusive relationship of 2020! You had to fight like hell to get his ass out of office, and he's still trying to control the loss! This is "grooming" on another level. I guess it's the nation's fault for not "choosing better". It's not about exposure, it's about truth, intention, boundaries, and accountability. It's about reclaiming what has always been rightfully yours. This isn't for the beautiful, brilliant souls that are good hearted out here. We're just doing the work that is required to make us better people. This is for the devils that blend in, preying on women and our children that they love to replicate their childhood traumas onto. It's not embarrassing, it's disheartening for me. Another's actions don't dictate who I am, I'm responsible for myself. I wonder who thought someone's stage presence on a TV Show would make someone a great leader? I hope folks will see the damage in labeling when it comes to topics such as this. I chose me first, as the American people did the same, fighting their way out of this madness of reality. I'm just as much appreciative of my circle of support, as we are coming together at the end of voting to see the outcome. The second coming has arrived, and I look forward to a healthier, vigilant, and happier four years dedicated to necessary changes.

April Carter is a Washington, DC - based writer, human rights activist, artist, painter, poet, business owner, and lover of positive vibes. Her email is april.carter@hotmail.com, and you can follow her on Facebook, https:// www.facebook.com/fearless258

FAITH FROM A DISTANCE
BY AVERY DANAE WILLIAMS
Age: 17

The world, ever since COVID-19 made its way into the country, stopped without warning. Although inconveniencing the public, such drastic measures had to be taken to prevent the spread of the illness. With over 15,000 coronavirus-related deaths in the state of New Jersey, no amount of effort to save a person's life can ever detract from how the word "unprecedented" has become a daily staple.

The beginning of the pandemic was a rollercoaster in some respects. I have never lived through such a fatal public health crisis before. Living through this historical event makes me realize how lucky I am to be alive. Many individuals in my county, Middlesex County, lost their lives due to COVID-19, and their loved ones will never see them again. Whereas, I am spending every day at home with my parents and twin brother, safe and sound. This is a blessing I will never put on the back burner; however, I did not heed advice such as, "Avoid contact gestures" at first. Everyday, Governor Phil Murphy repeats the term "social distancing" over and over again in his daily briefings, a term now ubiquitous in our vocabulary since COVID-19 commenced. It was something completely foreign to me, for I am one who thrives off of social interaction.

The only time I leave my apartment during the week is to buy groceries or take out the garbage. Hardly a day goes by where I do not feel lonely because of the quarantine. This is especially the case, considering the fact that I have been a fully remote student ever since September (my school, adopting a hybrid learning model at first, is now completely virtual as well). I value Google Meet and Zoom as much as the next person, because they help me to stay involved in extracurricular activities and school gatherings. I also don't need to worry about my long commutes everyday anymore, or the dreaded traffic congestion on the New Jersey Turnpike. Still in all, nothing beats physically hugging someone. Once America puts this series of unfortunate events behind us, I look forward to reconnecting with my Saint Dominic Academy sisters face-to-face. It has been far too long, and I want to ensure they are okay like they do for me regularly throughout the school year.

Proverbs 3:5-6 said it best: "Trust in the Lord with all your heart, and lean not on your own understanding." This Bible verse could not be any truer during the COVID-19 pandemic, in which so many questions remain unanswered. I have relished the idea of working from home since freshman year. The feeling of possessing absolute control over what work you do and when, while also balancing family and personal time is so rewarding (or whatever the feeling for you is). Even so, the voice in the back of my head telling me, "If you turn in this assignment late, your teacher will see you in a different light," crept up on me at times while working remotely.

As a sophomore, I still followed my regular class schedule. The only difference was that all my teachers set specific deadlines for submitting the assignments, which were normally on the same day as they were posted on Google Classroom. My chemistry homework, at first, needed to be done by 12:00 P.M., for example, and yet I knew I needed to start two hours earlier. The reason being is that chemistry is not a strong suit of mine, and it takes me longer to understand the concepts in class. So, if I needed help at home, I could ask my brother to explain it in a different way or search YouTube relating to the topic. I appreciated how the time constraints forced me to persevere in my weakest subject. This made virtually completing my other schoolwork not as intimidating, even if on some weeks the workload increased more than others.

Distance learning, despite the learning curve, did not drop my grades; I put forth the same effort as I would in a physical classroom. The same is true now as I continue meeting on Zoom for class, turning in homework assignments, and embracing student life in this "new normal." The situation we are in is by no means ideal, but I remind myself everyday that all things are possible with God. A vaccine will be made possible. A significant decreasez in positive cases and deaths will be made possible. Life as we used to know it will be made possible. We just need to keep the faith and trust Him.

Avery Danae Williams is a high school junior and writer from New Jersey. Her email is averydanaewilliams@gmail.com, and you can follow her on Instagram, @miss.universal.poet, to read her poems.

INSIDE 2020-EXCERPTS FROM A JOURNAL BY *CECELIA FALLS*

Wednesday

March 25, 2020

I just put on Spotify. I suppose I could listen to Tidal but it doesn't have this Meshell album. I really like her music—listening to *Peace Beyond Passion*.

I didn't follow my "flexible schedule." I'm still good though and practicing my breathing as I write. I also need to drink more tea. I lost my train of thought listening/singing. I want to pray on paper.

Lord help us to get through these times—we've never experienced this, here,

but all over the world people have known collapse, famine, war...

And we kept going.

said prayers while changing the channel or scrolling quickly as if death might be contagious *contagious*

like war might be contagious

contagious

why can't love be contagious?

Dear Lord help us through this time

even if we lived before w/eyes closed & hearts turned away from the sun

even if we went around the flames

refused to climb the mountain

or cross the raging rivers

Help us anyway God

even though we did not

HELP

or worse, we set the fire

mined the mountains

burst the dams

Love us anyway Lord

so that we may

so that we may

LIVE

I know that we won't learn though

not all of us

our eyes will close

we will play w/matches

and someone else

will be burnt alive.

Poems come. Pages call when you sit w/a pen w/teal ink.

Wednesday

April 29, 2020

It's the *1992 Uprising* anniversary and tomorrow is the end of the month. This month flew by in a way, not really. More like everything just—IDK —it's kind of a blur. It's also the 7th week of SIP (*shelter in place*).

Anyway, it's early and I am a little sleepy. I can hear the turkey across the street. He's safe for now. I want to think all the best thoughts. Things are pretty scary though. Leadership couldn't be worse. How does Fauci even stand up there w/that fool? And McConnell, Graham?

I've started watching the Roosevelts doc again—the interesting thing about history is that in their present time there were all the things we deal w/now—catastrophes, etc. It wasn't clear that things would be alright—there was greed, graft, poor decisions & then something would happen to make things better, not perfect.

Mom was watching this doc—I think it was the national parks series—and it was on the Florida Everglades and there was a part about some devastating floods in the 1920s and how each time there were man made issues that caused the deaths of a disproportionate number of Black folks. It was basically like the decision was made to sacrifice the Black folks and poor rural whites (only a few in this case) to make everything cool for the rich whites who might have experienced some flooding—but not the damn near massacre experienced by the Black folks. Most of them were migrant farm workers from the Deep South and the Caribbean.

Perpetually racist ass Florida that had once been a haven for the enslaved—turned into a living grave—just waiting for the last breath after being stolen. I'd never heard that story. It really made me sad. All those people from different places, going to pick fruit in Florida and gone—just like that—because a lake—like Pontchartrain—flooded the area and the government did nothing—Extermination by neglect, except it was calculated to a degree. They knew what could happen. MF's just don't care. And people feel like that now. If a bunch of Black & Brown people are the ones dying, "Oh Well".

The documentary is called "The Swamp" and it is a part of the American Experience series on PBS.

Saturday

May 30, 2020

Tomorrow is the last day of this long ass deadly month. COVID. Racial violence. Police killing people and now the country is on fire. Armaud Arbery, George Floyd, Breonna Taylor (March), 3 people in Indianapolis by police, Deasjon Reed 21, McHale Rose 19—then a white pastor lies on brothas while buying ass, a woman kills her autistic child and blames two Black men, Amy Cooper calls the police on Christian Cooper in Central Park, the "Off the Record" documentary, protesters—just too much. I have felt useless this whole week and not present. Haven't been journaling. My brain is tired. Why is it so hard to say what's on my mind?

Thursday

June 4, 2020

My mind is everywhere. I think I've typed something up about this. I feel like I need sections.

1. Coronavirus/COVID-19 Pandemic Issues

2. Ongoing management of *PTS

3. Ongoing "home" issues

4. Racial Violence

    a. 5.19 Macon, GA-56 year-old married teacher & youth pastor, Christopher Keys, falsely reports being kidnapped and robbed by two black guys to avoid being outed after being robbed while soliciting sex from a man he met on Craigslist. It is not clear if the robbers were Black men as they are described as "masked men".

    b. 5.21 Miami, FL-Patricia Ripley, who describes herself as "white Hispanic" murders her 9 year-old autistic son Alejandro by drowning him in a local creek. She falsely reports that he was abducted by two Black men.

    c. 5.25, NYC, NY, Amy Cooper falsely reports being threatened by Christian Cooper, an African American Birder who politely asked A. Cooper to leash her dog.

She actually threatened C. Cooper with calling the police and goes on to call and act as if Cooper is threatening to assault her with full on dramatics that are filmed.

d. 5.25, Minneapolis, MN George Floyd is murdered by white police officer Derek Chauvin, who falsely claimed Floyd resisted arrest, while his fellow officers held Floyd down. The incident was recorded by teen Darnella Frazier, as well as security footage from across the street. Prior to removing Floyd from the police vehicle, officers are seen assaulting Floyd in the back of the vehicle. He was initially arrested for using a counterfeit 20-dollar bill in a store across from his job. The officer who murdered him by kneeling on his neck for nearly 9 mins, also worked as security at the same club as Floyd.

e. 2.23, Georgia, Ahmaud Arbery, 25, murdered by a father and son while jogging in his own neighborhood. More protests are happening now regarding this case.

5. Ongoing protests and "rioting" across the nation, and globally

a. Militarized responses in urban centers with violence being exacted on protesters

b. 6.1 Louisville, KY well known resident David McAtee killed by police during protest. Officers had their body cams off.

c. 5.30 Omaha, NB James Scurlock shot by city resident Jacob Gardner, after a "scuffle".

d. 5.31 Davenport, IA Italia Kelly, 22. I haven't been able to find details.

e. 3.3 Tacoma, WA Manuel Ellis restrained and died in police custody-information becoming available.

f. 5.30 St. Louis, MO Barry Perkins, 29 ran over by a car

while protesting and killed.

g. 6.3 Iyanna Dior, a Black Transwoman was beaten by a mob of Cis Black men while Cis Black Women watched.

h. 5.27 Tallahassee, FL Tony McDade, a Black Transman was killed by police

i. Reports continue to pour in regarding injuries to protesters, including incidents while protesters are in police custody.

6. Release and viewing of HBO Max documentary "On the Record", which chronicles the stories of women "allegedly" raped by Russell Simmons. Deemed controversial anyway because of Oprah dropping out as a producer and the feedback of Black women filmmakers, it gets obscured because of everything going on. I don't know how to feel about the feedback. The stories are powerful and definitely took me back to the way violating women was so acceptable during that time. Hell, during this time! And we are expected to just operate around it. Very triggering. I was in my 20's in the 90's. I remember how things were.

7. Viewing of four-part documentary series regarding Jeffrey Epstein's sex trafficking ring that exploited teen girls in NYC and Florida. What was I thinking? I feel like I must not close my eyes.

8. Erasure of Black women killed by law enforcement.

9. Erasure of Trans people killed by law enforcement, harassed, assaulted.

10. Erasure of differently abled Black people killed by law enforcement. Mental health. So many ways to be vulnerable and ignored.

I keep adding to this list. I'm trying to do too much at this time. I can't even get all of it down.

PTS is post traumatic stress.

CeCelia Falls, MSEd Counseling, resides in Oakland, Ca. She is a Writer, Poet and Educational Consultant working to end sexual violence, particularly childhood sexual abuse, in the African Diaspora.

WHY???
BY CRYSTAL P. ANTHONY

June 19, 2020

Today is Juneteenth. A holiday, a day of celebration for African Americans. Here in the year 2020 African Americans are still being hung. That's right… Hung. It hurts my soul. Society asks why do we (Black people) tear up businesses, burn buildings? We are angry. We are tired. We are hurt. We didn't ask to come here. We were stolen from our homes. Forced to work. To build this country that your ancestors stole from others. And no matter what we do, we are hated, despised, mistreated, destroyed, assassinated and murdered. Even when we are in a small area doing our own thing, we are harassed. Our homes and businesses are burned. Our people are beaten, raped, killed…. And for what? Do you even know?

June 20, 2020

Juneteenth had me all in my feelings. I ask myself more often than I can count…. "Why Us?" I spend more time laughing to keep from crying. What did we do? And when we ask, we get no answer. No one can tell us why.

Crystal P. Anthony is a Long Beach, California based writer, realtor and property manager and author of the upcoming book Bitter Roots. *Her email is anthonycrystal1965@yahoo.com and you can follow her on Facebook facebook.com/cpanthony*

SO, WE ARE HERE
BY DANA SANABRIA

November 21, 2020 -

I learned today, exactly how many lights go on a tree that stands nearly seven feet tall. We typically ban anything holiday until mid-December out of respect for my son Maceo, who was born on the first day of the twelfth month. This season we're gonna set it off early. Thankful. Jubilant. Delivered. Our democracy intact - mostly. My optimism, still cautious. Heavy in spirit at the unending war America has with our people. Outraged at the willful ignorance that is the idiocy of the opposition. Missing everyone and everything. Desperate for lightness. Yeah, we're gonna need a bigger tree and ALL the lights it can safely hold. To be this excited about lights on a tree, a luxury pure and true in this time and certainly in this life for me.

My littles and me, we missed the ocean. My favorite place to shut out the world is by the water. When I need to be still, quiet my mind and seek the way forward, find me by the sea. Not much beats the ambient noise of the ocean greeting the shore. It calms. By now we would have been there already. But COVID-19. But the depths of Dixie dissent. Pre-2016, I never had fear about where or when I traveled. I wasn't sure how real things would get and if it was worth the risk. It felt selfish. I put some prayer on it, we went to the water, and we're all better for it.

We're on the cusp of the tenth month. At the time the pandemic hit I was already deep into my ritual of routine and fervent prayer. Near burn out, I had no room to add anything else. Does anyone ever, actually? I kept saying, "Not one more thing," and I feel like life kept saying, "Hold my beer," with each request for a lighter load. As things progressed I felt terrible for my ask - being that I was working, my kids were healthy, our basic needs - more than covered. Our immediate family and their families, good. But I began to ask myself, would we leave, could we leave if we had to? Never even thought about it outside of retirement, let alone planned or prepped for it. But it was on the table. Still is. Where would we go? Which place is less oppressive, more safe than here? Or would I be trading one set of oppressors' rules for another's but differently expressed? On a high-level I understood why people risk it all to escape war, famine, corruption. In no way am I comparing, but considering how close we came, a sneeze away from only God-knows-what as we witnessed our democracy being eviscerated across all available mediums. We've been holding our breath for a long while. Running from boogeymen coming at us from all angles. I resented these thoughts. Facing a somewhat similar decision I'm told, my great-grandmother put my then school-aged grandfather on a boat from Honduras to America in the 1930s. In these moments her reasoning was no longer abstract to me. Today I overstand.

Nostalgia creeps in. I miss those crowded holiday homes in St. Albans, Lakeview and sometimes Sag Harbor - with people holding plates sitting or standing along stairways and stoops. No less than five rice dishes as the Caribbean meets the Carolinas. Stuffing and dressing as north meets south. Rum-fueled debates on politics, music and how we spoiled American kids should be sent home to the islands or down south to be raised properly (but y'all raised us though). I remember one year the kids table was an ironing board draped with table linens.

My generation, we've become the tradition bearers. Our elders now supervise to make sure we get it right. Nana fusses at my mom for cutting the greens too small, and in the same breath asks for pie, but then reminds her that she's not a good baker. It still tickles me to hear my sanctified grandmother, an Evangelist who can preach a mighty word...caution my mother to mind the cinnamon because, "Nobody wants no black @$$ pies.". And then turn to me to make sure there is proper white rice on the table. Calling me by my whole government name she says, "Not yellow rice or rice with beans, peas and all them funny things in it like y'all make down to your father's people Dana Sheron.". And speaking of...you can only make Papi's-famous-chicken-on-the-grill if you use Adobo with the blue cap, by the company we no longer support. I'm sure he has a few bottles in supply, we have until the end of that last one to find a suitable sub. Politics found its way to our plates. *Shakes fist.

Dana Sanabria is a New York (born and raised) creative working in tech. She currently lives and writes in Atlanta. You can follow her on IG at @dalightmixtape.

DOWN AT THE SWAMP
BY DURWIN BROWN AKA BROTHA D

10/27/20

It's just days away and I feel extremely indifferent about the 2020 Presidential election. The fact that the overall theme of this election is centered around voting for a "lesser of two evils" says a whole damn lot. To compound all of this, is so utterly disappointing to me that we have a system which for all it is worth, only managed to produce two CAUCASIAN MEN over the age of 70 years old as the "best" candidates for the office of President in 2020.

11/4/20

"Dontchu' eva' fatten no frog, to feed no snake." These were just some of the oft-repeated wise words from a magical, melanated, sage of a woman, my Grandmother Mrs. Kate Brown. While observing the political, social, and racial rifts play out in 2020 specifically during the past few months, these particular words resonated in my head. In times of uncertainty, and confusion I could always rely on her to offer up some verbal soup to ease my mind. The aforementioned adage reminded me of good times and memories, like washing down her homemade teacakes with freshly squeezed lemonade.

As the voting numbers come in, it's becoming more apparent that Joe Biden and the 1st "Black" and female Vice President-elect, Senator Kamala Harris will attempt to take the helm of the sinking ship that is the U.S.S. Amerikkka. Folks are outside honking horns and dancing in the streets proclaiming we won, but there is also an uneasy calm before the forecasted far-right shit storm.

The frog's belly is full of ballots and the snake is surprisingly silent. Donald Trump has hunkered down and refuses to concede defeat. COVID cases and deaths are spiking and he's touting Wall Street record-high closing stats. Meanwhile lockdowns and curfews are about to be reintroduced here in the state of California. Biden is promising to put Amerikkka back together again. Humpty Dumpty. Remember how that worked out for him right? A scrambled mess. All of this shit has been about as clear as a jar of Everglades swamp water and just as unpleasant to the palate.

Durwin Brown is the founder of the Catalyst Foundation for Youth Development, an Oakland, California-based youth advocacy and wellness organization. He is a community activist, youth mental health specialist, public speaker, educator, and self-help writer, including his forthcoming How to Get Your Sh*t Together in 30 Days or Less: A No Nonsense Guide to Sensible Living. *His email is thecatalystfoundation@gmail.com and you can follow him on Instagram,* @hollaatbrothad

UNTITLED
BY ELAINA T. DARIAH

Syndemic date October 27, 2020

A week before the election...

Early voting did not seem real. The last time I felt this way was 1988, casting an absentee ballot from Spain. Difference being this time I am engaged. Much more now at 61, than at 29. Back then I ensured my vote. It was my right, my people died to give me the right. This time, as written on the sign I made for the "Sidewalk Solidarity," my church's 120-day protest..."My life depends on it."

I am not going to watch the results. Too much anxiety. I know there will be chicanery, foolishness and out and out lies! Number forty-five will try to steal this election. Point is, will the people be as complicit as they were before?

Syndemic date November 3, 2020

Election Day...

"Mom, do not go out on election day. There is no telling what these folks will do out there today." My 26-year-old son, with a degree in political science, living and working in DC instructs ME on election morning. This is a good day to go to the commissary, lines should be short. Why did I not listen?

Driving out of the commissary parking lot, I stopped, looked and proceeded. Next thing I know there is a white man, in an old Lincoln on my quarter panel honking and shouting..."NIGGER!!" as he runs me off the road. I stop short of hitting the back of a bus.

Syndemic date November 7, 2020

Still counting votes...

2016 we spent Veterans Day in DC. We made plans to do the same this year. Last time it was to celebrate the opening of the National Museum of African American History and Culture. I am happy this time to celebrate the Biden/Harris victory. As I watch my Twitter feed the results are in. Joe Biden has not only won the electoral college, but has flipped Georgia, Arizona, AND Pennsylvania!

My sister calls crying. The last election we cried together was November 4, 2008 for President Barack Hussein Obama. This time, they are tears of relief. I am going to DC to celebrate next Saturday!

Syndemic date November 13, 2020

On the train to DC…

What?! …a million MAGA march! I was nervous remembering election day. No anxiety, just nervousness. Looking over to my husband I ask, "Did you know the million MAGA march was this weekend?" He gives me that "Oh, Elaina" look as he says "no." You know what?... this is NOT about Donald Trump! We're meeting with my husbands' best friend Milt, from Philly. Sunday we will have brunch with my son to meet his new girlfriend.

We get past the rats running around outside union station. To the hotel, "We've never tried Westin before," he says. As we approach the front desk, groups of MAGA come off the elevator. Before we get on the elevator to our room, holding my hand my brilliant husband says, "They were losers when they came, and they will be losers when they leave." I love this man.

Syndemic date November 14, 2020

Black Lives Matter Boulevard…

Thank God, for Black Restaurant Week in DC! As if every day is not BRW?! The city is fifty-four percent black! P-Funk proclaimed them a "Chocolate City" in 1975. Stop trippin' Elaina. It was a beautiful morning for the brisk 3-mile walk. Breakfast at Busboys and Poets

NEVER disappoints, no matter the location.

My goal was to take a picture on Black Lives Matter Boulevard. It was daylight. I know what I know; the real foolishness will be after dark. Just like their ancestors, they will go get "likkered up" and that liquid courage will show their real reason for the loser march. I tell Milt, "It is not the men I am worried about, it is the fragility play of the women."

As we head to BLM Boulevard, I see individual black MAGAs. They do not disturb me as much as the Latinx delegation waving American flags, with MAGA shirts on, or the Asian family. Note to self… check the politics of the restaurants you patronize.

Finally arriving at the Boulevard, it is more than just golden words painted on a street. There are signs posted on the buildings around it. Colorful flags, with brown silhouettes music blaring, "…and the beat goes on, just like my love EVER-LAAASTING!" Hustlers with Biden/ Harris, #JusticeForBreonnaTaylor and I Can't Breathe shirts. At the other end of the street, counter-protesters chanting, "DONALD TRUMP YOUR TIME'S UP, PACK YOUR S**T AND GO!" There is a building with two BLM signs and in-between, as was the standard back when these buildings were constructed. The date of my birth etched in stone… 1959. How significant is this?! I must take a picture here and everywhere else I see these beautiful signs of support for me and my people.

These BLM signs are not just the words. They all have supportive national organization endorsements attached to them.

That night, after a great dinner at Nando's, while scrolling Twitter "White women tearing down BLM signs,"…at the very spot I took my picture! True to form. I watch a video of them ripping down the protest signs attached to the gates outside the White House. Audibly, I hear a woman say to the counter-protester, "We want to see OUR White House."

During his victory speech, President-elect Joe Biden said, "The African American community stood up again for me. You have always had my back, and I'll have yours."

This was not just a march about election results. It was a display of resistance and hate to the people who have been the backbone of this nation since 1619.

You may be 'coming for us.' Know that we are not our ancestors. Our concealed carry are PhDs, CEOs, Lawyers, Mayors, Governors, Sociologists, Microbiologists, Environmentalist, Soldiers, Sailors, Marines, Grocery Store Cashiers, Foodservice Workers, CNAS, Medical Doctors, Nurses, Busboys and Poets.

Elaina Dariah is a human services outreach specialist, retired US Navy, civil and human rights activist. Her email is dariahtracy@yahoo.com and you can follow her on Twitter, @ElainaDariah.

ELECTION TIME OBSERVATIONS: HEART V. MIND
BY ERZSÉBET KARKUS

27 October: Why does it feel like a Friday at 6:47pm in the office, when it's just after 11am on a Tuesday? Usually mid-mornings seem like mid-afternoons at the latest. Time is heavy. Election Day is one week away.

Nate Silver's projection that Biden is "favored" to win offers no comfort. His "FiveThirtyEight" election forecasting system was right before, though neither my heart nor head wanted to accept it. Now, my heart is all in, in the way it wanted to believe my junior high friend when she told me the boy who made me blush when his name was mentioned liked me, even though I didn't register in his world. My head resists. It is too afraid.

Things are swirling. I am anxious and afraid.

Afraid for women
who do not live in a
placetolerating choice.

Afraid for those
without power.

Afraid for people who
are not White.

Afraid harm will continue
if the results don't
go Democratic. Afraid if
they do.

Afraid we cannot stop
violence either way.

Afraid I will just stay afraid
and not fight.

Afraid to hope.

We have been here before. The outcome was far worse than many (including myself) expected it to be. Disappointingly, others found these years far exceeded expectations.

1 November: Leaving the Park, a handful of oversized pick-ups and an out of place SMART car (?!?!) troll around the Guggenheim, their drivers' palms resting heavily on the horns.

The Orange-a-tan's version of *Interahamwe* – the civilian bands that drove around Rwanda in Toyota Hilux pick-ups killing Tutsi?

Instead of banana leaves, they brandish flags and Orange-a-tan banners.

It's jarring to see this in Manhattan. If the aim is to bring unease, they succeeded. I am unnerved by their presence, even in such a tiny number.

These bully-mobiles almost certainly include law enforcement. Today, they intimidate; tomorrow, they patrol. How can we trust them to put aside amped-up aggression to peacefully protect us all? This question overlooks the fact that cops have no affirmative duty to protect, only a discretionary one – which makes it more distressing. [Of course, even with a duty to protect, we cannot count on it, as too many "bad apples" and willfully inattentive, enabling and/or impotent "orchard keepers" have shown us. An image of a worm-hole covered apple revving up a quasi-monster truck with a PBA sticker in the windshield just popped into my head *(pardon the mixed similes).*]

3 – 4 November, 2:48am: It's not over...My mind knew it wouldn't be, but I wanted a definitive outcome– A map covered in blue.

Obviously, I hoped: hoped for better from my fellow voters. Heart and mind conflict, bringing disappointment.

I've wondered if we murdered, mutilated or marginalized the person who could have cured cancer. This predates COVID and the Orange-a-tan – but my worry is elevated. We are not going to stop losing and will never know the extent of loss if this is not a one term blunder.

7 November: Exiting the Park hearing horns again, only without the apprehension from last week. The honking is spontaneous, unorganized and joyful, blending with bursts of celebration from pedestrians, bikers and apartment dwellers– including some jubilantly waving American flags, reclaiming them as a symbol of the democratic process and not a signal of aggression. This is all in response to the AP calling Pennsylvania for Biden.

I exhale longer than I have in a while, relieved.

Then, I remember: There are two winners...Biden and McConnell.

The head quickly resumes control. I cannot hope without reservations.

One person cannot repair everything alone, although another can continue successfully hurting many, doing so with unlimited callousness.

1,233,135 peoples' choice enables this Republican Shylock to hold the progress of 328.2 million *(including themselves)* hostage.

There is no compassion. Just disregard for the damage – much of it irreparable –his gnarly, grotesquely discolored hands have caused as he throttles power. All damage is valueless collateral.

It's the season of change. My favorite neighborhood tree, covered in reds and oranges just days ago, is almost naked.

Just a few leaves cling to what has been a full burning bush of color.

As swift as this change is, it is redundant and cannot be rushed.

Other change stalls or doesn't happen at all.

We have been here before too – with McConnell barricading action. While he may not live to see the end of his 7th term (*he's 78!*), that spark for potential change is neither certain, nor instant enough.

After 6 completed terms – 36 years – Kentucky is fourth from the bottom for overall poverty, even though it's second most dependent on Federal welfare funds.

I cannot imagine of the 1.2 million Kentuckians who voted for Mitch, none are living below the poverty line…Why do they keep sending him back? Do his *petit* strong man tactics fill their bellies or bank accounts?

Although I jotted "I am afraid to hope," I do hope for something at least restorative beginning 20 January 2021.

I want my heart to win. I think my mind would agree, but it's fighting hope, wondering: "How was it this close?" Over 73 million people voted for the Orange-a-tan. This number is so large, even the heart sees it will be very hard to pull out the win.

Erzsébet Karkus is a New York City-based writer, photographer, humanitarian, advocate, and attorney. Her email is ekarkus@yahoo.com and you can follow her on Instagram, @abanyuka.

PROTESTS
BY JASON RHODES

June 12, 2020

We're not listening (by that I mean some), nor are we moving closer to one another. Some of us are still holding on to the post. The post that says, "I'm right" and "what I believe is right." Some of us have our arms around the post gripped so tight and stick out our figurative legs and try to wrestle whatever tidbit, half fact, loose rationale to our side bringing it closer to our bodies, while we hang onto the post. Some even fish out representatives; Black or White that echo our position and then praise it, bow down to it, call it prophetic or the person prophetic; "This guy, this gal, should run for office;" it's almost like they're saying, "See this is 'one' of your own saying the same thing, I'm saying;" usually they're referring to somebody in blackface.

To that I say; "you're right; it is 'one' of our own, saying the same thing you're saying. I suppose that's all you need to negate what the rest of us are saying, as you keep gripping to that post."

There is willful blindness; there is fear, hyperbole and doomsday predictions, rationales rooted in privilege. Some don't want to listen, they don't want change; they want to prove they're right, point the finger, become personal, launch attacks, when the facts are irrefutable. As they make fun of those who are trying to listen, sarcasm drips from their mouths; they love their posts/positions. Of course this is done under the umbrella of Patriotism, Law and Order, Religion, and now Trumpism.

I think of my childhood, sharing the baseball diamond, the court, the football field, across cultures. From the playground, to the classroom, on field trips, in lunchrooms, we laughed, spoke, loved, and there were no outward politics to speak of.

How is it we've become weaker as men and women?

June 30, 2020

Trump the Magician-

There is something in our heart that calls out; seeks the truth and it is met by the world, with all its emotion, distortion and belief. Malcolm used to say; "Make it Plain," a call to strip it down to facts, leave the emotion out of it, the distortion, the belief. In the end, he realized, "We" are all human, and therein lies "the rub". We are susceptible to strong feelings, beliefs, prejudices, foundations built on mud, hate, lies. And to boot; something in us loves position; A raised fist, a flag, a statue, a knee on the neck, a hat, yes that's right "symbolism" another derivative, meant to speak to emotion. To make it plain, there is intelligence and there is emotion; fact and fiction. A great number of us become ideologues, believing in something despite the facts to the contrary, doing away with facts, coasting on emotion, seeking or trying to maintain position; what I've previously referred to as "holding onto the post," that's where prejudice lives, thrives, amongst other things. That's what makes racism so cancerous; it all at once encapsulates all the above. Good Magicians/Con men, make you believe you saw, what you didn't see, a flash of the hand, a perception, a variation of some truth. If done well; we applaud, crave more. We scream; "do it again, fool me again," because it makes us feel good. It is 2020; for the most part we now have 2,000 years of written history, but we don't look at the facts, we selectively pick and choose what to honor, discuss, teach, study, hold up, ultimately believe in, because it gives us the advantage, if not in reality, then psychologically. That is called "indoctrination" not "education".

Approximately 500 years ago; not 2,000; racism, on a wide scale, was introduced, practiced and then mass produced by countries. It took hold and hasn't let go since. Historians have pinpointed it to The Spanish Inquisition where "Race" became the driving factor and pseudoscience followed thereafter, in a willful attempt to legitimize it; the position, the lie, not the facts. And here we are; 500 years later, at each other's throats, idolizing position, bowing to symbolism, believing the lie, even voting for it. I applaud those who are trying to change, to answer that thing that is "calling out in their hearts" we can all learn from one another, if we just listen, then seek, then change. I had a conversation off-line about reaching this age and not being taught "Facts" in school. The person was White, I'm Black. "Racism" in this world can actually be pinpointed to time and place; which means it's not natural, it's learned, there is nothing Superior about someone's skin color; that is factual!

All else is just a Magicians' trick.

Jason Rhodes is an Attorney, LCSW, and Writer located in Baltimore, Maryland. Mr. Rhodes has just completed his first book. His email is jroanacy@aol.com and you can follow on Instagram, jason.rhodes.756

TREE RINGS
BY JENINA PODULKA

The limbs of the mulberry tree outside swing back and forth in the wind. The leaves are yellow and sparse. Just a few months ago I sat in this same window, soaking in the sun and looking outside at the green, lush leaves, and wondering why the sweetness of waking up on her chest was drenched in a distinct sadness.

Now I return to this place to make a new home out of it. A home for nobody but myself. For the first time in my life, when I close my door, nobody else can open it. Immersed in the task of building a nest for my soul, and trying to scrub the apartment and the neighborhood of the ghosts of a love that's come to an end, I've had no energy for the grief, the disasters, the new or intensified threats that have become a part of our every day. Everything is so, so loud. I know that there's beauty to be found in the upheaval, but all I want to do is catch up on 30 years of lost time with myself. The waves of uncertainty, instability, and empathetic pain wash over me as I root myself into healing.

I relish the silence and the space for my thoughts to unfurl. More than ever before, I listen to the feelings and desires sitting in the flesh of my consciousness. It feels both lonely and luxurious to keep all of that deliciousness to myself. And in this abundance of silence, now that I'm listening, the fear, the anger, and the echoes of old, old pain come through too. The story that they tell is meandering and long, but I have the time to follow it.

Although sometimes my healing may feel indulgent, or at odds with the chaos of what's happening around me, or tiny in comparison to it, something inside me knows that it's actually all one and the same. This is a time for healing deep into wounds that have never been allowed to heal properly. And sometimes that means breaking bones so that they can be reset. It's excruciating—but what could be more important?

I trust that inside the trunk of the mulberry tree, among the rings that record its growth, there will be a record of me too. Etched into the wood, a chronicle of us swinging back and forth in the wind of this season together.

Jenina Podulka (she/her) is a storyteller and nonprofit communications specialist based in Jersey City, NJ. She can be reached at jenina.podulka@gmail.com.

FAITH. HOPE. ACTION.
BY KATRINA HAYES

On March 17, 2017, I wrote to Kevin Powell. It went something like this. The subject was You Can Take the Girl Out of Brooklyn.

Hello there Kevin!

Thank you for evolving from a boy to a man and seeing the importance of supporting issues that affect sisters. A very smart man once told me one of the true measures of a real man is one who will genuinely serve the community.

A few things about me...

- I was born in Brooklyn.

- I have been honored as a Girls Inc. of NYC Volunteer of

the Year.

- I have done speeches on Autism Advocacy.

- I have earned a Masters Degree in Medical Biology.

- I have a fully stocked bookshelf.

- I know my rights.

...BUT despite all of this, I have still been treated like an outcast. Ignored when I have asked for help. Looked over as if Black Lives Don't Matter to them...or sometimes to my own people.

So, what haven't I done?

- I haven't told my experience of illegal injustice to those it would benefit.

In 2016 after my son was abused and deprived of an appropriate education; the school district set up a "mock hearing." After they were notified of the abuse the hearing was moved from a courthouse to a garage-sized community college room. The attendees thought I was coming alone. The attendees had at least 4 bailiffs in the room, on the left side of me. Most of the evidence was purposely left out. The rest of the evidence wasn't even considered. I was threatened with being arrested for advocating for the rights of my son. No appeal rights were given that day, but I appealed anyway. On every level, evidence wasn't considered, a hearing was denied, and appeal rights were not provided, or in the case of the state-level appeal...were insufficiently given. In the beginning, I felt diminished, but then I realized the pathology that went into these actions were only in the adversary's brain.

Unlike Sandra Bland...I'm still alive. My adversaries' greatest HOPE is for you to ignore this email.

Tons of respect + appreciation,

Katrina Hayes

BUT you can't take *The* Brooklyn out of the girl!

After 2020 Elections.

I haven't received justice yet. Though I am here. Taking the steps on this journey to sharing my story. The other day I received a postcard from the Biden Harris campaign stating that it's time that we have justice for our kids. A Black boy was on the postcard about the same age as my son. I'll keep knocking. I'll keep praying. I'll keep hoping.

To GOD be the Glory!

Katrina Hayes is a Special Education Advocate who resides in Cary, NC. Her email address is advocatehayes@gmail.com and you can follow her @SpeakUpAdvocacy on Facebook.

20/20 LOVE: A "NO OUTSIDE INTERFERENCE IN MY RELATIONSHIP" WRITING
BY KEPHRA AMEN

I gazed in love at my soulmate today the same way I did 25 years ago. Of course, by now there are a lot of new things in our life. New topics to debate. New recipes. New grandchildren. New places to travel. New goals. Let's not forget the new pounds to shed as well. Life! We're in love. Like most men in love, true love, we'll help our mates to no end. Love. We'll communicate. Well, at the least, try to communicate to reach a constant compromise.

Like any typical day, I may need to run an errand or complete a Honey Do List. 20/20, like no other year, adds a little bit of a twist to my typical day of errands. Maybe I should just call the days TWISTED! So,

I just came home from the grocery store. That lover of mine is heavily on my mind. I can't wait to see her. To hold her. To kiss her. To love her. See, our love is deep. It has wounds, healing, triumphs, understandings, fall-outs, make-ups, and "almost breakups."

Love! My wife, my lover, my queen, and I decided in the beginning that no matter what, we'd stay together. Not that cliché at the altar "I do!" either. Do what? You haven't lived life, yet you're telling the world in front of live witnesses what you won't do. Nawl. We're beyond that. Our love has been through tests. It's real. Our #1 rule? Never let anything on the outside destroy what's happening on the inside. We've stood on that. Preached on that. Counseled on that. Almost got divorced on that. Loved on that. Had attitudes on that. Saged our house on that. But in 2020, things have changed. I'm feeling some type of way right now. Another test! There's interference from the outside. I'm stand-offish. I'm hesitant. I'm cold. Shit, I'm scared!

I've never been concerned with the outside influence until now. I've seen some guys whisper in her ear. Send sneaky texts. Give me a shady look. Give her a seductive look. You know - Hater Shit! It's not limited to just guys either. When interference comes, it's dressed like the invisible man. Stealth. Covert. This invisible man is from now on henceforth a bonafide, pure Grade A, gen-you-wine ASSHOLE. The kind that don't stink but has a foul disposition.

During many nights of passion, I concentrate on my lover. I want badly to caress, massage, and stick my tongue…well, never mind that. I gotta deal with this fucking interference. I mean literally…"fucking interference." All the crudeness. The rudeness. The shrewdness. I refuse to let this cat win. I'll do whatever it takes to keep our love alive. To keep the interference at bay. I can't let this cat be a part of our life. Like a praying missionary from the Church Of God In Christ, I'm going in. Into my Heaven. Into my lover. Into my life. I grabbed her and brought her near. I'm reminded by the missionary's prayer of when I met my wife.

You see, it was all a dream when I used to read Word-Up magazine. She was there. I dreamed of her as a teenager. 15 years had passed, and I've had the dream many, many times. The dream would come randomly like a reminder of an old friend from junior high. Deja Vu had come. And then, like the footsteps in the sand, my love, my wife, my Queen appeared. My soulmate! My dream had become we.

The tumultuous mentally draining year is almost over. I just watched a squirrel bury some nuts. A reminder. Everything must and will change. That's what the squirrel whispered to me as I wondered about the interference in my relationship. The squirrel comforted me. I screamed in my head "I'm not giving up!" I'm in it for the long haul. I've heard it will get better with time. Well, I got time. Again, I brought my Queen in close. Hands. Eyes. Tongue. Flesh. We're one. Nothing from the outside will interfere with our Love on the inside. That's our rule. We let Love continue to dwell in our midst like the expanse of ether in time. The interference? It's gone. Evicted from the inside. We're moving forward with our relations. And so you know, and you should know for future reference this assholes' name.
The Trump Virus.

Kephra Amen is an Entrepreneur, Tech Consultant, Author, Humanitarian, Influencer, and advocate for the Black family. He's currently based in Minneapolis, MN. Kephra Amen can be reached at KephraAmen.com

JOURNAL ENTRY
BY KERIKA FIELDS NALTY

March 21, 2020

Oh shit, they officially shut the city down today. Helen called last week and told me to get ready 'cause they just shut down Cali. Lo and behold she was right 'cause the governor just announced today that NY is on lockdown. This shit is scary.

The disease itself is scary but scarier for me is OMG there's nothing to do, no place to go - everything is closed!! The library!! Bars!! The gym!! My three favorite places. Now I'm just gonna be…home. Even Carlton can't commute to Jersey for work. WTF.

Ok, ok Kerika, don't stress out. You have a roof over your head. You have a husband who loves you. You have food in the fridge. Thank God! You have your health (which is really the blessing right about now). You have everything you need so don't freak out. Just stay busy. That's what you've been doing so far. Folded all your sweaters! Watched a video on how to fold fitted sheets and still can't figure that shit out. Fuck it. You never said you were Martha Stewart up in this piece.

Main thing: write. You know that is what keeps you from going stir crazy. Maybe finally finish your books? What's up with "With Your Bad Self," the book about Gma Marie when she was a young girl in Bklyn? You started it back when you were staying at Ashland and working at Barclays Kerika, so maybe now take this time to finish already since you won't be schlepping to the city every day. You are not getting any younger. You just turned 50 earlier this month, March 9 to be exact. But because all that is going on? Didn't go anywhere! Was supposed to have a spa day with Skye but something-maybe all the news reports of ppl getting sick from this COVID told me to cancel. They hadn't even shut stuff down just yet but still I was like, nah. Not the time to be in a whirlpool or sauna with strangers.

So glad I stayed the hell home. Yup! Spent the big 50 home alone with a bottle of bubbles and old movies. It actually wasn't that bad. Gave myself a facial and did my own nails. But I was a lil sad. Sad might not be the right word. Lord knows I'm grateful to have made it this far. Melancholy maybe? That's the word.

Just reflecting on my life I mean—50! Where did the time go? Where did that girl I used to be go? I have no idea but I think that's why I've been avoiding these boxes of pictures and negatives I just got out of storage that I need to go through! I've got some good stuff but it's overwhelming. Like, who was the person that took all these pictures of all these people? Who ran around the city all energetic, excited? Who was at the parties and the concerts and the plays? Was that me? Thank

God for the pics cause they are proof that I DID THAT although just thinking about it now---just looking through them all—makes me absolutely exhausted. I had a ball though. If anybody enjoyed their youth it was my azz. And in NYC. The best city!! The best parties. The funkiest clubs. I wonder if the city will ever be the same. After all of this? Who knows? But the goal is to make it through this mess. This PANDEMIC. Now that's a word.

Now, what are we supposed to do? Wear masks if we go out, wash our hands like maniacs, stay the hell away from people? I can do it!

It's unfortunate tho' cause I had to miss dad's 80th bday. His was on the 12th and Marilyn had a whole party in the community center with balloons, food, the band, the works. You know how she do! But I was like nah, not going. I know she wanted me there to take pictures like always but not his time. I actually thought she was going to cancel but she didn't. It's all over the news. Stay away from old people and people with pre-existing conditions. My dad is old and I am overweight. So I took no chances. It would have been nice to celebrate my 50th and his 80th together but, oh well. If all I have to do right now is sit down, stay home, take a minute, take a breather, be still - then that is what I will do!

Kerika Fields Nalty, a Brooklyn-based writer, and photographer whose photographs and articles have been published and exhibited widely, is the author of He's Gone...You're Back! The Right Way to Get Over Mr. Wrong. *Please follow her on Instagram @flashandcircumstance and visit Withyourbadself.com to keep in touch!*

FROM MY HEART TO GOD'S EARS
BY LINDSEY "LYNMARIE" MORALES

11/7/2020

Dear Lord God,

I come to You, both proud and disappointed. Biden and Harris have won the 2020 presidential election. I know Your will be done regardless of who is in the office. I must admit however, I am happy about this win. To me, Donald Trump will always be a symbol of division, and he represents everything wrong in America. I believe Joe Biden and Kamala Harris are more equipped to run the country. I am proud that this win was largely due to Black women voting in such high numbers. Stacey Abrams and many others rallied to get people to vote, and 2020 showed their efforts weren't in vain. Biden's historic win in Georgia would not have happened without strong voter turnout. I think one reason so many people showed up to vote was because, like me, they were sick of the lack of moral character in this president.

As proud as I am, I am also disappointed. I am disappointed by the division I have seen in the Christian community, particularly between White Christians and Christians of Color. It was apparent that people who aren't from marginalized or oppressed communities failed to see how the words and actions of Donald Trump have caused so many people emotional distress and even bodily harm. I've witnessed so much condemnation on social media towards anyone in the Christian community who was not voting for Trump. I remember a person saying, "Please don't vote for baby sacrifice," in reference to the issue of abortion. Lord, I have counseled women who have gone through pain and suffering as a result of such a difficult choice, why do people feel it's ok to condemn them?

Why Lord, do many feel that supporting Trump is the Christian thing to do, despite all of his lies, adultery, misogyny, racism, and violent rhetoric? How is this Christ-like? I heard people saying he was to bring God back to the White House. With me being multiracial and Christian, I saw what the leader of the free world was saying about people of Color or anyone who

377

wasn't a White male. I couldn't find it in my right mind to vote for this man. It confused me why so-called Christians would campaign so hard for a man who admitted to sexually assaulting women, said that Mexicans are rapists, and many other ignorant and ugly statements. His actions, time and time again, show his self-interests for power and totally go against everything we as Christians are supposed to believe. So many online "prophets" predicted a second term for Donald Trump. I spent the night of the election crying out to You Lord that it wouldn't be so. I did my homework. I became educated on both parties. I watched, and I prayed. These people were saying Donald Trump is God's choice, but I just couldn't come to that conclusion.

So God, I come to You, praying for understanding. I believe You heard every one of my prayers for the president and the people of this country for the last 4 years. I pray You hear this one. I pray Christians can freely practice their faith. I pray that those called by You, seek Your face instead of man. I pray no matter what is popular or unpopular, I can hear and see clearly from You. I pray my tears and pain are not in vain and you show up mightily in my life. I pray false prophets are exposed, and You set free the people manipulated by their ministries. I pray this presidential transition is peaceful, efficient, and a good thing for the country.

I pray for wisdom, guidance, and direction during these times. I pray for courage and boldness. I pray for hope and for the future of the country. I pray for unwavering faith. I pray for spiritual eyes to watch and pray. I vow to watch and pray. I will study day and night the word and meditate on it. I will stand for what's right, even if I have to stand alone. I will love You, Lord, and I will love people.

In Jesus' Name

Amen.

Lindsey "LynMarie" Morales is a life strategy coach for women entrepreneurs, writer, and public speaker based in the Kansas City area. Her email address is writer@lindseymorales.com and you can follow her on Instagram @lindsey_lifestrategy.

BEFORE AND AFTER 2020
BY LISA T. DAUGHTREY

I am devastated, our virtual graduation for Black women and Black girls conducted through our non-profit organization was hacked. Today was supposed to be special, they have made major accomplishments in their lives: a few had battled cancer, mental illness, loss of employment and death. It's their day.

I am processing what happened…It's my turn to speak. I'm feeling excited looking at these beautiful women smiling, I notice a few are wearing their caps and gowns. My speech is interrupted by a noise, but I continue to speak. The next interruption, I hear 'you b*tch a$$ n*ccas". I stop to check and see who is speaking on my screen. I realized the call had been hacked but now several voices are yelling racist comments. All I can see is the graduates' faces. I am so angry right now. I feel like I'm having an out of body experience, but I have to think quickly, what do I do next? I just text the founder to disband the virtual call and I advise the graduates to look for a new email notification with a virtual link. My mind is running fast. I've never felt this much heat coming from my body so quickly. Within minutes, we resume the virtual call. First thing I said was "I am sorry; it's our fault and we have let you down."

So far 2020 has been a frightening nightmare with this global pandemic lockdown and a belligerent President throwing tantrums and creating chaos at the White House. I am looking at the graduates' faces and the disappointment in their eyes leaves me numb. I know how they feel.

I've been there. All I can hear are the voices running in my head. I have to take a moment and practice my breathing technique to prevent an anxiety attack. I am so tired of this, and I am ready to fight somebody. I'm emotional. It's that time of the year for me to grieve my son, he died by suicide and just recently, we lost George Floyd to police brutality. His death has started a global movement and I am mad as hell…right now. All I want is retribution. How dare you enter our sanctuary, our safe zone and try to demoralize Black women? How dare you target us? We were resilient. We ended the ceremony on a good note.

Our team posted a letter of apology via social media and we are still waiting for the web conference company to solve the hacking into calls.

I am praying that nothing triggers me while we're trying to salvage the ceremony, but I am having one of my flashbacks. Racism has been a part of my life. I was born and raised in Southern Virginia. Tourists would call my hometown Tidewater; but I always tell people that I was born under the Old Jim Crow Law of Southern Virginia.

When I was in college, I worked for a corporate bank. Being Black in Corporate America, you have to work hard and give 110%. You see, Corporate America always kept their knee on our necks. I made it a habit to limit my socializing with them, I always felt like I was going through a physical exam … they would push and prod with their eyes and cunning remarks. I never received a raise during my tenure. I had to apply for a new role to receive an increase in pay. My last role, my supervisor who was Black, reviewed my employment record with the bank. He was perplexed as well that I'd never received a raise. He advised me that he would schedule a meeting with the Vice President and ensured that I was compensated. When I heard the good news, I was on cloud nine and elated. In a day that all changed. I was on the elevator with the Vice President from our department. It was a quiet ride until he turned to me and congratulated me on the raise but informed me that I needed to show my gratitude. He stated that I was a little rebellious. I was never rebellious or unprofessional. However, I did not allow anyone to degrade me. The last few seconds on the elevator, I did not show any emotions. I remain poised and professional; however, my mind was on fire. I was not going to let him, or anyone else have power over me. I realize how important it is to be active and to advocate democracy for people of color.

October 24th, I cast my vote. The last few days, I've prayed and burned sage so much in hopes our ancestors and the most high hear our cry. It's November 7th, I need somebody to pinch me. It's official, Biden/Harris.

Lisa Daughtrey is a Washington, DC- based writer, motivational and public speaker, mental health advocate, activist, and a collaborating writer of Project Semicolon: Your Story Isn't Over by Amy Bleul. Her email is phoenixrllc4@gmail.com and you can follow her on Instagram, @one_phoenixrising

A LETTER TO DONALD TRUMP
BY LOLITA MAEWEATHERS

Dear Donny,

I understand you are not feeling too well. I know that you just lost your re-election bid and that as of January 20, 2021, you will no longer be President of the United States. I hear you are taking it hard. So hard, in fact, that you are willing to subvert the will of the people and stay in office. I have seen the tweets that you posted stating that you won the states of Georgia and Pennsylvania. I have even read one tweet that stated you won the election. If only tweets were policy. If only you could bend the country to your reality. If only you were celebrating that victory – waving to the crowds, dancing at the balls, bragging about how you won the election "strongly".

Donny, it is just a dream. It is time to wake up and go to school. Apparently, you have a lot to learn. Joseph R. Biden, Jr. is the President-Elect. He won by 6 million popular votes and he won the electoral college by 306 votes. That means that under the law, he won the election. Admittedly, some states are still counting, and the electoral college has not convened. However, there is no mathematical possibility of you winning. It is not possible to equal and surpass those 6 million votes. The opera is over; the fat lady sang. All the news outlets; ABC, CBS, MSNBC, CNN and even FOX, have called the election for Mr. Biden. Leaders from around the world are calling to congratulate him.

What I find hard to believe is that you did not see this coming. You are like a man who comes home to find his wife, his kids and his dog have gone and still believes they are coming back. America turned against you. They voted you out. This time your "basket of deplorables" could not save you. The sexism, racism, xenophobia, and homophobia that lives in the American bowel could not save you. You uncovered a great divide in this country. It was always there, lurking beneath the surface of civility. It is the divide between people who think they are better than the "others."

Donny, you convinced a nation it was ok to openly hate. It is ok to hate the immigrants who come to this country illegally to seek asylum. It is ok to separate them from their children. It is ok to hate gay people. It is ok to deny them the right to marry. It is ok to hate Muslims. Keep them out of our country. They are here to kill us. It is ok to hate Black people. Why do they give the cops such a hard time? It is ok if a cop shoots them. They commit more crimes. It is ok to hate everyone that is different from me. Because that was your message, people stopped looking at the inequality of the have and have nots and started hoarding America for their group, their tribe, their race.

You even taught Americans to hate their neighbors in the middle of a pandemic. We were told by the CDC, the WHO and your own COVID Response Team to wear a mask, wash our hands and social distance. However, you were never going to wear a mask. A mask was a sign we were giving up our freedom. It did not matter that it might save lives, no one tells us what to do. You divided the red states from the blue states by belittling governors in blue states. It was easy for you to politicize a health crisis. Remember your verbal assault on the governor of Michigan? The same governor who became the target of a right-wing militia. Less than two weeks later you encouraged your fans to chant, "lock her up."

I am mystified by the fact that you did not see any pushback coming. Did you believe that the country loved you? The entire country? I heard some of your fans remark that you had bigger crowds than Mr. Biden. That does not mean all those people voted. Any yahoo can go to a free rally and scream and shout. What you needed to win was the ability to capture some voters in the middle. Maybe if you had been less temperamental; a little less entitled. Maybe if you had not broken so many laws. Maybe if you had not been impeached. Most of all Donny, maybe if you had shown some sympathy for the more than 260,000 people who died from COVID.

However, that is not the reality. The reality is that the election was held and you lost. The American people have voted. That is a fact; not a tweet.

Lolita Maeweathers is a Bronx, NY writer who is currently working on her first novel. Her blog will be launched in 2021. Her email is lolitamaeweathers@yahoo.com and you can follow her on Instagram @lolitamaeweathers.

"PAN DAMN IT AND UNNATURAL CAUSES!"
BY MELBA JOYCE BOYD

I hate this shutdown. I know it is for the best, but I am as stir crazy as my 3-year-old grandson, Maverick, who stares out the window and whines because he wants to escape the house. My daughter answers his complaint and dresses him in a jacket. He runs around in circles with delight, and insists that I go with them. The governor's mandate requires a 6 feet distancing rule, and when in public spaces, you must wear a mask. But, this is only when you encounter others.

Maverick climbs into his red wagon that my daughter and I take turns pulling. It is sunny outside, and as we exhale and exercise our legs, we speak to neighbors, who likewise emerge to salvage sanity, to reassure themselves that the world still exists beyond the television screen, and that despite the terror of knowing tRump (Trump) is still the president, perhaps we will survive his demented derriere.

Detroit is a city of neighborhoods. Downtown skyscrapers, the Cultural Center and spaces of and near Wayne State University are defined by tall buildings, intensifying the proximity of populations. But here, children are playing in their backyards, and bicyclers peddle down streets, as we saunter down the sidewalk. We turn a corner and see a father entertaining his children with a remote-controlled toy car, zipping swiftly along a quiet street. We wave, and the toy crosses the avenue, and stops next to the red wagon. "Hi car." I realize that viewing animated children films has led Maverick to believe that this toy car is a living thing, and it can actually hear his greeting.

We wave at the smiling father, and yell, "Thanks," as we continue walking through our historic neighborhood, known for its architecture and century-old Oak trees that shade our homes. Evidence of this longevity is reassuring, especially when I see a robin nesting in my backyard in anticipation of new life.

I left my phone at home because I am fatigued by the endless group texts, posturing as socializing. But when I return, I succumb to habit and retrieve messages. My close friend, Alex, sent a text. "Julius is gone."

My cousin, Dr. Julius Combs, was a physician, known for his commitment to health care for Black people. He had been ill for some time, and was with his wife, Alice, in Florida, but she doesn't answer the phone. I call cousin, Jennifer and her father, Charles, who is also a physician, to report the sad news, and to secure some semblance of comfort in their voices.

Jennifer observes that today is Uncle Theodore's birthday. My birthday is tomorrow, and I am relieved that Julius did not die on that date, which is a selfish thought. But when death dates and birth dates coincide, celebratory activities are undermined by these parallels; subversive reminders of inevitability. The inability to close distances between loved ones is bizarre. We are like ghosts, unable to touch flesh, trying to evoke spiritual connections with our voices.

II

Madness begets madness, which spreads, like a virus. A group protested in front of the home of Michigan Governor, Gretchen Whitmer, accusing her of infringing on their freedom. They show up with their hunting rifles. It is curious that the State Troopers are not disturbed by this armed mob. This activity inspires other realms of idiocy, when a woman complains to her boyfriend that she was "dissed" when she was refused entry into a store because she wasn't wearing a mask.

"Three family members have been charged in the killing of a security guard who told a customer at a Michigan Family Dollar store to wear a state-mandated face mask. Calvin Munerlyn, 43, died at a Flint hospital after he was shot in the head," said Michigan State Police Lt. David Kaiser. Ramonyea Travon Bishop, 23, Larry Edward Teague, 44, and Sharmel Lashe Teague, 45, were charged with first-degree premeditated murder, along with other charges," CNN reported.

"Dissed" is a hood misconception that is as ill as those who claim to experience it. So, figure this shit out, Sharmel, while you're in lockdown in a jail cell that's rampant with Coronavirus because of disrespectful overcrowding, where you will wear a mask and be socially distanced for 20 years to life. You killed a human being, who was a father, a husband, a brother, a worker doing his job to protect you. You instigated a senseless murder, an evil act that your loved ones committed because you "got dissed." Listen to the Staple Singers, my sista:

"If you don't respect yourself,

Ain't nobody gonna give a hoot.

Respect yourself."

Though she would probably deny it, Sharmel thinks like the Wolverine Militia. These rusty, white men plotted to kidnap and murder the governor for "dissing" their "freedom." Considering all the lives Julius saved, he could not treat this violent illness. But I think he would agree with me: Take all the guns away, put them on lockdown and see how swiftly the deadliest pandemic in America ends.

Melba Joyce Boyd is an award-winning writer and editor of 14 books, 9 of which are poetry. She is a Distinguished University Professor of African American Studies at Wayne State University in Detroit. She can be reached at melbajoyceboyd@wayne.edu.

MY MOM AND COVID-19
BY MELINDA LIGHTBURN

When the pandemic hit in March, my mom was at a nursing home in Brooklyn. They had challenges prior to COVID-19. The lockdown only made it bleaker and frightening. As my mother's caregiver, I was alone and bracing for the worst. This virus blanketed NYC.

I couldn't turn on the television let alone watch Governor Cuomo's daily briefings, because I just couldn't listen to the daily death toll. The numbers were going up, people were dying from something we didn't understand. The media, I thought, kept saying again and again that the elderly were the bearers of this virus. My mother has dementia so when she last saw me, she thought I was going to return the next day. Repetition to a dementia patient is critical even though they're not aware of the day or the month let alone a pandemic. Playing out our last visit over and over in my head made me helpless and anxious. This lockdown was real and there wasn't anything I could do to assure her I would be back to see her. As the days passed, I kept waiting for word on how she was doing. I kept asking myself what I could do to help her.

Everything and everyone were at a standstill. I didn't want to be distracted even though my heart was pounding each day and my anxiety started again. I needed to be in the moment. When my phone did ring, and friends were calling to tell me of those who died from the virus, I hit the mute button and joined back in when I thought the conversation took a different topic. Not answering would seem like the easiest thing to do but where would I be during the shelter in place each time that they called. Then a friend whose mother was a few doors down from my mother's room called tearfully telling me that her mother died. Not from COVID-19 but that she stopped eating. I was speechless and couldn't move. That night I sat in silence and in the dark wondering would we ever get on the other side of this pandemic. I just wanted the days and hours to go by as quickly as they could so as to see how this story will end.

I decided to walk and went to the nearest park. As afraid as I was to go out, I had to and began to walk each day to pass the time. I kept thinking will we ever get through this? Will I ever see my mom again? When I did get that call from the nursing home, it was to tell me that my mom contracted the virus and that they would be sending her to the nearest hospital for treatment. My heart dropped and I couldn't think straight. She got pneumonia and needed oxygen to help her breathe. I called her doctors every day to check in on her and continuously thanked them for all that they were doing in this crisis. Knowing that she was probably scared and not knowing where she was, made me ask the hospital if they could play her music. They assured me that they would try, but because I knew they were dealing with a crisis, I decided to drop off a CD player with her favorite songs and leave instructions to play it for her so that it was familiar to her.

After spending two months in the hospital, she finally was released back to the nursing home after testing negative. With the CDC restrictions lifted a little, we are allowed to visit for 30 minutes as long as we have a negative COVID-19 test result. At 90 years old, she's coming along slowly. Looking back at those days a few months ago, I think that if there's a silver lining to her having dementia, it's that she doesn't remember what happened or that we're still battling COVID-19.

Melinda Lightburn is from Brooklyn, New York. Her email is Melindalightburn@gmail.com and her Instagram is @mrlightburn.

THE FREEDOM TO BE ME
BY MICHELE JONES

My anxiety is at an all-time high. I am so conflicted about this election and whether I should vote. Voting has never done anything for me and my people, so why should I vote? I have been questioning myself about this for these last few days leading up to the election. I'm torn because I know my ancestors died so I can live free. Free? Why don't I feel free? Free to be me, but not really me. Free to be the me they want me to be. I struggle with that thought often, and even more now. Watching these past four years unfold has been unbearable. Here we are in the middle of a global pandemic; the world is in chaos, and we have the worst president in history. It now falls in the lap of the people to get this raging lunatic the fuck out of office! My anger is temporary because I refuse to allow anger to consume me. Instead, I continue to focus on the me I want me to be. I will vote because it's my right, a right I choose to express. The lesser of two evils they say, but evil is evil right? So, who really wins? I'm conflicted yet determined.

After the Election

I voted! Now what? What changes for me? What changes for the country? The only thing I feel now is a huge knot in my chest. So now we wait, we wait to see who is next to run this country. I tend to try to look at things from a positive perspective, to always see the good in every situation. So, controlling those negative thoughts during this time has been a challenge. As we wait for the election results, I have decided to disconnect myself from all things election. I didn't have much luck in trying to dodge that giant bullet. As I found myself getting pulled back into the madness we called The 2020 Election. I started getting excited and realizing that at the end of all of this madness we could possibly have a Black Woman as the first Vice President of the United States of America. Then I thought, what does that mean for myself and my family? What is going to change except we were able to vote Trump out of office. The excitement only lasted for a moment. The anxiety I had in the previous months leading up to the election was back. No matter who wins I cannot ignore the killings of my Black sons, brothers, uncles, and fathers. I cannot ignore the killings of my daughters, sisters, mothers, and aunts. I will still be living in a country where I don't feel free. I watched as the results rolled in from state to state. It started to look like the lesser of two evils was going to win. The only thing I could think of is yes! Trump is out! It took some time for a winner to be declared, but finally the votes were in and Trump must go! I remembered back when Obama won for the first time, my emotions were uncontrollable, I really felt like a change had finally come. Today I'm not so sure.

Michele Jones is a NYC native, currently residing in NJ. She is a Customer Care Agent for USPS and hosts a podcast called Conversations with my Cuz. Her email address is michelejones40@gmail.com and you can follow her on Instagram, @michele_with1_ell

"MAKE ME WANNA HOLLER" JOURNAL
BY OMINIRA (CHIQUITA CAMILLE)

45 has insulted every race, gender, creed, including his own, expressed blatant racism nationwide and received threats of impeachment within the first three months of presidency with a downward slope from there.

I feel like I have experienced *The Matrix* these past four years. Many wondered is this the new norm of the type of leadership in the USA or is this an out-of-body experience taking place in a different dimension. Frequent conversations and posts included such phrases as, "your president" or "number 45" But STILL, the number of votes were close and still it took days to figure out who would become number 46. Similar to The Matrix, we had to select the blue pill or the red pill, the Democrat or the Republican, all the while contemplating what do each of us want as our reality and some of us still do not know what is real and what is fallacy. Finally, the results were revealed, the blue pill prevailed.

Does this mean that our votes actually counted...
But counted for what?!

Biden's Camp, I need a little more than, 'We Are Not Trump' to make me feel confident about what you are going to do for my people. Ice Cube had a great idea, a "Contract for Black America." I felt he was on to something, a written document to lead a pertinent conversation about the needs and expectations of people of African descent living in America. We do not have financial power, but we have voting power. So, before I darken the circle on the ballot, what are you going to do for my darkened race of people? If you cannot commit, neither can we...but what happened?! Where is the contract? Did it get hot? Did the Ice Cube melt? Here I am, once again, contemplating what is going to be our reality in these upcoming years. Number 46, if it is not a goal of yours to give true reparations to people of African descent, I cannot consider this a victory in these United States.

Ominira (Chiquita Camille), an actor, dancer and author of the award-winning children book, JUST BECAUSE, *is a Chicago native now based in Brooklyn, New York. Her email is chiquita@chiquitacamille.com and you can follow her on IG/FB @ChiquitaCamille*

COLLATERAL DAMAGE
BY PAULINE DENISE

Journal Entry – May 13, 2020

My baby brother is dead. Taken out by a sneeze…perhaps a cough. My mother no longer waits for the other shoe to drop. He's gone, she said. Her voice was laden with resignation.

His death horrifies me. So sudden. He will go from the hospital to the crematorium and then to a metal container. No service. Nothing.

So, I sit here, isolated, in my rage.

My rage at the dumb white bitch he lived with who lied about how sick he was. My rage at his gangster machismo that made him believe he could "ride it out." Am I wrong to think a "sister" would have made his ass go to the hospital sooner—even if it pissed him off?

My rage at his children for their indifference. (I can't say I blame them, though.) He was a daddy-less boy who became a fucked-up father. But was he irredeemable?

My rage at all the men who passed through my brother's life and did nothing for him (or any of us, for that matter).

My rage at my mother for beating him down…for not living up to her hopes and dreams. She said she doesn't live in regret. I think it's too painful for her to face.

I remember he was a cute, happy baby. He had that sweet baby smell. Pink-ish, small and scaly like a salamander. He grabbed my lips in his tack sharp nails when I puckered up to kiss him. (He never did like anyone up in his face.) Did he really make her fear calling an ambulance? This makes me crazy angry…and sad.

He's now a memory…reduced by the world, to a sad statistic; T-Rump's collateral damage. Another black man destined to die young.

But what do I do with all this rage?

Pauline DeNise is a freelance writer in the New York City area who spends her days masquerading as a public employee. Her email is pddaniels28@gmail.com.

FLIGHT OF THE SOLO TRAVELER
BY QURELL-AMANI WRIGHT

2016.

Me: What is our Plan B if Donald Trump wins?

Him: He's not going to win. You always think the worst.

It was at that moment I knew, sooner or later I would be alone, that Plan B would be Plan Solo.

So, I renewed my passport and quietly began to search for a new home country.

The obvious choice – Canada

November.

He wins. My "I told you so" comes in the form of brushing up my resume, adding a Canadian alert to my Indeed profile and registering for the CELPIP English language test. Although I score sufficiently, Express Entry is a no-go. Age of the applicant is heavily weighted. Here is where the realization hits that migration to Canada is not intended for Gen Xers. The generation on the cusp of retirement and bad knees. The generation one diagnosis away from taking more from the healthcare system than contributing to it. Maybe it's a blessing in disguise – it's too cold up there anyway.

3 years later, minus 1 boyfriend – Plan Solo.

In the midst of stocking up bottled water and canned goods (because we all know Trump is going to piss off both our allies and our enemies and we'll be lucky to find a decent apple when this is all over), I venture to South Africa for a much-needed vacation.

South Africa – Beautiful Black people to the left of me...Beautiful Black people to the right of me. This...Is...It. It feels like the umbilical cord has been reattached to the mother. And it doesn't hurt that the locals constantly speak to me in one of the several native languages; that is until they notice my "deer in headlights" look in response.

Me: It's pretty cool that you thought I was African.

Random woman in the store: You ARE African.

Why yes, yes I am.

Research, research and more research brings me to the tiny country of The Gambia; The Smiling Coast. The internet streets say one can rent a 4-bedroom house, correction, 4-bedroom **mansion**, for less than $500.00 per month. South Africa was beautiful but The Gambia may be a more economical way of moving to the continent.

Me: The Gambia? Ya think?

Myself: Hey, why not? Let's check it out.

I: Well, alright! Let's do it! But why not stop off in Mexico first and celebrate our birthday?

All: Sounds like a plan! Wait, what's that Mr. Cuomo? A novel virus you say? We have to stay inside, you say? Ok, it's all good. This will be over in a few months. We'll celebrate our birthday and head to the motherland.

Flights and lodging booked. Now we wait. And we stress.

The sounds of ambulances pierce the otherwise eerie quiet all times of the day and night. Hours run into days, and days run into weeks. The banging of pots and pans and the cheers of the neighbors leaning from windows and standing on fire escapes marks the 7pm essential worker shift change. Every day another prayer request:

"You remember so-and so? She came down with The COVID."

"Brother so-and-so's mother is on a ventilator."

A trip to the grocery store changes everything.

Me: Where's Manuel today?

Cashier: He passed away last week…it was COVID.

I hear his voice all night – "Thank you Mami," when I'd drop my change in his tip jar.

"Thank you Mami."

"Thank you Mami."

"Thank you Mami."

And Breonna Taylor

And George Floyd

And Elijah McClain

A few months later we flatten the curve. WE flattened the curve. Other states, at the thought of wearing masks, are acting like small children who are told they can't have that strategically placed candy at the check-out counter. And the world is noticing. The Gambia closes its borders.

Cue major panic and depression, the need to get out of dodge...NOW. Expressing my anxieties brings out the typical:

"Why are you running away?"

"It's bad everywhere."

"It doesn't make sense to leave right now."

"Be careful."

Be careful. That's a rather odd statement from those living in a country where Black people are hunted like animals; a country plagued by a virus too many don't take seriously.

Me: Mexico is still open.

Myself: Let's get the hell out of here.

I: Don't tell anyone, let's just go.

So here I sit, in Mexico, with no idea what's next.

Feeling free yet isolated. Happy yet melancholy.

They think I'm crazy for leaving.

But I'm safe...

Safe.

And that's the most important thing.

Qurell-Amani is a writer, actress, producer and director based out of the NYC area. She is the writer of the one-woman show Panther Woman *and can be reached at: producer@pantherwomantheplay.com.*

UNTITLED
BY REGAN KELSO-SPELLS
November 23, 2020

It's 4:30 pm. Feels late. Daylight savings time has concealed all evidence of a sunny California day. Thirty scrawny minutes stand between me and punching the time clock. Mentally, I checked out twenty minutes ago. I should clock out now, but this chair cradles me, and my desk supports the weight of my emotionally drained body while collecting my puddle of tears, keeping them from falling on the floor.

I dedicated my workday to looking for emergency homeless shelters for an unemployed, single mother with two kids who could not afford another night in a motel. I made phone calls to all of the homeless shelters in our area. Most shelters were either waitlisted or closed due to the Coronavirus pandemic. My final call of the day was to inform the single mother that the closest shelter still open was an hour away. At the beginning of this pandemic, furloughs smoldered under "Shelter-in-place" orders and ominous shutdowns. Before global protests sparked for racial justice and the smoke of California wildfires strangled us under N-95 masks, before my job was labeled "Essential," working at a doctor's office was enjoyable.

I will never forget the day when a peacock appeared outside of our office window. Like eye-catching graffiti, the peacock was colorful and not supposed to be against the brick wall. Intrigued by its mid-morning cameo appearance, my coworkers and I ran outside to look for clues about the peacock's presence, only to discover it had disappeared. For the next ten minutes, we talked about the "Orange Is the New Black" episode when Piper, the newest inmate at a Women's prison, thought she saw an uncaged chicken running around the prison yard. We joked that the peacock, like the chicken, was a figment of our imagination, helping us to cope with the flood of phone calls from patients reporting symptoms of the virus. We researched the symbolism of peacocks and found several meanings. That was about two hundred and forty-eight days ago.

A lot of things have changed in eight months.

A third of our office staff have been furloughed. Out of the few employees left, some people are out sick or on 14-day quarantine precautions due to virus exposure. The rest of us are thankful to have a job but work under the anxieties of possible exposure and whether our kids logged into school. I keep reminding myself that the grass is always greener on the other side, but lately, it seems like dog shit sprawled across both sides of the lawn.

Today, I called the local three-digit resource hotline designed to connect people to resources within their local communities. I hoped that the resource specialist would be a liaison between myself and the mom, but nope. An unfriendly specialist answered and tried to rush me off the phone. In her defense, I heard a crying toddler in the background, a reminder that everyone is stretched thin. The communication between the specialist and I was cloudy.

We attempted to give each other grace by softening the impatience in our dull voices. Honestly, I was less upset with the inflection of her voice and more appalled by the lack of information she had to give. The closest shelter is 39 miles away, too far for someone with inadequate transportation. Also, no gas or motel vouchers were made available.

My mind funneled with swirling bouts of confusion. I do not understand why our city has a lack of available resources during a pandemic. Was our city not given federal funds from the Cares Act? I cannot fathom how many times this specialist has had to navigate people to dead-end resources. The final recommendation was to encourage the mother to apply for cash aid from the county to get help with housing. This option could take weeks. A storm of tears replaced my whirling thoughts. I could hear the resource specialist crying too.

The office feels lonely. Everyone has gone home for the day. I do not mind being alone so that I can process my thoughts through journaling. Writing is my way to check-in. I am thankful to have rediscovered my love of writing this year, during the quarantine.

It is already time to clock out, but I feel guilty. I will go home thinking about this mom all night. She was so grateful and humble for my efforts. I am slightly relieved to learn that the mom has enough gas to drive 39 miles. If not, she will split the rest of her money between food and gas. In the morning, I will resume a resource search.

I read that peacock sightings serve as a beacon of endurance and courage during dark times. Tonight, I am praying this mom gets shelter, food, and any small symbol of hope.

Regan Kelso-Spells proudly represents her Southern California, Inland Empire roots where she works as a Community Health Worker. You can email her at Regans.kelso@gmail.com or follow her on Instagram @itspellsregan

CHALLENGING, BEAUTIFUL, BREATHTAKING
BY REGINA DAVIS

Saturday. 10.24.20. I got up at an ungodly hour for me on a Saturday and went to meet my best friend for a hike. The drive was 45 minutes outside Newark. Just as I saw her car, we were approaching a red light in front of us and the beginnings of a Trump rally to our left. We met eyes and it wasn't the unspoken language of best friends that communicated both disbelief, confusion and a hint of fear but also a slight bit of humor. It was more the unspoken language of kinfolk. Kinfolk who questions how people, educated people, God-fearing people, people with children could champion this individual whose behavior defies all logic and reason.

The hike was good. At times it was challenging, beautiful and breathtaking. I felt like it was never going to end but, in the end, the 12k+ steps by 12pm felt rewarding. In some ways, the hike represents 2020 so far- "challenging, beautiful and breathtaking". I just pray that in the end I can say it- "felt rewarding."

I had all but forgotten about the Trump rally until it was there, now on my right, now a full-on rally complete with police, an overwhelming crowd of people and passersby honking. Were they honking because they loved Jesus? Were they in agreement with the shenanigans or signaling their protest to this sign of support for this divisive leader? I don't know but I felt safe once I was past it all. Until I began thinking, did I really have to drive 45 minutes away to see this display of what I would call ignorance? Was this in my own backyard? Were there skinfolk that I, all but assume, are against this nightmare of an administration? I don't know. But what I know is before going home I had a stop to make. I had brought my mail-in ballot with me. I had not yet mailed it because I feared it wouldn't be counted. I struggled with the uncomfortable thoughts of actually voting in person. Not just around other people but inside of a structure that wasn't my home. I thought putting it in the dropbox would be a safer decision but ultimately knew, however it got there, it needed to be done. I slid that ballot into the mailbox and prayed it would make a difference.

Tuesday. 10.26.20. Today I shed tears, not because my vote made a difference, I don't know that yet, but because it was received. In all the years that I have voted I never really questioned my vote being received, but looking at that screen showing the life cycle of my mail in ballot made me shed a tear. Then instantly I was gripped with fear. I hadn't asked the newest voter, my 18-year-old nephew, if he had even registered to vote or for that matter if his older brother had voted. I sent out two texts to ensure that they understood this was their right and they needed to exercise it, in spite of, heck because of the year we are having. Both assured me they were prepared and had voted, respectively. All we could do now is wait and pray that everyone else showed up.

Tuesday. 11.3.2020. We have a new president. This should be a relief. I don't feel relieved. January 20th, 2021, inauguration day when Trump is officially no longer the President of the United States, I will begin to feel relieved. There will still be angst over whether the most important of promises will be kept. The words "I'll Have Yours" in reference to having the back of the African American community who supported, perhaps carried this campaign on their backs, were felt deep. A betrayal of that would be devastating especially with a running mate that represents, at face value, that community.

President Obama gave hope for a world I never dreamt of, only to be faced with the reality of a world 8 years later, that was worse than some nightmares. We don't need to get back to normalcy; we need to get to a place where hope materializes into our reality.

Regina Davis is a North Jersey-based full-time Business Systems Analyst, part-time Virtual Assistant and, writer. Her email is: iwrite424@gmail.com and you can follow her on Instagram @dreamwriter424

COVID CHRONICLES
BY R. UMMI MODESTE

3/31/2020 6:45am

As an unapologetic believer in the Most High, I think it's fair for me to address my fellow believers who object to the closing of houses of worship due to the spread of the coronavirus. People, the building is not the church, the synagogue, the masjid or the temple; WE ARE. Sure we love our edifices, but we can worship, take care of each other and pray without going into a building. God created science and medicine, and the leaders of those communities tell us that it's unwise and unhealthy for us to touch or congregate, so stop it! Stay home, wash your hands and worship. Stay home, wash your hands and praise! Stay home, wash your hands and pray!

There are plenty of online worship opportunities; take advantage of them. If you know someone who doesn't have access to the internet, stay home, call them on the phone and pray with them! We BELIEVERS have to be the leaders in stemming the tide of fear and in flattening the curve!

03/31/2020 3:30pm

Three things I've learned during the Coronavirus crisis:

1. How to assemble a small piece of furniture following directions that have no words on them

2. How to get spilled candle wax off of a wood surface (with a blow dryer and a wet rag; thanks, YouTube!)

3. Even during a crisis, some men will try to mack a woman in the street, a woman in baggy sweats, a hoodie and a mask, who is minding her own business, just trying to get to Family Dollar for some toilet paper and Clorox wipes.

04/01/2020 6:30am

I was gonna complain about my wonky Wi-Fi, but then I remembered that I am grateful to have internet capability, a safe, clean apartment in which to have that wonky Wi-Fi, all the food and supplies I need and resources to obtain more; healthy family members, access to health care if I need it and, thankfully, no current need for it. So I told myself to shut up and go read a book.

R. Ummi Modeste is a Brooklyn-born-and-raised educator, college and career advisor, writer, mother and Grammie, and the author of Because I Knew, *a collection of poetry. You can reach her at musecitypress@gmail.com and follow her on Instagram @BecauseIKnew.*

"VOTER REGISTRATION DÉJÀ VU" BY SAFIYA E. BANDELE

"Dump Trump 2020" was on my mind when I volunteered to do voter registration in Bedford-Stuyvesant, but at the appointed time I stayed home. I rationalized that my few hours of service weren't really needed, that there would probably be a surfeit of volunteers, and that some folks would be maskless and social-distancing averse.

My voter registration effort began and ended fifty-two years earlier - April 4, 1968 - in rural North Carolina near the city where I was a junior at a Historically Black College. My German- Jewish philosophy professor had requested student volunteers to conduct door-to-door voter registration. We left campus in a two-car caravan for the 15-minute ride, parked, exited and gathered around Professor Bohn for last-minute instructions. He was cheerful as he led the six of us to the unpaved entrance of what looked like a third world settlement. Unsettling because the community looked "foreign" though located not far from our beautiful, leafy, stately historic college buildings. Unsettling, too, was the realization that in comparison, my segregated childhood community in a small southern Black town was loving, self-sufficient and more alive than these sad-looking houses. Unsettling, too, was the fact that the white professor was leading the voter registration project and not any of the black professors at our Historically Black College.

We spread out in pairs. My partner Chet and I approached the first of the identical, small, gray houses separated by a narrow walkway. I took the lead and climbed the three wooden steps leading to the small porch. Before I could knock, a middle-aged Black woman appeared on the other side of the screen door. The house was quiet behind her.

"Good evening Ma'am. How are you?" I asked respectfully, following the script Prof. Bohn had given us. Assuming her non-response was an invitation, I continued: "My name is Raine and this is my classmate Chet. We're doing voter registration and if you're not registered, we would be pleased to assist you." I lifted my clipboard as proof. Still encouraged by her non-response, I went on, "This presidential election is important and we hope Black people will register to vote. Are you registered, Ma'am?"

"No we not." She replied softly, looking over my shoulder at Chet standing at the bottom of the steps.

"Would you like to?" I begged.

Her soft but definite, "No, not today," precluded further questions.

"Yes, ma'am. Well, thank you for talking to us."

I turned in defeat and went down the steps to join Chet for the walk to the next house.

Just as we were about to critique our unsuccessful effort, we heard a loud "No!" The professor was screaming: "They killed him! The stupid idiots killed him!" Years later I wondered why he called the killer(s) "stupid idiots" and not the more obvious label, "murderous racists." The six of us gathered around him. Our faces asked the question and he replied shakily "Dr. Martin Luther King, Jr. - they shot Martin Luther King, Jr.!" We were speechless; our new-found Black-is-Beautiful afros and Black Power attitudes arrested on the spot. We stumbled back to the cars, and drove back to campus in silence. There we were met by groups of students on the quads and walkways - shock and disbelief quickly turned to anger. The semester, scheduled to end the following month, was a washout as some of us concluded that pursuing an academic degree was, well, useless. Voter registration efforts were abandoned. ..

My 1968 nascent radicalism was unbothered by my secret admiration for this white German- Jewish male teacher. I had often wondered about his route - which he never discussed - from Germany to small-town North Carolina. Not even on the occasion when he invited several students to his house for dinner. A first for me! Dinner with a white family! Professor Bohn's gracious wife and two small boys presented the almost perfect blond tableau.

I subsequently lost interest in philosophy. In my ignorance, I equated his teachings with a way of life for whites who could afford the luxury of contemplating existentialism. A *Pox* on Sartre.

A few months later, Republican Richard Nixon received 301 Electoral votes; Democrat Hubert Humphrey 191 and Southern Democrat George Wallace 46 votes.

Rabid Dixiecrat George Wallace: The progenitor of Donald Trump.

Safiya E. Bandele is a Brooklyn, New York based educator, public speaker and Ida B. Wells activist/performer. Her email is safiya.bandele@gmail.com.

2020 SHOWED OUT
BY SHERRING DARTIGUENAVE

Silly me. I thought I was really doing something by avoiding the news on Election Day. The results wouldn't be called that night, but I preferred to protect and maintain my sanity. I didn't want to see *that man* in the lead. I didn't want to see the numbers tick up, up, and up. Self-care, I convinced myself, and watched DVR'd shows to avoid breaking news cutting into my regularly scheduled programming.

My BFF aunt called me from Boston, TV volume blasting. Election updates on her end drowned out her voice over the line.

"Can you turn down the volume?" I pleaded.

"I need to know what's goin' on," she whined in her thick Haitian accent. Over thirty years in the U.S. and that sucker wasn't budging. She droned on, telling me about another aunt taking my 98-year-old grandfather to vote early that morning.

"I don't want to talk about politics."

She disregarded my wishes. We had switched roles. I was attempting to be zen-like: face mask, hot shower, sweet-scented body butter, and cozy pajamas. She was the hot mess, her buzzing energy palpable through the phone. I urged her to take a shower and drink tea. She refused to peel away from the TV. I told her I had to go.

2020 showed out. It barely gave us one good month, before it sucker-punched us with Kobe's death in a helicopter crash. Still catching our collective breath, the world shut down due to a boogie monster airborne disease. Held hostage at office-school-gym-home, (white) people were forced to pay attention to Black men and women's recorded murders. Things bubbled over. Too paranoid to leave my apartment to check mail and throw out trash on a daily basis, I now felt compelled to slap on a mask, make a Black Lives Matter sign, and attend one of the many daily protests that erupted countrywide—worldwide. Just one. The country was literally on fire with West coast wildfires, yet talking heads on cable news argued that everything was fine.

On Election Day 2016, I would've bet money I'd be toasting to America's first woman president. I asked a friend to meet me at Vodou on the corner of Nostrand and Halsey. The Bed-Stuy bar was a short walk for us both. I wanted to share the historic moment with someone. Eight years prior, I had celebrated Obama's victory with two cousins at a Boston bar. I imagined starting conversations with: "Remember how we celebrated when Hillary got elected?" Instead, we giggle and sigh. My friend's stomach began cramping when it became evident that Clinton wouldn't win. We left the bar to watch the dismal results at home. Alone.

This year, I planned to early vote to avoid the Election Day rush. Nope. News reports chronicled hours-long waits at various locations. Long waiting lines in the midst of COVID-19? Did I make it this far to be taken down voting in an election that might leave me with stomach cramps and COVID? I still planned to vote, but I wasn't excited. Not like when I cast my ballot for Obama, Clinton, or Sanders (in this primary). Wednesday night's gloomy weather matched my mood en route to the polls. I cheered up in the quick-moving line. I pocketed my "I Voted Early" sticker and "Vote NYC" pen and walked to the bus stop.

The Saturday after the election, I was chatting with my cousin during a quick break from the fourth annual Well-Read Black Girl Festival. Damn pandemic. Festival was virtual. I was stuck on my couch, glued to my laptop screen. In previous years, I attended in person. As I paced in my bedroom in the front of my Brownstone building, I heard cars honking and cheering outside. I thought it was a drive-by birthday party, as I had seen on the news and social media. The ruckus continued when I moved to my living room in the back. I thought the caravan had wrapped the corner.

We hung up about thirty minutes later. I checked the text and WhatsApp messages that had been pinging during our conversation. I'm in more group texts than I care to count. Nonsensical things like cotton candy-flavored grapes and binge-worthy TV shows are discussed. The last message received and the first one I read said: "And now the court battle conspiracy to stay president will begin." Huh? I clicked over to the WhatsApp chain reserved for sharing pictures and videos of my cousin and his wife's almost one-year-old daughter. A 2:53-minute video. His mother and others were clinking champagne glasses and woo-hooing like college students at a homecoming game. "Hallelujah!", "Thank you, Jesus!" and other chanting in Creole and English erupted as they danced in front of a large screen TV.

Holy shit! Kamala Harris, a Black Woman Vice President, is headed to the White House.

Sherring Dartiguenave is a Brooklyn-based blogger working on several writing projects. Follow her on @sher_ring and check out her musings on Just Sherring.com.

GLEANING ELECTION HISTORY
BY S. PEARL SHARP

I have to do it. This election day 2020 it's even more important to keep the tradition alive. So, I put on ground-to-head COVID protective gear: closed-toe shoes, socks, long pants, long sleeves, neck scarf, beret fully covering my hair, and finally a lined face mask topped with a plastic face shield. On the way to my voting site, just six blocks away, I'm walking and singing out loud the names of those who sacrificed and suffered so I can take this easy saunter to a school gym turned voting center. There's no stress at my voting site. Tradition fulfilled.

Back home, I turn off the TV and radio to let media's non-stop talkers have their all-night revel. I'm determined to maintain a personal peace. It's going well until the next morning when the ancestors, tricky folks that they can be, intercept. I'm online looking for one thing and they drop the Colfax Massacre right onto my screen. I had not met this piece of our history before.

April, 1873. This is back when the political landscape was reversed. The Republican party was favored by Blacks back then because of its role in the abolition of slavery. Abraham Lincoln and Frederick Douglas were Republicans.A hotly contested governor's race the previous fall was narrowly wonby the Republicans, but the Democrats' protest against the results, simmered right through the winter and exploded on Easter Sunday in Colfax, Louisiana. When it was over, one-hundred-fifty Blacks had been murdered.

Now my talkin' box is showing supporters of "electoral Trump" (as I've chosen to call him) taking to the streets, victorious, as his initial surge in Georgia is announced. Then I feel their attitude shift as that count, generated by in person voting, begins to recede and mail-in ballots supporting Biden increase. Among the rallying are Americans who thought it was alright to block a Biden election bus during the campaign, brandishing weapons and threatening harm. Among the watchers are politicians and election officials who used their power to make it as hard as possible for certain groups to cast their votes.

Between the election reports I return to Colfax, to 1873, trying to absorb more of the story from the few websites that include it. Apparently Black state militia and volunteers were asked to help protect the Colfax courthouse and its white officials. But three hundred armed whites formed their own militia and attacked them. Then the murders spread beyond the courthouse. And, much like our circumstances today, no one was ever held responsible for this massacre.

As the vote count tension builds in Pennsylvania, Arizona and Georgia. I'm focusing on the faces on the screen, reading the banners, noting the weapons, the seething, the resolute anger and yes, hatred emanating from the president's "base" which he has empowered to unleash and act on their true feelings. This moment does not feel good. Or safe. Or possible to fix.

I see strong flashes of Colfax in the genes of these protestors. As someone who wants to learn and benefit from my history, I find myself suddenly praying that the tribes of rifle carrying militants will not remember or benefit from their history right now or over the coming months.

S. PEARL SHARP creates cultural art for eye, ear and heart as poet, playwright, filmmaker, essayist and artivist with a mission to illuminate and instigate. Her short fiction is in Uncertain Rituals. *Her essays/commentaries have been heard on* NPR *and are collected in* The Evening News. *www.spearlsharp.com*

ELECTION EVE
BY TARA D. SMITH

11/2/2020

The skies are blue.

Listening to talk radio, Thom Hartman and Heather B Live on SiriusXM. The discussions center on caravans of trucks blocking a Biden campaign bus on a highway in Texas this weekend. People seem shocked (but this is Texas...heavy sigh). Tensions are certainly high.

On my way to deliver an iPad to my parents so that we can have contact with them from afar. COVID-19 is still running rampant across the nation. I haven't seen them in almost a year. I'm already mentally ready for how hard it will be to train an 82-year-old how to use technology. I have to do what I must, because I'm not sure what these election results will mean for the reaction in the streets. I need to be able to see my people. (Daddy wanted no parts of learning how to use the iPad...btw.)

Back at home, I turn the television on MSNBC. Tensions still high; the anticipation of trouble is on the horizon. I reflect on the Bible verse that describes how the world mourns Babylon's fall in Revelation 18:9-20. I know that no man knows the hour Jesus will return, but could this be it? Feels like the end times. We are so ill-prepared.

I voted on the first day of early voting. I stood in line for four hours to ensure my vote would count. This time, will it?

11/3/2020 – ELECTION DAY

Wow. Another beautiful day out.

I worked today. Tried to tune out politics on television as in previous days. Listened to Karen Hunter, Clay Cane and Lurie Favors on SiriusXM with election coverage into the night. Results began pouring in for senate races. Mitch "Turtle Man" McConnell kept his seat, and so did Ms. Lindsey Graham. President Trump got on the mic and lied to his supporters that he won. The votes are still being counted for the presidency. Even if Biden wins, with a Republican majority in the Senate, we can expect more gridlock. With all that was on the ballot, more of the same or worse.

The faith of the saints will have to get me through.

At least my grandbaby is doing well. Gotta think about the kind of world she will grow up in. The future just doesn't look as bright as it once did. Racism is the disease that continues to pervade society, on a global scale. What do you do? Where do you go?

11/4/2020 – THE DAY AFTER

Yet, another beautiful day outside. Sipping on my coffee and eating breakfast, thinking.

It's 10:42 AM and election results aren't back yet for the president; news is not what I've wanted to hear. Election results so far show that America has indeed voted for racism. I'm disappointed in the narrative, post-election. Trying not to digress.

These deceptive ass wolves are out here in these COVID streets, saying they voted one way and actually voted the other.
The media is horrible.

I'm considering moving. I actually want to leave the country.
Where would I go?

11/5/2020 – THE DAY AFTER THE DAY AFTER

The count continues...

11/6/2020 – THE DAY AFTER THAT

And it continues...

Joe gave a speech tonight which put my heart at ease. I think I'll get some rest. I believe it will happen soon. Peace is on the horizon.

11/7/2020 – GOD SHOWED UP

11:03 AM - My God, my God!

They did it!! They won the election.

Joe Biden will be sworn in as the oldest President of the United States and Kamala Harris will be sworn in as the first woman
Vice President, and she's Black/South Asian and my Soror.

I glanced at the television as I passed and saw the projection. I wasn't relieved until I saw the notifications coming through confirming everything, filling my heart with gratefulness.

Today is indeed a BEAUTIFUL day!

At night, we got to witness the first woman VP give a speech that was amazing. I can now envision a world where my great-niece (Skylar) or granddaughter (Kya) can grow up to be president!

Tara D. Smith is an entrepreneur and freelance writer based in Houston, Texas. You can follow her on Instagram at @taradsmith_IG and contact her at tdsmith1908@gmail.

DEAR NOVA
BY TATIANA RICHARDSON-NARELL & ELIJAH NARELL

Dear Nova,

What kind of world are we bringing you into? This has been the question on my mind since me and your mother found out we created a life. Because your due date was in November 2020, your arrival was tied up with that year's election. I was hoping that by the time you learned the name Donald Trump, he'd be a disgraced, criminally-convicted former President. I didn't want to think about what would come next if he won, and how I would balance my two great responsibilities - keeping you safe and doing my part to fight back against the rise of fascism.

I wasn't a fan of Trump's opponent either. Before I knew you existed, I went to boo Joe Biden when he came to Oakland in early March because I saw him as an emblem of the failed Democratic leadership that led us to Trump, eight months later, with you set to be born any day, I watched anxiously as the election results rolled in, praying that Biden would pull it out. So much had happened between those two dates, and I had adjusted to new realities. Just one week after I found out your mother was pregnant, mass outbreaks of COVID-19 began. Since then, we've mourned so many deaths while waiting for you - those dying from the disease, those murdered by our racist police forces, and those killed in the wildfires raging across California. Again, I thought about bringing a child into a world being destabilized by climate change, where even in the midst of a deadly pandemic, police continue terrorizing Black communities, and humans are caged in overcrowded prisons with no way to protect themselves from infection. But I also saw reasons for hope - the strength of your mother as she battled through the rigors of pregnancy, the courage of activists facing down militarized police in the streets day after day, the kindness of people setting up mutual aid networks to step into the breach where the government was failing, and the promise of a younger generation that is ready to cast aside old, destructive ideas. Trump's election loss wasn't an end to our problems, but maybe it will create an opening for change. I'm sorry you are being born into the proverbial fire, but a beautiful movement is forming, and the world needs people like you to help save it. So after waiting what feels like an eternity for your birth, I will cherish the moment and then begin the essential and interconnected work of fatherhood and of transforming the world.

Love, your father

Dear Nova,

Finding out about you in March was my dream come true, but I didn't believe it was real until I saw your little body growing, and heard your heart beat so strong. You were the light in my life, providing the hope we all needed. As you will find out when you grow up, 2020 brought so much chaos to this country and the world. Your mom is pretty tough, but this had me scared, and your father worried about our future. President Trump had spent the last four years bringing all the country's ugliness to the surface, and then a global pandemic hit right when we found out about you. By November, there would be over one million dead worldwide. America likes to think it's the greatest, but we led the world in deaths because we foolishly thought we were invincible. During the summer, millions of people in the U.S. and worldwide protested police brutality, and were pepper sprayed, tear-gassed, and beaten down by police. Because you were growing inside me, I had to make the selfish decision to not let your father be out there. I needed to make sure our family was safe, and was scared something might happen to him, or he might bring back the virus and get us sick.

I feel like I spent the whole summer trying to keep you safe, barely going outside for months trying to not breathe in the smoke from the wildfires. There was one morning where we woke up and the whole sky was orange - it felt like the apocalypse. There have been small wins but it's still a struggle. Trump lost the election but refuses to concede. The movement to end racial injustice and police brutality is growing, but we have so far to go. But you, my little star, are done cooking and will be out in this world soon enough. You are the hope we need to keep fighting. I got through this year because you were a part of me, and I'll get through the rest of my life knowing you are here to make this world a better place.

Love, your mother

Elijah Narell is an Oakland-based EMT, writer, and owner of Hot Sauce for the People. He can be reached at enarell@gmail.com and you can follow him on Twitter, @peopleshotsauce.

Tatiana Richardson-Narell is an Oakland-based student in the progress of getting her Masters in Expressive Arts Therapy. She can be reached at nelsyr2@gmail.com or you can follow her on Instagram @peekaboo231.

2020: THIS MAKES NO SENSE
BY TONY THOMPSON

5.08.2020

I started this pandemic with the mindset of beating procrastination. I got up every morning and worked out. I made a budget. Stuck to a diet.

I read. And I did everything I said I was going to do to better myself. I lost 25 pounds. I decided to be happy. Then as the pandemic went on, I found myself slipping back into my old ways and habits. And in a week or two, things felt…difficult. I became depressed. Not sure if it's being stuck in the house due to the pandemic or the fact that it's giving me more time to think about my life and how it's nowhere near where I want it to be. Or could it be that this pandemic signals the end of the world? So much of what is happening is Biblical. I am angry and confused. I have made so many mistakes, wasted so much time and now it's all coming to an end. I have not yet begun to live. I have let so many opportunities go by. Combined with the murder of Amaud Aubrey, my emotions have me stuck. I have not been able to do anything. I'm just feeling overwhelmed with grief, stress, anger, disappointment, fear, and doubt. God, please help me.

5.27.2020

I made the mistake of watching the George Floyd video in its entirety. I have not been sleeping for days. I was up late the night it happened and saw the video on Instagram. I was traumatized. Literally traumatized. I was crying…shaking…furious! And like him, I could not breathe. I was still. I sat still. For days. Angry. Confused. Hurt. I stopped reading; gained back the 25 pounds I lost. Trying to find my way back. Trying to get the knee of oppression off my neck. They don't see us as human. They despise us. When they see us, what do they see?

Sometime in July…

By May, the pandemic had already taken its toll on my psyche. And at some point, we found out about Breonna Taylor. It's been weeks of protests, and I am numb. I couldn't tell you what has happened the past couple of months other than what people tell me. I don't watch the news. It only serves to take me deeper into depression. Most days I lay in bed not sleeping. Just an endless cycle of loud silence. I must break out of it. I did catch Jumaane Williams on Instagram saying, "I am not ok." I'm not…not sure if I ever will be again. I watched it over and over trying to gain strength from knowing I wasn't alone. That it was ok not to be ok.

There is so much hate floating around on the internet, it's painful. I can't believe that former co-workers, classmates, and castmates not only harbor these feelings, but are bold enough to display them online for the world to see. Before the pandemic, I had a Trump loving coworker tell me to look at it from his perspective. He was a 63-year-old White guy, and they are forgotten about. That they didn't count anymore since Obama. Wait, so because of a Black man who was intelligent and articulate, who put other Black people in leadership positions who were also intelligent and articulate, you felt like no one cared. That explains a lot. You people (pun intended) are so used to being in charge, of being in power, the moment someone Black shows we can do it too, you can't handle it. Obama was a man who tried his best for the country, not Black people. But because we were inspired, motivated, you got scared. Makes me wonder, what do you see when you see us?

8.20.2020

Looking at my last entry, it reminded me of some encounters I've had over the years. I'll never forget one night when I was working on the Upper Eastside. I worked late and when I came out it was pouring down raining. Dressed in a suit and tie, it took me almost an hour to get a cab. This was years ago, before Uber. Cab after cab went by. One stopped and told me that he wasn't going Uptown. I said neither am I, I'm trying to get to Penn Station to catch a train to Jersey. He drove off. I was pissed. Another one stopped, looked me up and down and said he was going to the garage in Queens and wouldn't let me in. Finally, one stopped. He, like the others, was Arab. I can't remember which country, but after I was securely in the car and heading to Penn station, I started going off about his Arab brothers. "I can't believe in this day and age a Black man can't get a cab in New York!!" In a very thick accent, he said "my friend, don't be mad at my fellow cab drivers. It's not their fault. In our countries, the Black man is, how you say – the devil." What?? WTF did you just say? He said, "Please let me explain." He said that where he comes from, and neighboring countries, all the tv shows, movies, and stories portray Black people as criminals and scoundrels. By the time they arrive here, that is their perception of us. Our blackness is equivalent to evil.

Since I'm not sleeping, I started watching tv. There's an NYPD Blue marathon every night. At one point I watched for a couple of weeks straight, and I became angrier every day. People who watch certain things on tv and in the media view us as these criminals, murderers, and, like the cab driver said, "the devil." I had this conversation with a friend about how we are portrayed in the media. He said who cares what people think about us? If people from the other side of the globe think that way about us, imagine what those in middle amerikkka think? We must care about our images. Otherwise, they will always fear us, they will always get the benefit of the doubt, and they will continue to have an excuse to see our Black skin as a weapon.

Tony Thompson is a New Jersey based actor, writer, and producer. His email is tonythompson06@gmail.com and you can follow him on Facebook at https://www.facebook.com/tony.thompson.562/.

HAPPY BIRTHDAY, HAPPY BIRTHDAY TO ME!!! *BY TRACY CARNESS*

November 28, 2020

9:59 pm

What a difference a year makes. Same time, last year I was riding five deep in a dilapidated Toyota Corolla, with a quartet of grumpy, sand-covered Millennials. Us 5 had spent the day traveling the winding and very dangerous roads of the Hana Highway in Maui and I am sure four of the five, were high (them, not me). I just can't seem to catch them when they are" partaking", but let's just say, they all went through our snacks quickly and they just could not stop laughing, even when we were terrified as the rickety car careened a bit too close to the edges of many cliffs. Some of the curves on the road were so sharp we had to pull over to gather our courage and breath. I should be upset that they put my life in danger, but I was not - it was a good day.

A year ago, the Hubs (the boy child) and I had traveled to Maui to spend time with his twin sister, Kuka (the girl child) and her boyfriend, Nature Boy.

365 days later, Kuka and Nature Boy are no more, and she is back in the City of Angels, now with Beautiful Boy. The Hubs has released his first album, Cassowary, and is constantly checking his Spotify numbers - he's at a million. ...and I am 54.

It's my birthday today and I have been gifted the following:

- 2 white ice trays

- 1 bolsa de Frida Kahlo

- 2 tablespoons of medicinal Lion's Mane mushroom powder (an apparent - but not so apparent - super food)

- 1 photo of a tricked out 64 Volkswagen Bug

- 1 $25.00 Amex gift card

Happy Birthday to me!

Last year I received

- 2 containers of freshly made Huli Huli chicken from a woman barbequing on the side of the road to Hana. Tried to tell her I was vegetarian and the Millennials are vegans, so she only gave us two containers instead of the 3 she first offered. The chicken was enjoyed by four of the five (them, not me).

- 1 box of tea - thank you Hubs

- 1 birthday letter - thank you Kuka

I am always thankful and don't expect anything, so this year's bounty was abundant.

The two ice trays were a gift from my brother-in-law. He likes ice. He did not like my old, malfunctioning ice trays - you put the water in and it ends up on the bottom of the freezer, creating ice sheets that do not fit neatly in cocktail glasses, even after you hammer them into shards because that's the only way you can remove them from the bottom of the freezer. He seems happier with his properly squared ice cubes. Thank you!

The bolsa de Frida Kahlo. Thanks Hubs. I will store this lovely gift with the Frida playing cards, Frida coasters, Frida key chain, Frida compact, Frida commemorative box, and small black-light Frida painting.

It's too cold for smoothies, but I will make a smoothie and I will put all 2 tablespoons of this dank mushroom powder into it, and I will drink it knowing that it is good for me. I will - but I just don't remember where I put the baggie of mushroom powder. Thank you Kuka.

When Optimus (a former) student called me and asked for my address, I thought he was going to send me a card. Our birthdays are in the same month. Instead, his mother drove him to my house and he and his sibling, Bumblebee (current student) put a very large photo of a tricked out 64 Volkswagen Bug and a $25.00 Amex gift card into the mailbox. Thank you - but I am hoping I don't get written up by the administration at my school because students came to my house, on a Saturday morning, during a pandemic. They told me they knocked on the door and waited for me to answer. Thank goodness, I wasn't home to open the door. When Optimus asked for my address, I guess I should have asked him why… I just hope I don't get written up, again…

…and why was I not at home? I was running. The SRLA (Students Run Los Angeles) debacle has been settled and my team and I are training again - virtually. I send running reminders to seven 8th graders and one 7th grader and they send back pictures of themselves running, along with screenshots of times (could be their times, could be someone else's - who's to know). On my birthday we were scheduled to run a 20K in conjunction with our "sister" organization Students Run Philly Style (SRPS). A 20K is 12.42

miles. I was ready. I only overslept by 45 minutes and instead of getting started at 5:00 am, I made it out of the house at about 6:15 am. I had my bottle of water, a small bag of Trader Joe's trail mix, my running buff and my running course charted. I am more determined than speedy as a runner, so I knew I'd be at it for a few hours. I started at 24th Street and Raymond. Traveled east to Hoover, then South on Hoover to Jefferson, ran the perimeter of USC to Figueroa. Ran Figueroa south to Exposition. Exposition west to Obama (formerly known as Rodeo Road) until it ended at La Cienega. North on La Cienega to Jefferson and Jefferson back home (via a few additional side streets). This was my 20K, 12.42-mile route. I ended up running 15.34 miles. 15 plus miles on my 54th… Happy Birthday, Happy Birthday to me.

Nine months in - and we are still in a pandemic. Usually, I have lots of plans and spend some time reflecting on goals and writing my yearly "to-dos". Not this year. This year, year 54, my only plan is to stay alive.

I wonder, where can I find a Frida Kahlo face mask?

Tracy Carness is a Los Angeles-based educator and writer. Her email address is teachertracy@mail.com.

AN (NOW) OPEN LETTER TO MY FATHER
BY TRACY MACDONALD

Dear Dad,

2020 is truly testing my strength. Last night in the throes of insomnia (again), I was thinking about the power of memory. I mean, really, most (if not all) of who and what we are, collectively and individually, is made of memory. Our family was particularly good at making memories, and like most families, and people, we forgot, or chose to forget, what rested just outside the edges. Inside the edges, though, there was always love. All that love.

Do you remember the old carousel slide projector? I'm pretty sure you guys still have it in that antique trunk in the family room, along with God knows how many boxes of old slides. Decades worth. Anyway, in some of my favorite memories, we're all gathered in the family room - you sitting behind the projector with its quiet hum and hot dusty smell, mom and Craig and Scott on the couch, me in my green vinyl bean bag chair, Mopsy and Ming, and eventually, a rotating cast of boyfriends and girlfriends, husbands, and wives, and then, the grandkids, all of us watching the big screen pulled down from the ceiling, mesmerized by memories so perfectly captured and projected. There we were.

So much of family is rooted in memory. Do you remember that time, this time, the other time, the last time? And so, it's natural for me to ask you.

"Hey Dad, do you remember the time you died?"

Do you remember how the stupid fucking Peter Pan Bus drove right by me and left me at the airport? The last bus of the night? Do you remember how we laughed when I finally made it home? Even though it was one AM, and even though we knew you only had a couple days to live? Oh my God, we laughed so hard. Stupid Peter Pan Bus line. Do you remember the day or two following? You were so happy, the way your family and friends drifted in and out. (Spoiler: they weren't so happy). They each hesitated at the bedroom door when it was time to go, and then again when I walked them into the foyer, because who wants to say goodbye for the last time, especially when they know it's the last time? Everybody loved you so much, Dad. I mean really, you were the best. You were the steadiest, the fairest, and the most honest man I've ever known.

Of course, I can't ask you to remember any of this, and I know that. But still, I'm going to ask you here, because you always did love my letters, and you always wanted me to write about my memories and experiences. Dear Dad. Dear Dead Dad. Here's that letter you won't be reading, from your daughter who recently became a member of a club she never wanted to join. Ha ha, sorry. I'm getting a little morbid and melodramatic (it IS death, to my defense), so I'll get back to my point, the point of this letter, really.

Dad. I sure could use you right about now. 2020 has been… clarifying? Terrifying? It's been a hope and a prayer, a shudder, a sharp inward breath, a slow hissing release, an awakening for some, and for others, a continued practice of love and resistance.

Dad!!! Donald. Fucking. Trump. And his cronies. And his minions and his enablers. It's been dark since you died, and without you here, 2020 feels even darker. I try to remind myself of the power of resistance and of love, to root myself there. And in family, always in family.

Alice Walker once suggested that resistance is the secret of joy. Nobody in this country has been rooted in the joy of resistance the way Black folks have, at least in my humble (and white) opinion. I think white people are finally starting to see that we can't claim to love Black culture and hate Black people and still call it fair. Of course, I can only speak to the resistance I have come to know and understand, which is resisting white supremacy as a co-conspirator (do you know what I mean by that? I'm not sure). And of course, I can speak to resistance with absolute clarity, as a woman. Daddy, I don't know if you understand this, because you were all about equality, but you didn't really have much of a feel for equity, and how equality can't really exist under the circumstances in our country as it's been and as it is. And as it goes for race, so it goes for gender, albeit in very different directions. And so, you, being you, always told me that if I wanted something, I should just go for it, that nothing and nobody could stand in my way if I worked hard enough. What you didn't understand (and it's really ok, Dad) is that for girls and women, simply existing is an act of resisting. And while resistance, individually and collectively, might very well be the secret of joy, it's sure exhausting.

There are many things I didn't tell you about myself over the years, or more accurately, there were many things I didn't tell you about others. Other men. This, despite the fact that I loved and trusted you completely. I didn't tell you because I was embarrassed and ashamed, although I should not, need not, feel this shame. Why should the hateful and violent acts committed BY OTHER PEOPLE cause me to feel shame, right? That's what you would ask me, if you could, and you would be right to ask. You were perhaps my greatest cheerleader. But what you couldn't see (can't see?) is that which exists for women around our edges, in the edges of memory, or in the actions and words of our friends and lovers and family members and co-workers, and also, that which exists deeply, painfully and quietly inside of us: the little voice that whispers, "You will never be enough." Or the other voice that whispers, "You don't matter." Or the quietest and most insidious voice of all (which is our own) and which hisses slyly, "Are you sure it's not your fault. Are you sure?"

The fatigue of resisting these voices is constant, at least for me. Maybe I couldn't/didn't/wouldn't tell you because this resistance, my existence, took all of my energy. Maybe I was afraid it might break you. It broke me, that's for sure. They BROKE me, Dad. They totally broke me, over and over again, although nobody - not even you - could see it, expert as I was at quietly sewing myself back together with tiny, hidden stitches.

2020, though. 2020. 20/20. Perfect clarity. Perfect vision. There's no way to deny what's come into focus. The stitches aren't holding. Some are small and some are big and ugly and all of them are there for a reason and those reasons are what make me whole.

Are you ready? Here it goes. Mr. Gray. I think I was 8? He had a pool. Stitch. The guy at the town beach, Dustin. He was 19 and had a mustache. He wanted me to be his girlfriend and told me he had dated lots of 12 year olds. Stitch. The guys in the pick-up truck who ran me down on my bike. I hit the street hard and fractured my chin. Mom had to take me to the doctor for stitches. Do you remember those assholes? You don't, because I told you I fell off my bike, which I did. I just didn't tell you why. Stitch stitch stitch. Matt C., Chris P., Larry D. That guy, this guy, the other guy, all the guys. Remember this? Remember that? Remember when? Look closer. See them? All the stitches, all those names? I don't want them there anymore. 2020 has done that for me, at least. I'll chew them out myself if I have to. I don't want you to worry though, Dad. 2020 broke me. It did. It broke me for reasons I haven't even told you, not even here; a Mother's reasons. Those reasons, if I shared them, would definitely break you. It's not even that, though, that keeps me from sharing them, because I'm pretty sure you'd want to help me carry this particular burden. It's just not my story to tell you, or anyone, at least not yet. Maybe she's already told you herself. If she hasn't, I'm sure she will, in her own time and way. She loved and misses you so much.

Do you remember, Dad, how she was there for you? How she held your hand and sat by your bedside? And not just her, but all of them, all three of the kids. Even Sal. Do you remember how we were all there together that night? It's such a beautiful memory, so whole, so perfect, with no edges. There had been a blizzard. The power was out and we had to start the generator. It was dark and quiet in the woods and in the house. We could hear the hum of your oxygen, and Mom finally let me turn it off. I cracked the bedroom window so we could smell the snow. I laid against your chest. Crazy as it seems, I wanted to feel your heart fade. I wanted to feel that last beat. Do you remember how Mom spoke to you in soothing tones? Her voice was so quiet, Dad, and we all know she's never quiet. Do you remember how loving and present Matt was, the way he sat beside Mom on the bed quietly holding her hand, his head bent, his other hand resting on your leg? Scott with one hand on my back, as if to say, not to worry, not to worry. And Craig, sweet Craig. He was there, too. Do you remember that moment Dad? The snow and the dark and the quiet, and the love, all that love? What I remember most is the way that even in our brokenness, we were whole. We were perfect. There we were, and everything else just fell away.

Tracy MacDonald is an Emmy Award winning writer, director, and producer for television and film, as well as a feminist, a mother, and a proud Armenian. You can follow her on Instagram, @dotelltracy

20/20 ELECTION : BLK WMN SAVE AMERIKA . . . AGAIN
OR
WE GOOD, WE BEEN HERE BEFORE
OR
IT'S LEVELS TO THIS THING
OR
ALWAYS CENTERING OURSELVES IN OUR EXISTENCE DAILY LONG FORM BULLET JOURNAL ENTRIES
BY VERONICA PRECIOUS BOHANAN

:: Sat, Oct 31

We sat on my sectional. Vote-by-mail ballots balanced on laps. Easily accessible screenshot of *The People's* sample ballot. Started with judges...so many. Retain, yes or no?!?! Slow and methodical—telling Mama which oval to perfectly fill black. Flipped back to vote for Kamala, Joe, and the Fair Tax. Signed & Sealed. USPS unreliable. We'll drop them off at a polling site.

:: Sun, Nov 1

10am CST. Zoom. Entered into a hug of light joining the *Adura Prayer Circle*. Reassuring melanated faces welcome connection. India Arie sets tone: " Every one of us is worthy . . ." Our worth untethered from election outcomes. During prayer my wandering mind recalled Ntozake Shange's: "i found god in myself . . . i loved her fiercely"

:: Mon, Nov 2

- Field songs blanket early morning musing. Fannie Lou Hamer belted love notes to her parents and the land. *Woke up this morning with my mind . . .*

- Sent mass email to Sis, *U Belong Here.** Reminded them of our collective asè.

- Mama and I had a date with a secured blue box. We returned our ballots at BAC.* 115th St. early-voting site. Rocking my signature green Chucks. Mask & matching headwrap. M4BL* white tee with Shirley Chisolm keeping my spine erect and herstory near. Sliding our ballots into the box—this moment felt big—like our ballots were our 2020 *pop of color.*

- Celebrating our vote, we went to Fairplay. Mama laughed as I gathered groceries, dancing up & down aisles to 80's music: avocados, broth, lentils . . . frozen okra—I'll make soup. Grocery shopping during Rona is a cautious, yet coveted, outing.

- . . . just finished guest lecturing—Antioch U, Seattle. Focused on socially just art therapy. Negotiated screen sharing slides with being conversational on gallery view. Relieved. Most videos were on. I relished talking to faces with blinking eyes, not at names, fur babies or that professional profile pic that everyone repurposed from their LinkedIn account.

Georgette Seabrooke, Dr. Lucille Venture . . . Cliff Joseph . . . spoke names of Black art therapists upon whose shoulders I stand. The smiling eyes of the only Black student kept me intentional. My existence reflected her presence in this graduate program and profession. She knew Black art therapists existed, but I was her first.

:: Tues, Nov 3

They can't have it: My spirit. My safety. My vibrato. My shea butta'd elbows. My oil'd scalp. I bless the spirit of my head. Sit with ancestors. Fresh water on altar. NO outside voices. NO social media. NO news, today.

:: Wed, Nov 4

- Re-elected. Cook County State's Attorney Kim Foxx. They tried to reduce her to Jussie Smollett, but she was raised by Chicago's hawk, so she knows how to survive the wind of Illinois politics.

- Still, no projected winner. Maybe we'll have a president by Black History Month.

- Finally watched City Treasurer Conyears-Ervin & Congresswoman Kelly "SGRho* Stroll to Poll" video. Get it soRHOrs! EE-YIP.

:: Thurs, Nov 5

I ask Earth's forgiveness as I absorb November's globally warmed 70+ degrees. The day 44 won, it was also unseasonably warm. I worked Obama's 2008 campaign that day, calling residents of a neighboring state. white farmer told me: "I like that Obama . . . I just can't vote for no white nigga." Not so funny Chicago's, Rahm-manufactured, bad reputation for violence—that's NOT the Chicago I know . . . but that midwestern farmer is probably considered harmless, patriotic and non-violent, right?

:: Fri, Nov 6

PJs & sparkling cider. Video off. I settled comfortably into this evening's virtual soul care fête. Noor curated an interactive Freedom Friday session for BIPOC, sponsored by ATN.* Jones-Bey guided us in remembering when we've felt most free in our bodies. Concerts: a normal I long for. My body misses live music—nuzzling with the rhythm of the pocket.

:: Sat, Nov 7

For this post-election woosah, I welcomed them into our virtual sista-circle. Blk Wmn draped in yellow & white. Grand Rising delight. 8am CST. Glowing. Camera ready. Videos on. Sis, U Belong Here . . . I thanked them for voting. Yet again, gathering themselves to save democrats. We breathe'd. We tapp'd.* We ki-ki'd. And for turning Georgia blue, we embraced Stacy Abrams as a shero.

Zoom ended.

TV on.

Responding to the projected vice-president elect, Blk people disrupted isolation with HOPE...JOY and Wobble'd throughout these COVID streets. One time for all rewired boomboxes & woofer speakers. Strolling social media, AKAs, Alphas...all D9 were cutting up. Blk sista-greek headed to the WH. Duplicity of relief. Anti-Blackness remains and our work continues, cuz Harris is a prosecutor and Biden, a politician.

We demand that this administration centers Black humanity and invests in Black communities.

---

*Sis, U Belong Here - a monthly sista-circle for Black Women, sponsored by create.heal.share, and curated by me.

*M4BL - Movement 4 Black Lives.

*BAC – Beverly Arts Center

*ATN – Abolitionist Teacher Network.

*SGRho – Sigma Gamma Rho Sorority, Inc.

*Tapp'd – EFT meridian tapping.

*AKA – Alpha Kappa Alpha Sorority, Inc

*D9 – Divine Nine. Historically Black sororities and fraternities.

veronica precious bohanan is a Chicago-based art therapist and writer. She is the founder and curator of create.heal.share.*, a self-expression and wellness community for Black Women. veronica's poetry can be found in* Home Girls Make Some Noise: Hip Hop Feminist Anthology, Check the Rhyme: An Anthology of Female Poets and Emcees*, and in her debut book of poetry and prose,* OM: My Sistagyrl Lotus. *veronica can be reached at veronica@veronicabohanan.com and on Instagram @createhealshare.*

Made in the USA
Columbia, SC
17 March 2021

34585512R00241